Undertold Texas
Volume 2

Mike Vance

Dos Dogs Press

Also by Mike Vance

Please enjoy these other titles by Mike Vance. They are available where books are sold and also at www.mikevancewriter.com

Non-Fiction

Undertold Texas Volume 1

Getting Away With Bloody Murder

Mud & Money: A Timeline of Houston History

Murder & Mayhem in Houston (with John Nova Lomax)

Houston Baseball: The Early Years, 1861-1961

Houston's Sporting Life

Stand-Up Stories: Tales from Behind the Microphone

A Fire to Kindle (Two volumes)

Brenham

Fiction

The Devil's Lease

A Convenient Scapegoat

Wingo: The Remarkable Story of an Unremarkable Man

Wingo's Redemption

Zeke Gets Glasses (with John Swasey)

LCCN pending

ISBN (hardback) 978-1-965272-15-2

ISBN (paperback) 978-1-965272-16-9

ISBN (ebook) 978-1-965272-17-6

Contents

Foreword

The first half of this foreword repeats and expands upon what I wrote in earlier volumes. Hopefully it will answer the most common questions which I've created for myself.

The selection of topics for all volumes of Undertold Texas are entirely subjective. They are not, however, random. I'm hopeful that some of these smaller stories might illuminate a bigger picture. Above everything else, I'm seeking to present a diverse range of stories that reflects the faces of all Texans, both present and past. It is vital that history is preserved in its entirety without kowtowing to politicians who don't understand history in the first place or sanitizing the truth for everyone because a few folks don't want to face it.

Human beings do good things and bad things. All of us do. It is important that we learn from our mistakes and do better as a species. That's why you'll find some people in these pages who you might think are more admirable than others. If we keep in mind that history is the story of an often tenuous humanity taken in context, it becomes very entertaining. History is also a good reminder that, even in our darkest times, we have been resilient as a nation and as humans. Just as nature demands, we evolve.

Please note that the stories contained herein are undertold, not untold. The goal is to present stories from Texas history that will be new to the reader, or at least expand their knowledge on a given subject. I took the two most famous Texans of all time and tried to present a lesser known aspect of their tale or tie them in with much more obscure folks who intersected with their lives. If a name is widely recognized, I hope that I will present new details or add context that might help the reader better understand the story.

In short, some of the chapters may be familiar to some of the readers, but, in Lincolnesque terms, not all of the chapters to all of the people. Much of that will likely be regional. What is known in Dallas is less known in El Paso. Our state is a big place, just in case no native has reminded of you of that lately.

In the foreword to Undertold Texas Volume 1, I mentioned that I was eyeballing a four-volume series. That is now looking like six volumes. I will again say if you don't see your favorite undertold story, it may be coming up. Or drop me a note at mike@mikevancewriter.com to run your idea by me.

One story in this second book is worthy of a comment here because it is so instructive. For those people who believe that history is a static thing, consider the tale of WWII hero Doris Miller. I had already written his story and had moved on to later chapters in this volume when the current presidential administration ordered all biographies of people of color removed from the Department of Defense's extensive historical websites. I read about the removal of the most famous ones in various newspapers, but the *New York Times* did a story on Miller specifically. I went to the US Navy website and found the notice of removal with my own eyes. You may read the chapter to learn the details on Miller's story, but don't ever forget that there are those small people who will happily cleanse history to fulfill their own cowardly agenda. Telling the true, unvarnished, complete stories of Texas is my biggest goal in this book and all of the history I write about.

Lastly, on a much happier note, think of this book as an introduction to new history trails to follow. Texas has a past that is more diverse than any other state, and anyone with a healthy curiosity will enjoy a little virtual off-roading through those tales. It may even inspire you to make a real road trip and see where some of this undertold history took place.

Mike Vance

2025

www.mikevancewriter.com

West Texas & The Panhandle

Guadalupe Peak. Carl Carlson IV via Wikimedia Commons

Chapter One

Satanta

Not all history storytelling is created equal. Some people leave a much wider paper trail than others. The most difficult historical figures to know are often the indigenous and the enslaved. In the case of the former, since American Indian tribes disseminated history by oral tradition only, much of what we know is told by outsiders or even enemies and captors. For Texas Indians, it was not until the middle 19th century that Whites began regularly noting personal details of their mortal enemies.

One of the earliest indigenous leaders to be written up in the Texas newspapers was the Kiowa war chief Satanta, or White Bear. He was born at his people's winter camp grounds along the Canadian River in the Texas Panhandle between 1815 and 1820, during the height of power for the Plains tribes. For Texas that primarily meant the alliance of the Comanche people and the Kiowa people. As soon as Anglos began to arrive in numbers, those Plains people entered a steady decline.

Most tribes had multiple chiefs and factions. War chiefs were often different than the wise elders who served as principal chief, but the Kiowa of the early middle 1800s were united under Chief Dohasan.

Dohasan had risen as a young war chief and became a member of the Koitsenko, an elected council of the top ten warriors from among all the Kiowa bands. By the 1850s, Satanta had emerged as a sub-chief to Dohasan and was also honored as a member of the Koitsenko, literally translated as the principal or top dogs.

Satanta was the son of a chief named Red Tipi and a Spanish woman captive, and his skills included more than just fighting his tribe's enemies. Satanta was also esteemed as a great and stirring orator, something that the American press noted. The *New York Times* wrote in 1867 that "in cunning or native diplomacy Satanta has no equal in boldness, daring and merciless cruelty."

He first came to the notice of Whites only three years prior to that, as one of Dohasan's trusted sub-chiefs at the First Battle of Adobe Walls. The place was the ruins of William Bent's adobe trading post and saloon on the north bank of the Canadian River. All of the tribal groups, including the Comanches and Kiowa, were supposed to be living on the reservations in modern-day Oklahoma by the late 1830s. The land was to be theirs alone to hunt and control, but White hunters continued to traverse the reservations and kill the buffalo upon which the tribes relied for survival. In retaliation, raids were frequently launched into Kansas and Northwest Texas and against wagon trains on the Santa Fe Trail. When the U.S. Army's attention became focused on the Civil War in the early 1860s, the Kiowa and Comanche only increased their attacks.

General James Carleton, commander of the Department of New Mexico, reached his breaking point in November 1864 and dispatched Colonel Kit Carson, one of the best known frontiersmen of all time, to lead a force against the winter camp grounds of the troublesome Indian tribes. Carson departed from Fort Bascom in Tucumcari with 260 cavalry, 75 infantry, and 75 Ute and Jicarilla Apache scouts.

Carson also took two mountain howitzer artillery pieces and 27 wagons. They headed east along the Canadian River into the very heart of Comancheria.

The Ute and Jicarilla scouts covered the army's flanks and ranged far ahead to check the path forward. On November 24th, the column reached Mule Springs, 30 miles west of Adobe Walls. Carson left the infantry to guard his wagons and supplies and continued forward. Just past daybreak, entering the floor of Palo Duro Canyon, they found Chief Dohasan's village with 176 lodges. The occupants fled, their escape covered by warriors under the sub-chief Guipahgo. Carson continued to Adobe Walls and had his small force dig in there at mid-morning. The cavalry troopers quickly found that several bands of Comanches and Plains Apache were also in the area. Soon the Army was besieged by twelve to fourteen hundred attacking Indian warriors. Carson dismounted his cavalry and arranged them around the two artillery pieces, weapons that lobbed shells into the groups of attackers.

Though later reports by Lieutenant William Pettis claim that the numbers of the Kiowa and Comanches soon reached 3,000, that seems doubtful. Either way, they greatly outmatched the 330 surprised soldiers and their Indian scouts. Pettis wrote of warriors "mounted and covered with paint and feathers . . . charging backwards and forwards . . . their bodies thrown over the sides of their horses, at a full run, and shooting occasionally under their horses." With every bugle call Carson ordered blown, Satanta, possessed of his own bugle, gave a contrary call, further confusing the Army's defense. By afternoon, following more than six to eight hours of continuous attacks, Carson's men fell back to the captured Kiowa village. The Comanches and Kiowa set grass fires to block the retreat, but Carson had his men set backfires to give them a path out.

Once back at the village, Carson ordered it burned, including one tipi with Chief Iron Shirt, who refused to leave, still inside. Four elderly Kiowa were killed and their bodies mutilated. A single Comanche scalp was taken by a soldier. The following morning, Carson's men packed up many "finely finished buffalo robes" and retreated back to New Mexico. It was the final time that Plains warriors would drive the United States Army from the field. The Cavalry tried to claim a victory based on having killed more people than they lost, but the annual record of the Kiowa, recorded on a buffalo skin, noted the time as "muddy travel winter, the time when the Kiowas repelled Kit Carson."

Dohasan died in 1866, and the Kiowa were never again united under a single leader. Along with Tene-angopte, Satank and Guipahgo, Satanta emerged as one of the Kiowa leaders. He negotiated several treaties with the American government including the Little Arkansas Treaty and the Medicine Lodge Treaty in which the Kiowa agreed to move onto the reservation near Fort Sill. Competition between the chiefs fomented more raids, however, and an estimated 250 Whites died before the matter was settled.

The army mounted a campaign against the Indians of the Southern Plains in the winter of 1868-69. It was notable for the destruction of the tribes' homes. It was during this cavalry campaign that George Custer murdered dozens of women and children on the Washita River. Satanta and Guipahgo came to Custer under a flag of truce, but the officer arrested the two chiefs and held them for three months, until the Kiowa returned to the reservation.

At times, Satanta tried to assert his leadership to keep the peace. When a Kiowa warrior was killed at the civilian camp near Fort Zarah, Kansas, Satanta defused his followers who gathered for revenge. In spite of that, the cavalry attacked the Kiowa camp later the same day. Throughout these years, Satanta continued to lead raids on wagon trains and once even took a family of White prisoners to Fort Dodge to sell them back to the Americans.

His downfall began in present day Young County, Texas in May 1871. Waiting for a richer prize, the Kiowa and Comanche party allowed an Army ambulance wagon to pass, not realizing that head of the Army William Sherman was riding inside. The bigger fish turned out to be the Warren Wagon Train that was headed to supply the Texas frontier forts. The wagons were drawn into a defensive circle, but the Indians triumphed, capturing all of the supplies and killing and mutilating seven wagoneers. General Sherman and Colonel Ranald Mackenzie vowed to find those responsible. The threat proved unnecessary.

Satanta posing in captivity. Library of Congress

Satanta foolishly bragged to an Indian agent that he, Satank, and Ado-ete, known as Big Tree, had orchestrated the raid. In spite of a brief armed defense, the three were arrested by General Sherman himself. A murder trial was held at Jacksboro, but Satank never made it. He told his friends that they could find his body along the trail. During the transport, he gnawed his own wrists to the bone so he could escape his shackles. Stabbing one of the guards, he jumped from the wagon and was shot dead. His body lay for some time by the roadside.

The Jack County jury sentenced Satanta and Ado-ete to death, but Governor Edmund Davis, under pressure, commuted the sentence to life in Huntsville. Satanta was temporarily paroled to Fort Sill after two years as a condition of Guipahgo leading a Kiowa delegation to Washington to talk peace with President Grant. A year later, with the Red River War underway, the army accused Satanta of taking part in attacks on buffalo hunters and being present at the Second Battle of Adobe Walls. The Kiowa adamantly held that the old warrior had given his war lance to younger men and was merely an observer, but his presence was viewed as a violation of his parole. He surrendered in October 1874 and was returned to the penitentiary at Huntsville.

Prison guards reported that the aging warrior withered away inside the walls. For a time, he worked on a chain gang that built a portion of the MK&T Railroad, otherwise, he sullenly stared through prison bars toward his people's hunting ground to the north. The long accepted story is that Satanta, unable to accept confinement any longer, dove head first from a high window in the prison hospital on October 11, 1878. Many Kiowa believe that he was murdered since taking his own life would rob a warrior of his place of dignity in the afterlife. His body remained in the prison cemetery for almost a century before his grandson received permission to move it to Fort Sill, Oklahoma. In 2000, his shield, bow, arrows, and quiver were returned to Fort Sill and dedicated in a ceremony that included Kiowa veterans of the U.S. military.

Chapter Two

Lubbock Glider Museum

General William Westmoreland called gliders "the only aircraft built to crash," and that train of thought might not have been especially encouraging to the men who rode in them. Even before Pearl Harbor, servicemen were already calling them "flying coffins." They had no power of their own to accelerate out of trouble and possessed only limited ability to control their precise destination. By nature, they were constructed of light and flimsy material. Since the troops contained inside had to be ready to fight in an instant, they wore no parachutes. In spite of all the negatives, the U.S. military bought 14,612 of them during WWII.

It was a successful 1940 German glider attack on an "impregnable" fort in Holland that captured the attention of the world's air forces, but it was the United States Army Air Force and Marine Corps that capitalized on the idea on the grandest scale. The Air Corps' commanding general, Hap Arnold, ordered the design and build of an assault glider force in February 1941, well before the United States officially entered the war.

The concept was for aircraft that held 15 men. Without engines to deal with, one would assume that they would be easy to build, but that did not prove to be the case, at all. The trouble was that the nation's largest aircraft manufacturers were already at capacity supplying planes for the British and looking ahead to American involvement in the war. Other firms believed the gliders were risky and untested, and declined to get involved.

Several designs were tried, but Arnold selected one from the Waco Aircraft Company, pronounced differently and not associated with the Texas city. The name was a distillation of the Weaver Aircraft Company of Troy, Ohio. The Waco gliders could haul the 15 men, two pilots and 13 infantry, plus either a Jeep and four passengers or a 75MM howitzer, 18 shells and a three-person gun crew. It was constructed on a metal-tube frame, had a wooden floor, and was covered with fabric and plexiglass. The Waco gliders were 48 feet long with a wingspan almost twice that length. Though it was intended to land intact and be used in the next assault, landings generally took a high toll.

The glider design was from the Ohio firm, but several companies cranked out the machines according to their specs. The Army Air Force paid $15,500 per craft. One of the manufacturers was a piano maker in Connecticut. Another assembled planes in a circus tent. Four had no previous experience building airplanes. Though a few of the manufacturers trained pilots and other facilities were situated around the country, most WWII glider pilots passed through the South Plains Flying School in Lubbock, Texas.

The city was a going concern at the start of the war. It had grown by a full 50% since the 1930 census. Texas Tech University was sneaking

up on 20 years old and had just over 2,800 students. Cotton farms
and large ranches surrounded the area, and agriculture-related industry
dominated the economy. For a decade, Lubbock had been recognized as
the cleanest town in Texas. KFYO was the city's lone radio station, and
the county was dry, as in no legal alcohol could be found.

Finding pilots for the gliders proved to be a problem. Newly trained
military fliers wanted to be placed in fighter planes or bombers. The
gliders were considered more dangerous and much less sexy and exciting.
Many of the glider pilots were transferred to the program by orders,
not choice. Compared to the pilots of conventional aircraft, glider pilots
were younger and much less experienced. The oldest ones were those
who had been released from or flat washed out of other flight programs.
They were brawlers who were light on discipline but craved the thrill of
combat.

Jump-ready soldiers and glider. Silent Wings Museum

South Plains Flying School was the second Army training base in
Lubbock. There was an air base west of town. The glider training took

place at the city's municipal airport, a facility the city loaned to the Army. There were concrete runways already in place, one sheet metal hangar, one brick hangar, a control tower, and an airport manager's residence. Housing for the cadets sprang up quickly, and the base became a sprawling beehive of activity. Within a year, Lubbock became the only advanced training base for glider pilots. More than 80% of the American trainees spent time there.

The reality of flying gliders proved to be every inch as dangerous as it looked on paper. Six thousand glider pilots were trained, and 203 of them were killed in action. Another 140 died in training. There were several other things that failed to build confidence. As one instructor leaned against the wing of a glider while he lectured, the thing fell completely off the fuselage. When pilots graduated from the program at South Plains, they received wings with a large G in the middle. The wags among them said it stood not for glider, but for guts.

The first time the Allies tried a large scale glider invasion was in Sicily in July 1943. They were towed across the entire Mediterranean from Tunisia only to meet anti-aircraft fire, including some from Allied gunners on ships offshore. The navies had not been informed about the Army planes. High winds whipped up Sicilian sand and obscured visibility, but the worst was when the tow planes, both American and British, released 65 gliders too early, dropping them into the sea. More than 300 soldiers drowned. Of the 25 American glider pilots sent from Tunisia, only two made the shores of Sicily.

On D-Day, gliders landed six to ten miles inland from the coast to support the American landing on Utah Beach. Though the casualty rate among the infantrymen aboard was a terrifying 11%, some 4,000 of them landed behind the line along with 100 artillery pieces and 300 tons of cargo. Gliders were used in the assault on the French Mediterranean coast, and bought supplies to besieged Americans during the Battle of the Bulge. A very large number went into the Netherlands as part of the ambitious Operation Market Garden. As always, consistently finding the landing zones and springing from the aircraft to fight at an instant were issues that took a terrible toll.

The largest and costliest deployment of gliders came in the last weeks of the war when more than 600 C-47 transports towed over 900 Waco gliders to landing zones on the German side of the Rhine. Half the planes towed more than one glider. It was in support of British General Bernard Montgomery's crossing of the river. Coded Operation Varsity, the glider operation took place in broad daylight for the first time, and anti-aircraft guns extracted a heavy cost.

The Pacific Theatre also saw glider use. British and Indian Chindit troops used them to move around Burma and to set up weather stations on a remote part of New Guinea and land the men and supplies to build an airstrip in the dense jungle.

When the war ended with the Allied victory, the dollar-a-year contract with the Army stipulated the return of South Plains Flying School property, a total of 1,600 acres, to the City of Lubbock. Trouble was, even though they had no plans for it immediately, the Army did not want to give it back. It took four years of wrangling by local officials, but the federal government did return the base along with a new terminal that went up in 1950. It served as the city's airport until the mid-1970s. Today, that terminal building is the Silent Wings Museum. It is dedicated to the history of the thousands of U.S. Army Air Force glider pilots who trained on the field. At its centerpiece is a restored and intact Waco glider.

Chapter Three

Gordon Wood

One of the lynchpins of Texas culture is high school football. Perhaps nothing else can unite a community like the Friday night gridiron. It was the subject of a hit movie that in turn spawned a primetime TV drama. It is fodder for rancorous debates over public expenditures. High school football rules over every small town and midsize city, and friendships and grudges developed as players or cheerleaders last a lifetime. Whether they were in the marching band or the pep squad, millions of Texas natives recollect those Fridays, with chili pie at the concession stand and postgame Cokes at the pizza place, as their glory days.

High school football is also a source of civic pride like nothing else, and many dozens of Texas towns welcome drivers to their municipalities with billboards boasting of their state titles. It is as sure as the precipitous drop in speed limit and the cop hiding behind the Dairy Queen sign.

Among the folks who follow such things, there is another surety – those rural fans can rattle off the names of the state's winningest coaches and the programs they led to greatness. Phil Danaher at Calallen. Randy Allen at Highland Park. G.A. Moore at Celina, and others in towns such as Daingerfield and Albany where the first bell that rings for thousands of Texans is the one connected to high school football.

Another immortal name is Gordon Wood, who currently sits fourth on the all-time victory list among the state's high school football coaches. When he led his last game, though, Wood sat at number one, not just in Texas, but in the entire nation. He won more than 80% of his games, and everyone else who had ever blown a whistle, ridden a blocking sled, or drawn up a play in the dirt held him up as the best there was.

His personal story is quintessential West Texas. Wood was born in Moro, a farming and ranching community 28 miles southwest of Abilene in Taylor County. It was not a place on the upswing. The primary commerce was breeding and dealing livestock, and before Wood reached the age of 10 the town's post office was gone. Today there is only a Baptist church and a cemetery.

The first game of football that Gordon Wood ever saw was one he played in. His junior high did not offer the sport. He commuted to high school in the big city, and the travel meant that he played in only five games for Abilene Wylie, but he returned to Abilene to get a physical education degree from Hardin-Simmons in 1938. He also played end on their football team. As things were done at the time, that meant on both offense and defense. He boxed, too, and compiled a record of 27 and 4 in those bouts.

Though Gordon Wood is most often associated with Brownwood, he had coached for two full decades before he moved to his final stop. He began as an assistant at Spur then took the head jobs at Rule, Haskell, Roscoe, Seminole, and Winters, never staying for more than three years. Between Haskell and Roscoe was a stint in the United States Navy during WWII. While stationed in San Diego, he met a Kansas girl named Katherine Boyd. They married and stayed together for 59 years.

For city folks unfamiliar with the expanses of West Texas, the names of those towns where Wood coached his way through the 1940s would likely produce a blank stare. Winters is still probably best known as the birthplace of baseball Hall of Famer Rogers Hornsby, and Seminole produced Tanya Tucker. Otherwise, they were not far off the movie sets of Hud or the Last Picture Show.

In 1951, Wood took the job to lead the Stamford Bulldogs. The town's population that year was 5,800, the biggest it would ever be. Wood stayed there for eight seasons and compiled a record of 80 wins against just six defeats. The Bulldogs won district five times and had back-to-back state AA titles in 1955 and '56. They reeled off a string of 35 straight victories in the process. The team that Wood had coached up took state the year he after he left, and would've made that two if they were not disqualified after winning the 1959 championship game.

Gordon Wood was gone by then, hired away to coach Victoria in 1958. When he took that job, he brought along Morris Southall who had served as his assistant at Seminole a decade earlier and had taken over the head job there when Wood left. Their record in Victoria was 12-7-1 over the next two years. They were winning seasons, but it was not the house afire that the people and the school board expected. Maybe they believed that Wood was a small town phenomenon who was not cut out for bigger places like Victoria. Maybe the South Texas coastal prairies were just not the same as West Texas. Victoria had never won their district before, but their vaunted new coach did not get it done, either. Gordon Wood and the Victoria Stingarees parted ways.

In 1960, the school board at Brownwood gave Gordon Wood another chance for greatness, and he embraced it fully. It might have seemed like an odd choice for a coach who had never experienced a losing season. The previous pinnacle of Brownwood's gridiron success was a single district title. The hometown paper called the team's 1960 outlook "below average." That publication listed the squad's main weaknesses as "lack of experience, speed, size, age, and strength." Other than that Mrs. Lincoln...

Wood brought along Morris Southall and the same style of coaching that had served them at previous stops. It was less stringent than many coaches used in those days. His predecessor in Stamford was a man who ran his team through three hour daily workouts without benefit of water breaks, but Wood believed that football teams could be forged without "blood-letting." In his first season in charge of the Brownwood Lions, with only six returning football lettermen, just two of them starters, Wood's team won the state title.

Gordon Wood had a reputation for clean living, and he expected the same in his players. He taught ethics through the game of football. He talked up honesty and eagerness and dispensed discipline mixed with praise when he thought each was warranted. He preached that coaches and players must believe in one another always. A sign inside the fieldhouse door read "Wood Tough." It is still there.

Twice his peers in the state named him coach of the year. The Texas Sports Writers chose him for their top honor four times. He was elected to a spot in the Texas High School Coaches Association Hall of Fame and its national counterpart. May 15, 1971, was declared "Gordon Wood Day" in Brownwood. Lieutenant Governor Ben Barnes was there along with Texas Longhorns coach Darrell Royal and former President Lyndon Johnson "to honor a man with a record in athletic leadership without a parallel." There was a sold out dinner in the Brownwood Coliseum, and more than 1,500 fans joined the bigwigs. Former players flew in from as far away as California and Colorado to fete their old coach. Charles Coody, a Master's golf champion, sent a telegram to speak on behalf of the men who had played under Gordon Wood at Stamford.

Coach Gordon Wood. Courtesy Brownwood Bulletin

That might have been the high point and a fitting end for Gordon Wood's coaching career. Just a few years later, four members of the Brownwood ISD board got it into their heads that the coach was over the hill. He was about to turn 65, and that was the mandatory retirement age for district employees. Though most of the townsfolk vehemently disagreed, it appeared that Gordon Wood was about to be aged out of a job.

Then a serendipitous thing happened. Ronald Reagan, campaigning for a presidential nomination he would lose to Gerald Ford, made a stop in Brownwood. Some in the audience asked him "if (he) had a football coach who had won seven State Championships at two different cities and was renowned as one of the great coaches in the State of Texas, and was still active and still winning at... sixty-five, would you fire him because of his age?" Reagan, who was just about that age and wouldn't occupy the White House until he was almost 70, blasted whatever idiots had made such a suggestion. The school board duly changed their policy to reflect an annual assessment of an employee's work, and Wood coached for another decade.

Gordon Wood's record upon retirement in 1985 was 255 wins, 53 losses, and 7 ties at Brownwood. There were seven state titles there to go with two he won at Stamford. Two of those came after the school board tried to let him go. Brownwood was also state runner-up once.

Wood's name is on the stadium in Brownwood today. It is not a gleaming modern 20,000 seat venue like those in places such as Allen, Mesquite, Odessa, or Tomball, but with a capacity of 7,500, it holds its own. Roughly 40% of the town's population can fit inside. Still, it has a certain old school vibe that suggests the values of its namesake.

Brownwood has not won a state title since Gordon Wood's then-record seventh championship in 1981, but they are still rabid about the Friday night games. There is still respect and reverence when the long-timers talk about "Coach Wood." (His wife was known around town as "Mrs. Coach.") Many locals readily refer to him as "the most important person in the history of Brownwood." Those Lions football teams were about the only time the town ever hit the statewide, and sometimes national, radar.

Wood averaged more than one all-state player per year, a number unheard of at his retirement. His former players agree that Wood was the best motivator they ever encountered, and that Coach Wood understood each player as an individual and could wring the most talent out of his kids. Most of all, those old players still talk about, and tear up at, the arm Wood draped around their shoulder "when it was over to let you know he loved you."

Chapter Four

Billie Sol Estes

When Billie Sol's back was hard up against the wall in 1962, famed writer Tom Wicker of the *New York Times* described Estes as a bit of a romantic outlaw: "Billie Sol Estes is a product of the limitless plains of West Texas and the limitless spirit of the American frontier... And though it is many years since there was 'no law west of the Pecos,' some of the old frontier freedoms remain — the right of a man to dream of new worlds, for instance, and to set about finding them the quickest way he can." The victims of Billie Sol's confidence games probably failed to see the panache.

The story of Billie Sol Estes began with inspired ingenuity and old fashioned hard work. Born into a religious farm family near Clyde on the east side of Abilene, his wheeling and dealing started at age seven when he asked for and received a lamb for Christmas. Billie Sol named her Merry and bred her with a neighbor's ram. By the next spring, the boy owned two lambs, and soon there were two more. He got up at three in the morning to work a before-school job at a dairy farm for 50 cents a day, and invested the money into more stock. He began skipping school to sell wool at market, and long before he entered puberty, Billie Sol was paying his brothers and sisters to do his farm chores, freeing him up to run his business.

His first scheme involving the government happened when he was a teenager. Billie Sol wrote President Roosevelt asking what the United States could do to help drought-poor farmers in Callahan County. His desire to help the poor was a lifelong calling. The answer came back from the White House that there was surplus grain available at a low cost. Billie Sol sold 100 sheep for $3,000 and borrowed an additional $3,500 from a local bank. With that money he bought 17 train carloads of grain. After he carved out plenty to feed his own stock, the boy sold the rest to his neighbors at a tidy profit. The *Abilene Reporter-News* ran a feature story on the business boy wonder, and he was named the top 4-H Club boy in America. At age 18, when he joined the Merchant Marines, Billie Sol, even though he was overdrawn at the bank, had compiled $38,000. It was more than the young man's father had ever made in a lifetime.

With WWII ended, and Billie Sol returned to civilian life, he picked up right where he left off, once again seeing money to be made on the fringes of federal programs. He started buying surplus Army barracks and converting them into small houses which he sold to returning GIs. In 1949, he sold his home in Clyde and moved to Earth, a town near Amarillo. He brought in irrigation to improve the property value then sold his Earth holdings to acquire cheaper land in the rugged, arid spaces around Pecos. Again, he sought to better his low cast acreage. This time he used portable tanks of anhydrous ammonia fertilizer and was soon buying more land and filling it with cotton and grain. The *New York Times* reported that at his zenith, he owned 26,000 acres around Pecos.

By the early and middle 1950s, Billie Sol Estes was pure-D rich. In addition to his straight up farming operations, he owned grain elevators, a farm equipment business, a trucking company, a newspaper, and a mortuary. One story opined that "he had bought every viable business in Pecos." The U.S. Junior Chamber of Commerce agreed, naming him one of the 10 outstanding young men in America.

"Everything I touched made money," he later told a reporter.

He was in his mid-thirties, had an estimated 4,000 employees, and a net worth of $40 million. Still, he maintained his lay preacher status at the local Church of Christ and railed against drinking and dancing and cussing. Behind the scenes, though, Estes had assembled the proverbial house of cards. There were sketchy loans and under-the-table buy back operations, and those arrangements were multiplying.

None of the illegalities worried Billie Sol because he thought he was under political protection. He had begun making campaign contributions to seemingly every politician he could find. They were mostly Texas Democrats at first, when that was the only party that mattered, but there were later Republicans from as far away as Minnesota. He threw lavish parties with politicos invited to his home, the largest one in Pecos. It had a waterfall in the living room, and out by the pool, the one in which boys and girls were not allowed to swim together, was a barbeque pit big enough to accommodate multiple steers at one time. Soon his walls were lined with autographed photos of the likes of John F. Kennedy, Harry Truman, and Lyndon Johnson. A combination of those Texas politicians and various bureaucrats helped grease the skids for Billie Sol to lease some of his grain silos to the government.

Then in 1961, bad rumors began to circulate about Bilie Sol's business dealings. A federal investigator named Henry Marshall came down to look into the Estes cotton business. Supposedly, there was an offer of promotion if Marshall would stop his digging and return to Washington, but the man said no. Not long afterward, Marshall was shot five times in the stomach. The death was initially ruled a suicide by the locals, but was later changed to homicide.

A year later, Billie Sol's wheeling and dealing became national news. The editor of the *Pecos Independent and Enterprise*, a semi-weekly that competed with the local Estes-owned daily, wrote a multi-part expose. Though it did not mention Estes by name, it garnered the small town writer a Pulitzer Prize. More importantly, it spawned a veritable avalanche of other stories. There were books, songs, jokes on late night television and in nightclub acts. In May 1962, Billie Sol Estes, with his horn-rimmed glasses and a dimpled smile, was on the cover of *Time* magazine.

Behind him on that famous cover was a liquid fertilizer tank. That was the scheme that brought him down. He had gone heavy into promoting the fertilizer tanks that nursed crops from the dry soil of the West Texas borderlands. The rub was that his tanks did not actually exist.

Billie Sol had been borrowing money based on other farmer's financial statements then kicking back 10% of the loan. Instead of manufacturing the entire number of promised tanks, he was only making metal tags with serial numbers. After all, the tanks were portable. When a lender came to inspect the operation, Billie Sol showed off a thousand tanks on his own property. A few days later, the same banker saw the same tanks at a different location, but this time, they were sporting alternate tags. By the time the newspaper stories broke, Billie Sol had swindled about $24 million based on 33,500 tanks that just did not exist.

It surprised exactly no one when politicians in Washington, Austin, and beyond quickly began to distance themselves from Billie Sol Estes. Seventy-five FBI agents were assigned to the case, and President Kennedy, his Attorney General brother, Bobby, and their Agriculture

Secretary Orville Freeman, were put on the defensive by "almost daily revelations."

JFK told reporters, "This government is staying right on Mr. Estes's tail."

Three agriculture department officials were fired for taking bribes. An assistant secretary of labor admitted pocketing money and resigned. There were at least three suicides including the man who had kept Estes' books. Another figure in the cases died in a plane crash. Conspiracy theorists had a field day.

Billy Sol Estes before an investigating committee. United States Senate

In addition to the phony mortgages on imaginary fertilizer storage tanks, there were illegal transfers of federal-compensation rights, lands taken under eminent domain, kickbacks for bankers, and bribes handed out in Washington. His network of fraud extended into Oklahoma, Georgia, and Alabama. As the *Times* wrote in Billie Sol's obituary: "The scams were so complex that prosecutors eventually had to break them down into 50 state and federal indictments."

When the verdicts were read, Estes faced 24 years in prison. That was shortened to only 15 years thanks to several State of Texas charges being jettisoned by the U.S. Supreme Court. He went through a tangle of appeals, served six years, and was paroled in 1971. Before the decade was over, Billie Sol was convicted of mail and tax fraud and went back inside for another four.

It was during his legal process the first time around that Estes began to peddle assassination plots and other theories. As he kept talking, the stories involved Jimmy Hoffa and Fidel Castro, Jack Ruby and Lee Harvey Oswald, and especially Lyndon Johnson, the man who Billie Sol had assured his family would finagle a pardon if Estes ever went to prison. LBJ, Estes said, had ordered seven or eight murders, many to cover up his ties to Estes, and Johnson's aide Mac Wallace had carried them out. Wallace had even fired a bullet that hit President Kennedy in Dallas. When the Justice Department asked Billie Sol for details, he said he would happily provide them in return for total immunity and a perpetual get out of jail free card.

In 1984, after getting out of prison for the second time, Estes got his immunity from a Texas grand jury and repeated all of his allegations, even adding the eighth alleged murder to Mac Wallace's resume. As with virtually all conspiracy books and films, there was no proof. The *Times* pointed out that "everyone else, except Mr. Estes, was …dead." Billie Sol subsequently repeated his allegations in a pair of books. There was even talk of writing "one hell of a movie script" with Fred Michaelis, a former hairdresser turned Austin street hobo who spent four years living in Estes' Abilene house and chauffeuring the big man around in a 1974 Cadillac. Estes needed his stories to pay off.

Though Estes always maintained that he was a close friend of Lyndon Johnson, others whose relationship to the late president is well documented put the talk down to the Estes ego. There were definitely contributions and a spendy trip to the Kennedy-Johnson inauguration in 1961, but a Texas oilman who was one of Johnson's biggest donors said that "Johnson hardly knew who Estes was." Another pol from Pecos said of Billie Sol, "He's a hopeless name-dropper. Lyndon Johnson might have known him, but I don't recall he knew him that well."

As for LBJ himself, the only time Billy Sol Estes' name appeared in the thousands of hours of Oval Office tapes was a handful of occasions when Johnson discussed rumors that Republican Barry Goldwater, his presidential opponent in 1964, had offered Estes a pardon and a million dollars for dirt on the sitting president. Goldwater's running mate, William E. Miller, did bring up Estes on the campaign trail.

With Pecos long since in the rear view mirror and two jail stints behind him, as well, Billie Sol Estes settled near Abilene. He became popular with the pastor and congregation at the Church of Christ. He was still hatching his schemes, and he had an affair that threatened his longtime marriage. As he told *Texas Monthly*, "I love putting deals together and watching them run." In 1987, Estes was being investigated for yet another large scale fraud, this one involving stolen blueprints for cargo trailers and a deal to sell $5 million worth of them to a government agency near Corpus Christi.

Billie Sol was also helping the poor, his lifelong crusade. Family members and friends said that "in the beginning, he gave money away because it made people like him," but that does not explain his later generosity, especially toward Blacks and Mexican Americans. At the height of his riches, he and his wife Patsy sent some forty minority kids to college. His entire foray into the funeral home business had started when the White mortuary in Pecos had refused to bury local minorities. It matched the ideals that Lyndon Johnson preached, and the famous Three Rivers case that LBJ championed as a young senator. The backing of minority causes cost Billie Sol a spot on the Pecos school board, and it meant that many parents refused to let their children play at a house that welcomed Black ministers.

In Abilene, post-prison, Billie Sol continued trying to help the downtrodden with whom he identified. Estes begged food from grocery stores and restaurants and drove it to the Black side of Abilene. He sent his limousine to drive those minority children to school when it rained.

To the end, though most considered Billie Sol Estes a criminal mastermind, he still maintained his charms to many who knew him. He remained friends with his Abilene mistress, Sue Goolsby. She told the *Texas Monthly* columnist that Billie Sol was a wonderful person who once confided to her "that there is no secret." Her memories were fond ones, but she also added, "Billie's problem is that he's a liar and he just can't help it."

Chapter Five

Anton Friedrich Wulff

Most who recognize the name of Anton Friedrich Wulff will see him for the San Antonio story that he is, and deservedly so. That is where he made his lasting mark, and the only spot to find his tangible remains. Yet Wulff's tale is also a wonderful illustration of the plight of the recently arrived German immigrants before and during the American Civil War, and to find the ground where that part of his life took place, definitely his most drama-filled years, one needs to journey 60 miles south of Marfa to a border town west of Big Bend and then cross the Rio Grande into Chihuahua.

Wulff's American saga begins similarly to thousands of other German immigrants to the United States. By the end of the 1840s, newcomers from the various German states and duchies were rivaling the numbers of incoming Irish. One of those arrivals was Anton Friedrich Wulff, a single man who left the big city of Hamburg in the summer of 1848 for the bigger city of New York. Work in Manhattan was nearly impossible to find, and the population density, at more than 65,000 people per square mile, was the highest in the city's history. Wulff kept moving in search of gainful employment, first to Cincinnati, a hotbed of German settlement, and then down the Ohio and Mississippi Rivers to New Orleans. He finally ended up broke in San Antonio where he found a job as a clerk for five dollars a month.

Like most immigrants, Wulff was not afraid of hard work. He soon had a job working for Joseph Landa on the city's Main Plaza that increased his salary sixfold. He also had the good fortune to become friendly with James Sweet, a Canadian immigrant who utilized funds from his brother-in-law to set up a retail store. By the beginning of 1852, Wulff was involved in the business, moving to Fredericksburg to open a mercantile that no doubt relied on the patronage of the overwhelmingly German population there. It was a big year for Wulff. That November he came back to San Antonio to marry María Guadalupe Olivarri, a descendant of the city's original Canary Islands settlers. Two years after that, he was naturalized as an American citizen.

On paper, things seemed to be going swimmingly for Anton Wulff, but serious trouble was brewing for San Antonio's Germans, a population that had surpassed 7,600 and made up a third of the citizens in Bexar County. They were especially insular, but they were also well educated and increasingly successful in the city's business community. As if that in itself did not rub Anglo settlers the wrong way, the Germans were overwhelmingly anti-slavery. Some were moderate in their views and sought only to preserve the Union. Others, particularly the Forty-Eighters, intellectuals and failed revolutionaries who had fled Northern and Central Europe out of fear of persecution, were adamant abolitionists.

Perhaps the most vocal of those Forty-Eighters in San Antonio was Adolph Douai, an educator from East Prussia who had served prison

time for his revolutionary activities. When he was freed, Douai moved to
Texas. After a year teaching in New Braunfels, he took over as editor of
San Antonio's *Zeitung* and turned the German language newspaper into
a persistent voice for abolition and advocate of an America comprised of
"free tillers of their own soil." Douai was even so bold that he called for a
separate free state to be carved from the western areas of Texas. German
political leaders held a convention in San Antonio and declared that
"slavery is an evil, the removal of which is absolutely necessary according
to the principals of democracy."

In the face of this strong sentiment, the Anglos and soon-to-be
secessionists pushed back hard. The *Texas State Gazette*, a widely read
pro-slavery newspaper out of Austin, wrote editorials which called out
the *Zeitung* by name. The *Gazette* and other Texas press published stories
that painted German immigrants with broad, negative stereotypes.
Threats were leveled against the Germans to such an extent that
members of the San Antonio Turnverein, a German athletic club,
volunteered as a protection detail for the *Zeitung* offices. In 1856, the
pressure against Adolph Douai grew so hot that he sold the paper and
fled to Boston.

The name of Presidio del Norte de la Junta de los Rios was changed
in 1865 to honor Manuel Ojinaga, the governor of Chihuahua who was
executed by the occupying French army under Emperor Maximillian. A
century prior, it was established by the Spanish as a protective garrison,
and the families of the soldiers built up a nearby villa. It retains a rural
feel even today. Ojinaga is best known for being the hometown of several
famous Norteno musicians and as the site of a 1914 Mexican Revolution
battle in which Pancho Villa's army crushed the Federales to take control

of the Northern Border. It is also perhaps where the famed American writer and satirist Ambrose Bierce may have lost his life.

In 1857, though, Presidio del Norte, which is on the south side of the river from Texas, was a sleepy border trading town on a very sparsely populated stretch of frontier. That is where Anton Friedrich Wulff chose to take his family for safety's sake. His chain of dry goods stores with James Sweet had the primary San Antonio location, the one in Fredericksburg, and others in Laredo and Coke County, north of San Angelo. Wulff opened one in Presidio del Norte. It was across the river, and presumably away from the rabid secessionist madness.

That notion was put to a test in early 1861 when Texas voted on the issue of secession. Though the statewide total was 75% in favor of leaving the United States, 18 counties voted against seceding. Another 32 of the newer counties, all in the western part of the state, either failed to hold election, did not submit returns, or, if some outcry is to be given credence, suffered ballot suppression. In Wulff's former home of Bexar County, the official vote favored secession, but just barely – 53.8% to 46.2%. Those on the losing side cried foul.

In the elections aftermath, newly-empowered Confederates vehemently harassed the Unionists across Texas. It led to mass murder in Gainesville and a massacre of Germans from Comfort. As a group, Texas Germans were targeted especially hard. Some of the most zealous of the rebellious leaders sought scapegoats and people with whom they could settle old scores.

In a time of brutal White supremacy and taking affront with a hair trigger, John Robert Baylor was an overachiever. Most in the rebellious states found the man to be a rabid fighter, but not everyone approved.

After he declared himself governor of Arizona and New Mexico, without ever setting foot in the former territory, the newspaper editor in Mesilla, New Mexico launched a series of attacks on Baylor including calling the lieutenant colonel "incompetent and utterly unfitted for the high position which he holds." Baylor, who had once published his own newspaper called *The White Man*, was outraged. When he encountered the *Mesilla Times* editor Robert Kelly in a store, Baylor instigated a fight, and though Kelly was armed only with a knife, Baylor shot him full of enough bullets that Kelly died within a fortnight.

After he was pushed back into Texas, Baylor was commanding the Second Texas Mounted Rifles at Fort Bliss, the U.S. Army post at El Paso that had been seized for the South. It was there that Baylor set his sights on Anton Wulff. The German had been operating his mercantile business in Presidio del Norte and supplying both U.S.A. and C.S.A. garrisons north of the border with various goods including corn and hay. Baylor declared Wulff to be a spy. In October 1861, Baylor ordered Captain W.C. Adams to kidnap Wulff into Texas where he could be arrested, placed "in irons," and presumably hanged. Adams, in turn, dispatched Lieutenant Emory Gibbons, an Arkansas native who grew up near Uvalde.

On October 16, six men crossed into Presidio del Norte to take Anton Wulff. Lt. Gibbons later told Benigno Contraras, the top civic authority in the villa, that their purpose was to attend a dance and socialize. At three o'clock in the morning, four of the Confederates slipped away from the dance and knocked on various doors at Wulff's home, pretending to be friendly Americans looking for a place to stay. When Wulff reluctantly opened up, two seized him by the hair, and all four dragged him, screaming, out the door. Maria Wulff and one of her brothers also yelled for help, and a party of several Mexican neighbors, armed with pistols, followed the kidnappers toward the river demanding that their friend Wulff be released.

As the two Confederates who had remained at the dance slunk across the river, at least two of the kidnappers fired pistols toward the armed Mexican civilians. Fire was returned, over 50 shots in all. The two Confederate shooters were killed along with one Mexican civilian. Another Mexican was seriously wounded. When Lieutenant Gibbons wrote to Contreras feigning total ignorance of the matter and inquiring about his two missing soldiers, he was politely informed that the criminals had died and were already buried "on this side of the river."

Wulff himself wrote an indignant letter to Captain Adams at Fort Davis laying out all the particulars of the crime. One of the dead men, a hefty, red-whiskered fellow named Tom, Wulff recognized as having run a bar near the Main Plaza in San Antonio some seven years prior. The merchant also reminded Adams that he had been furnishing the captain's post with hay for their mounts and had an order for 1,000 bushels of corn and some wood. "But considering my own life in my own house has been exposed as it has been," Wulff wrote Adams. "I will be unable to fulfill any contract for your post." To add one last insult, Wulff noted that he pulled two due bills totaling $110 from dead Tom's pocket and that he would hold onto them in Mexico until the captain might come get them.

The failed errand he ordered against Wulff had no effect on John Baylor's career. In December, he was promoted to full colonel. John R. Baylor remained obsessed with the killing of Native Indians, however. He may or may not have led a murderous raid south of the border into Chihuahua after Apache warriors. There are no records to back his claim. It is undeniably known that soon thereafter Baylor issued an order to his troops that they should use "all means to persuade the Apaches or any tribe to come in for the purpose of making peace, and when you get them together kill all the grown Indians and take the children prisoners and sell them to defray the expense of killing the adult Indians." Though there is no evidence of those extermination orders being carried out, the low brutality of it didn't sit well with Confederate political leaders. They relieved Baylor of his duty and his officer's commission.

As for the target of Baylor's attempted kidnapping, after the first failure, Anton Wulff did not wait to see if there was a second. He moved deeper into Mexico, getting a house at Monterrey. In 1863, still fearing for his family, he took them back to his birthplace of Hamburg and safety.

When the Civil War ended, Wulff and his family resettled in San Antonio once and for all. He operated a wagon train between his hometown and Chihuahua City and served as the local agent for the stagecoach that ran between the two places. He was elected alderman for the largely German 4th Ward and utilized his passion for gardening to beautify several public spaces at his own expense. The San Antonio mayor rewarded Wulff's work by naming him the first parks commissioner. When the city paved Main and Alamo Plazas, Wulff, now an alderman at large, pushed for landscaping there. He oversaw design and execution personally and was honored for transforming Alamo Plaza "from an unsightly mudhole into a circle laid off in an artistic manner, and planted with trees, rare shrubs, roses, and other flower-bearing plants."

The most visible reminder that Anton Friedrich Wulff left a positive mark in the Alamo City is the limestone house he had built at 107 King William Street. Italianate in style, it was completed in 1870 on property that was traceable back to the Mission San Antonio de Valero. Wulff's construction included a bathhouse and boathouse for use on the adjacent San Antonio River. The family sold the property in 1902, so they were not present for a major flood in the 20s that led to rerouting the watercourse in the name of flood control. The landmark house went through permutations as individual apartments and a union hall before becoming the headquarters for the San Antonio Conservation Society in 1975.

Wulff House. Wikimedia Commons

Chapter Six

Judge Roy Bean

How can the story of a person who was portrayed in movies by Paul Newman and Walter Brennan be under told? The answer lies in the difference between fact and legend, though in the case of most "Wild West" stories, it is next to impossible to completely separate the two. Roy Bean's exploits and rulings made good copy for contemporary newspapermen, and embellishment was stock in trade. Luckily for modern day history fans, the judge was plenty colorful enough in real life to make for a great story, and if some myth creeps into the telling, little harm is done. In case anyone was curious, Bean looked much more like Brennan than Newman.

Roy Bean's journey to Texas fame was filled with crime, fraud, and trouble of his own devising. Born Phantley Roy Bean, Jr. in Mason County, Kentucky, he moved to San Antonio to join up with his brother Sam, possibly out of legal necessity. At the conclusion of the Mexican War, Sam and Roy set up a trading post in the Mexican city of Chihuahua. After Roy murdered a local there, he beat a hasty retreat to California where he hooked on with his other brother, Joshua, who had become mayor of the small hamlet of San Diego. Again, Bean scarpered after shooting someone, and he and Joshua set up shop at a saloon in San Gabriel, California. When Joshua was murdered, the business became Roy's, but he killed once more. This time it was a Mexican officer who had married Bean's "girlfriend." He escaped a lynching attempt over the incident, but Roy Bean was done with the Golden State.

He headed back to brother Sam who had become sheriff of Dona Ana County in New Mexico Territory. They might have succeeded with a store and saloon in the burg of Pinos Altos, but the Civil War intervened, and Roy headed for Texas and a chance to capitalize on the hostilities. Bean found a place as a teamster hauling contraband cotton from San Antonio to Matamoros where it was shipped out for Britain on non-American ships. When the war ended, he stayed in San Antonio, supplementing his haulage income with schemes that included selling watered down milk and rustled beef. There Bean married a young girl named Virginia Chavez, and they had four children, Zulema, Roy, Jr., Sam, and Laura, but the match was not a happy one. Bean earned an aggravated assault charge against his wife after just one year. The family lived in a Mexican American slum near South Flores Street that was for a time called Beanville. It took two decades of strife and nefariousness before Bean was once again pushed or pulled out of town. He sold his possessions, left his wife, and headed for railroad camps down toward the Mexican border. It was a largely unpopulated area the Spanish called the Despoblado, perhaps the most perfectly apt placename ever created.

In 1882, he was operating a tent saloon at a railroad construction encampment nicknamed Vinegaroon after a type of scorpion. When the bridge was finished, Bean moved his operation to another Pecos River encampment called Eagle's Nest. That was where Texas Ranger Captain T. L. Oglesby described this scene: "Upon my arrival here on June 29, I visited all the railroad camps and scouted the country thoroughly.

There is the worst lot of roughs, gamblers, robbers, and pickpockets, collected here I ever saw, and without the immediate presence of the state troops, this class would prove a great detriment towards the completion of the road." The closest courthouse was 200 miles distant in Fort Stockton, and Oglesby told his superiors that he would find a magistrate to introduce some order. He settled on Bean.

Thus was born Judge Roy Bean, partially self-appointed. Eagle's Nest was renamed, likely for a Southern Pacific Railroad foreman named George Langtry. When an election was held two years later, Bean won his post with legitimacy. He lost the race after that, but then was reelected to a precinct in the newly created Val Verde County and won every contest for the ensuing decade. The new magistrate owned one law book, a copy of the 1879 *Revised Statutes of Texas*. It was the only one he ever used. The story is that when newer ones arrived, Bean burned them.

Roy Bean soon made an enemy of a powerful local landowner named Cesario Torres, but the judge circumvented that problem by setting up his saloon on railroad right-of-way, the only property Torres did not own. Soon there was a wooden building which Bean christened the Jersey Lilly after beautiful British stage actress Lillie Langtry, someone who Roy greatly admired through carte de visite photographs. Sadly, Bean misspelled her first name. Langtry was not Lillie's birthname, nor was she related to railroad man George.

The bar at the Jersey Lilly, or sometimes the front room of his later adjacent home, doubled as the local courthouse in the one-street town, and the juries were comprised of Bean's hardest drinking customers. Sometimes Roy Bean presided from a seat "on the billiard table," a true work of art with iron lion's head legs. Other occasions saw him pronounce judgment from the bar's front porch. There was no set schedule for court hearings. They took place when need and mood coincided. The justice of the peace did not allow hung juries or appeals. Like marked down merchandise, all verdicts were final. Since Langtry did not have a jail, punishments inevitably consisted of fines. Especially egregious offenders were sometimes handcuffed to the town's tree. Frequently the tariffs of sin included purchase of a dozen or two beers for all assembled. In either event, the money found its way into the pockets of Judge Roy Bean.

Unlike his fictional counterparts, the real Bean was not given to hanging people. In his entire time as magistrate he meted out only two death sentences, and one of those men escaped. Though horse thievery was a hanging offense by Texas statute, Bean did not agree. He demanded only that the culprit return the animal, and of course, pay a substantial fine to the court. Likewise, Bean occasionally disagreed with the many laws that forbade carrying a firearm. He once freed a man by saying, "If he was not standing still, he was traveling, and it's legal for travelers to carry weapons. Case dismissed." In a contrary case, the judge was summoned to officially pronounce the death of an area cowboy. After observing that the man's coat held a six-shooter and $50, Bean fined the corpse $50 for carrying a concealed weapon.

His rulings often held a measure of common sense, deliberate humor, and at least once, a heavy dollop of self-preservation. When an Irish worker named Paddy O'Rourke murdered a Chinese laborer, more than 100 of his countrymen filled the Jersey Lilly demanding that O'Rourke be freed. After thumbing through his 1879 statutes, Bean announced that he could find no specific law against "killing a Chinaman." It no doubt helped that the Irish workers were drinking heavily at the bar.

Though his court had no jurisdiction to grant divorces, Bean did so with some frequency. Divorces cost ten dollars and weddings five. Slightly less, if the circumstances demanded. Bean was even known to get out of bed in his underwear to perform a midnight marriage for those who had a sufficient fee. His weddings usually concluded with the words "and may God have mercy on your souls." On one celebrated occasion, two Tejano sheepherders came to the judge and confessed that they had fallen in love with each other's wives. Bean divorced the four then promptly married them to the spouses they desired.

Roy Bean with white beard at the second Jersey Lilly

It is easy to imagine the liberties and exaggerations devised by reporters in the name of humor, and to see why that makes the historical record of Roy Bean so challenging to decipher. One tale involves a horrible accident related to railroad bridge construction in which ten workers fell into a deep ravine. Bean rode a balky mule to the site where he swore that all ten men were dead. The fly in the ointment was that three were still breathing and moaning. Bean looked them over and said that they probably would die, and he did not want to make the trip twice. Fortunately for them, the men recovered.

In 1896 he won the vote, but Val Verde County authorities decided that Roy Bean did not meet the qualifications to continue as justice of the peace. The office was officially declared vacant and a man named Torres was appointed to fill the post. Roy Bean refused to hand over the seal of office and continued to try all cases north of the railroad tracks and west of the Pecos. That state of affairs continued for two years until Bean's son, Sam, killed a man named Upshaw, and J.P. Torres was compelled to hold an inquest.

Also in 1896, Roy Bean pulled off his greatest promotion – a heavyweight boxing match in tiny Langtry, Texas. Since prizefighting was illegal in the state, Bean set up a ring on a sandbar on the Mexican side of the Rio Grande River. He then arranged for hundreds of spectators and writers to train in from El Paso. The fight itself was a lesser spectacle. Freckled Cornishman Bob Fitzsimmons, who held the world middleweight title but was moving up to top heavyweight contender, knocked out Peter Maher in just 95 seconds. Fitzsimmons would defeat Gentleman James Corbett a year later to win the heavyweight crown.

The original two-story Jersey Lilly burned in 1896, a big year for Langtry, and Bean rebuilt it as a two room single floor building with a generous front porch. It is not large. The barroom may be 30 x 18 feet, and the attached billiard room is even smaller. Bean had lived upstairs before the fire, but he constructed an adobe house behind the saloon. He called it his opera house and crowed that it would someday be a performance hall for Ms. Langtry, but it held only his iron bed and clothes.

With his days as J.P. behind him, Roy Bean spent most of his days on his porch spinning tall tales, drinking, and cradling a shotgun, just in case. He was also known to provide charity to area people in need. After an especially long turn at drinking, at age 77 or 78, his heart and lung troubles finally caught up with Roy Bean while he slept in March 1903. He was predeceased by his pet bear, Bob.

Newsmen in Texas and beyond reveled in the creativity and orneriness of the Val Verde County Precinct 6 J.P. Some cast aspersions on him, saying that he was "no more a justice of the peace than the first jack rabbit to be met in the Big Bend brush." The *Southern Mercury* of Dallas called him "better known by far than the town in which he lived and its only claim to fame was that he lived there." The same remains true even now.

The Jersey Lilly, Bean's house, and a terrific small museum, all operated by TXDOT since 1959, still welcome visitors to Langtry. The alleged, but almost certainly not, namesake of the town did make a stop there, though not until a year after the smitten judge was in his Del Rio grave. The famous actress was touring between New Orleans and Los Angeles and made a stop in the rustic hamlet that had become associated with her name. She listened to town folk's stories about Roy Bean and later described her experience as "memorable." A letter of hers regarding the judge is on display along with Bean's guns, his Edison phonograph, carved walking stick, handcuffs, and his lone law book.

Metroplex & North Texas

Red River. Anka0380 via Wikimedia Commons

Chapter Seven

Amon Carter

Since the start of the nation, certain newspapermen have wielded outsize influence in politics and government affairs, and several people fitting that description have been Texans. No other likely rose to the heights of Fort Worth's Amon Carter, however. He built a city, cajoled a president, pioneered communications, started a great university, helped create a national park, made a personal fortune, and left a legacy that keeps giving to this day. And he did it all with magnificent Texas flair.

Carter was born in the town of Crafton, a hamlet in northwestern Wise County that likely never surpassed a high water mark of 200 residents. The family home was a one-room log cabin. Carter came along only a matter of months after Comanches had been removed from the area, and a year before the community earned a U.S. post office. He was born with the first name of Giles, but he liked his middle name better, so early in life, he changed it. Amon Carter quit school at age eleven to go to work, washing dishes at a hotel, selling chicken sandwiches to railroad passengers in nearby Bowie, and then pursuing opportunities in Oklahoma and California. In 1905, he was back in Texas and had chosen Fort Worth for his new home.

He got a job at the new *Fort Worth Star*. At age 26, Amon Carter was the startup paper's advertising manager and a favorite of the money behind the enterprise. There were two other daily newspapers in the market – the *Telegram* and the *Record*. The latter was owned by William Randolph Hearst. The *Star* was innovative in their approach. That included running an optimistic quarter page ad in the rival *Record* to announce how well they were doing and ask for 14 boys to take over new paper routes. Behind the scenes, Carter fomented much bigger plans. In 1908, looking to cement his position, Amon assembled a team of local investors to buy out the *Telegram* and merge the papers into the *Fort Worth Star-Telegram*.

Five men held the bulk of the stock in the new corporation. Carter was one of them as was Louis Wortham, a veteran newsman who was installed as editor. One of the backers was Paul Waples, a wholesale grocer who put up at least a fifth of the $125,000 incorporation funding. A few years earlier, Waples had been a major booster of the Fort Worth Interurban railroad. Ironically, Waples died in 1916 when one of those trains T-boned Waples' auto. Carter and Wortham became the name partners, and by 1923, Amon Carter stood alone at the corporate helm.

Carter was an inherent promoter. While Fort Worth itself could be viewed as a mid-sized city, Carter turned his vision to the west. The *Star-Telegram* soon had a string of different editions that went out across West Texas. Carter, who paid to bring the first airplane flight to Fort Worth in 1911, soon had bundles of his papers being transported through the air. By the 1920s, Amon Carter was arguably the most powerful man in the western half of the state.

The understanding of where his bread was buttered led Carter to create a slogan for his city – "Where the West Begins." Stoking a burning rivalry with his North Texas neighbor, he often added "and Dallas – where the east peters out." Though he was not especially fond of cowboy boots, he wore them for public appearances along with a diamond tie pin and Stetson hats which he frequently gave away. There was also an ever-present large cigar. He created a Texas cowboy businessman persona and expanded on it over the rest of his life.

Will Rogers, Jr. and Amon Carter. Library of Congress

In 1925, Carter bought a farm on Lake Worth. He called the 780-acre property Shady Oaks. Over the years, he added buildings and even moved in a cabin that had been home to Cynthia Ann Parker. The biggest thing to know about Shady Oaks was that the most influential Americans across three decades came to pay homage to Amon Carter. That certainly included Will Rogers, arguably the most beloved figure in the country and one of Carter's closest pals. It was through Rogers' syndicated newspaper columns that all of America came to know Carter as the most iconic Texan of the day.

The same year he acquired Shady Oaks, he bought out the Hearst paper in town and eliminated his last competition. Three years earlier, he had started WBAP, the first radio station in the city. The newspaper business might bring a certain power, but it was not going to make Amon Carter filthy rich. His first big business expansion followed his interest in aviation. By the end of that decade, he was part owner of American Airways and quickly convinced the company, which is today American Airlines, to headquarter in Fort Worth.

American Airways was not the only company Carter lured to his town. When oil was discovered in North Texas, he, as the youngest ever president of the Fort Worth Chamber of Commerce, got Sinclair to come. He encouraged rich men to finance skyscrapers in downtown and wheedled new oil millionaires to move to "his" city. In the late 1930s, Carter brought Convair and a huge aviation complex that became General Dynamics. After mergers and buyouts, that giant concern is now Lockheed.

In 1935, Amon Carter invested in his first successful oil well. The well was at Mattix Pool in New Mexico, and it would not be his last. Carter later claimed he had financed 90 dry holes before one hit, but it was betting heavily on oil that secured most of his many millions of dollars.

From early in his ascent, Carter proved to be civic minded. The *Star-Telegram* led a campaign for "a great state college on the plains." In 1923, he became the first board chairman of Texas Technical College, today's Texas Tech. There were anonymous gifts to the poor in Fort Worth and decades of service to the Southwestern Exposition and Livestock Show. He became the president of the Texas Big Bend Park Association that succeeded in establishing the national park. When it was finally a done deal, it was Carter who presented the deed to the land to President Roosevelt. At Christmas, Carter saw to it that every resident of his city's orphanages and senior homes received a crisp five dollar bill.

Franklin Roosevelt's New Deal had a fan in Amon Carter, and the president was a personal friend. Will Rogers even suggested that Carter might gain a cabinet appointment from FDR. The humorist said of his friend: "He is mighty well-liked by the Democrats and 50 percent of the Republicans. Well, I will say a dozen anyway."

Amon Carter, the master marketer, did not shy away from a good feud. He and Texas governors Ma and Pa Ferguson loathed one another, and on multiple occasions, there were turf wars at Texas political events. Pa Ferguson once offered $500 to any policeman willing to arrest Amon Carter. There were no takers.

The largest and longest of his grudges was against the City of Dallas. It was so serious that when business required him to travel to Big D, he brought a sack lunch rather than spend good Fort Worth money in a restaurant there. A high point of the rivalry is what happened in 1936.

Texas was ready to celebrate the centennial of the Republic, and its three largest cities were bidding to host. Logic would award the event to San Antonio, but the prize went to Dallas, a city that did not even exist in

1836, by virtue of the largest pledge of money. Fort Worth had not even been involved in the competition, but when the centennial was awarded to his nemesis, Amon Carter opened his wallet to steal some thunder from Dallas.

He decided to supersize Fort Worth's modest Frontier Days event. Carter paid a cool hundred grand to Billy Rose, the country's most famous producer of show business extravaganzas. The Fort Worth brain trust opted for salaciousness and fun. That started with gambling and giant neon signage shouting "Wild!" and "Whoopee." Rose hired Jumbo the elephant, and provided nudity in the form of scandalous fan dancer Sally Rand who had recently set the country on its ear at the Chicago World's Fair and the equally famous Ziegfield girl Ann Pennington. Carter built a jaw-dropping outdoor amphitheater and restaurant, the original Casa Manana. It boasted the world's largest revolving stage and used a wall of fountains as the stage curtain. The water cascaded into a moat.

Not that he needed any justification, but he employed his favorite phrase anyway: "You'd think Dallas invented Texas, just because they bid higher for the centennial than any other city. But we're going to put on a show of our own and teach those dudes over there where the West really begins!"

At the end of WWII, Carter, now swimming in oil money, established a foundation and earmarked large amounts of cash for a variety of cultural, medical, and educational causes. He gave to schools, hospitals, symphonies, museums, churches, parks, and camps. He sank funds into medical research. He was tireless in his civic boosterism, always wanting Fort Worth to have the best. None of it hurt his own bottom line, of course. At the very least, he was getting new subscribers to his paper, new listeners for his radio station, and new viewers for the television station he started in 1948. It was the first TV outlet in the South and Southwest and eventually changed its call letters from WBAP-TV to KXAS.

Carter had another figurative blood feud to fight with Dallas, this one over airports. In the 1940s, the federal government told the two Metroplex cities to work out a joint airport venture. They were tired of supporting both Meacham Field in Fort Worth and Love Field in Dallas, but the deep pockets in each city were not ready to settle. After years of maneuvering, Fort Worth, supported by Carter, created Greater Southwest International Airport at a Tarrant County site not far from today's DFW. Dallas continued to pump money into Love Field. Great Southwestern was renamed for Amon Carter in 1950, but the ongoing controversy remained unsettled until long after his death.

Carter is a fine example of money buying respectability. In a day when it was uncommon, he divorced twice then chose a woman 25 years his junior as wife number three. He loved to drink. His boozy parties at Shady Oaks always lasted into the wee hours. There was no beer available. Carter did not like it, but according to *Time Magazine*, there was Texas corn liquor and good Scotch to be found "in abundance." When he reached a certain limit, he was fond of pulling a revolver and shooting the joint up wherever that establishment might be. That included a Rice Hotel elevator at the 1928 Democratic Convention in Houston. At that same conclave, Carter threatened to beat up a Protestant minister who dared oppose the Catholic Al Smith as the nominee.

Amon Carter's hard living caught up to him eventually. He had a series of heart attacks starting in the early 1950s, and by the middle of the decade, he was gone.

It is tough to miss the name of Amon G. Carter in North or West Texas today. It's on buildings at Texas Tech and A&M, and it graces the football stadium at his beloved TCU. There is a lake in Montague County and a high school in Fort Worth. His hometown is also home to one of the top art museums in the state. Carter's daughter, Ruth, opened the Amon Carter Museum of American Art in 1961 to display the phenomenal collection of western paintings and sculptures that her father had amassed. The incredible showcase for the works of Frederic Remington, Charles M. Russell, and the like draws people from around the globe, and all of them are admitted free of charge.

There is even a one man play about Amon Carter. The author was enchanted by the iconic man and underscored his importance by saying, "He ran Fort Worth for 50 years. He ran the city. He ran West Texas. He was the dominant figure in this region for half a century." The play debuted in the 2020s, but it might have summoned a twinge in the man himself since the playwright, Dave Leiber, lives in Dallas.

Chapter Eight

Dallas Freedman's Cemetery

The paving over of history is nothing new. It happened to monuments from ancient Rome and Constantinople. Untold treasures of our past lie beneath every major city on Earth, and so do millions of past inhabitants. In the United States, we have readily poured asphalt atop historic cemeteries. It happened in such enlightened places as Boston, New York, and Philadelphia, and across all of Texas. Sometimes it was for new construction. Developers in far flung suburbs are still bulldozing graves today. Very often, in times not that far gone, cemeteries disappeared when city fathers simply decided they were sitting in their cars too long. Something had to be done about their inconvenience.

Without exception, the largest cities in modern Texas purposely routed their new expressways through the hearts of neighborhoods of color. In Houston, Austin, San Antonio, and El Paso, it was the same story. Many minorities did not own the dirt they lived on, and those that did would sell it cheap. Perhaps most importantly, they would put up less of a squawk. So it was with the building of Central Expressway in Dallas.

The highway, U.S. 75, ran north of downtown Dallas along the line of the old Houston & Texas Central tracks. Modern freeways often do that because railroad right of ways are long, and they go places. They connect major towns, and contracts to get them are easy to negotiate. Buying from one entity is infinitely simpler than haggling over a thousand small real estate deals. But those strips of land are also narrow, and the government usually needs to acquire land on one side or another. These projects aim for an impossible goal of relieving traffic congestion. To paraphrase singer Robert Earl Keen, the road goes on forever, and construction never ends.

To get the land for the original Central Expressway, TXDOT planned to pave over a solid acre of Freedman's Cemetery, a space of such historical, spiritual, and cultural significance that it is tough to quantify. More than 1,500 homes and businesses would also meet the wrecking ball in the name of Central, almost all of them belonging to Black families who had lived in the neighborhood since Emancipation. Lest anyone think that there was widespread concern over these developments, the *Dallas Morning News* wrote in 1946: "It is hoped that no unwarranted delay in the removal of tenants and city-owned houses will upset the schedule in beginning this work."

Road crews in the late 40s used many of the stone and concrete monuments paid for by grieving families to fill ditches and other low spots, then they poured tarmac over the top. Central Expressway opened in 1949, and presumably, the first traffic jam on it occurred about a week later.

Freedom Colonies sprang up around the South in the months and years following the end of the Civil War. As Black families left their former plantation homes, they needed somewhere to live. They sought work and protection amongst each other, and new communities were created in rural areas and adjacent to larger towns. Before the 1860s ended, many of these new settlements had added churches, schools, and cemeteries.

North Dallas was one of those enclaves. It sat roughly two miles north of downtown Dallas, a village founded in 1841 where two Indian traces forded the Trinity River. Dallas grew quickly as Americans flocked to perceived opportunity first in the Republic of Texas and then the state. During the first quarter century, a fair number of new Dallasites brought enslaved Africans with them. Some scholarship suggests that when their property died, the slave owners allowed them to be buried on the fringes of the Old Dallas Burial Ground which was a few blocks north of modern-day Dealy Plaza. There were possibly slave burials in what would become the North Dallas community as early as 1861, but evidence of that is mostly anecdotal.

The first recorded transaction came in April 1869 when Sam Eakins, "a trustee for the Colored people of the Town of Dallas," paid $25 for an acre of land as "a burying ground for the free people of color and his successors." That confirms an active burial ground at least by 1869. An additional three acres were purchased a decade later from what was likely the same Bowles family. By that time, the Freedman's Cemetery had an official board of trustees.

One name on that board list was A.R. Griggs. He had been brought to Texas from Georgia as a nine-year old enslaved boy, but upon gaining his freedom, Griggs sought an education and became a Baptist preacher. His was one of the first two congregations in North Dallas, a number that eventually rose to seven. The first schools in the neighborhood were associated with those churches.

Even a decade or two after Emancipation, a steady stream of freed people were still settling in North Dallas. The community developed like those in every other large city across the United States. Denied full rights from the White business community, a parallel economy arose. There were Black-owned groceries, livery stables, and tailor shops, Black doctors, dentists, metal smiths, and teamsters. When the H&TC railroad passed through, many of the residents latched on to employment there. As Megan Kimble of the *Texas Observer* pointed out, "it was a place of hope and growth."

Not long after the 20th century opened, St. Peter's Academy, a Catholic boarding school for Black children, began operations. North Dallas got a movie theatre, a Knights of Pythias Temple, and a small slew of music clubs, especially during the dawn of jazz. Many cultural historians place North Dallas in the same breath as the thriving Black social scenes in New York, Los Angeles, Houston, Chicago, and Memphis. But the grim reaper of progress comes disproportionately for communities of color.

Freedman's Cemetery's activity began to decline, and the last recorded burial there came in 1925. By that time, three large White developments had sprung up immediately above North Dallas, and they seemingly encroached on the edges of the cemetery. The purchases of expanded right of ways for the railroad and new and rerouted surface streets took more of the community. Then came the expressway. By the early 1950s, the majority of the old Freedom Colony had been eaten away. In 1965, the last descendants association of the cemetery deeded their interest to the City of Dallas. The city put up a sign and a few concrete benches. They mowed the grass, but they never did get around to erecting a promised fence. A full generation passed by. And then the forgotten was rediscovered, accidentally, in the name of progress.

In 1987, The Texas Department of Transportation decided to widen Central Expressway. American society had evolved a bit in the previous 40 years, and a state archaeologist was sent out to do a survey. They noticed a sign that said "Freedman's Memorial Park," and that brought more archaeologists and a hold on the work. A largely ignored report that a city road crew had found five bodies under the pavement when they widened Lemmon Avenue again saw the light of day. So, the archaeologists dug, and they found bodies. Singly, in groups, and in droves. A total of 1,157 of them, many of whom were born into bondage and died as free people. TXDOT decided to exhume all of them and reinter them in what would become the Freedman's Cemetery Memorial.

The work required a team of archaeologists and researchers along with a very talented shovel operator who could pull levers that scraped his big metal bucket across the ground with tolerance within one half inch. Given that the century old wooden coffins were already deteriorating, that precision was important. The team determined that about a quarter of almost 7,000 burials had been paved over for the expressway. The rest had been stripped of "all physical above-ground reminders" and covered in fresh sod for a park.

The state's effort was remarkable for both its size, it was one of the largest such projects ever undertaken in the United States, and its duration, the work lasted almost six years in total. It also tried to fill in the gaps of an historical wrong. None of the graves were identified with headstones, so researchers set out to learn as much as possible from the contents and context of the burials. James Davidson, who wrote his master's thesis at the University of Texas about his work on the excavation project, said that each burial site generated an average of 29 pages of documentation. That meant analysis was done on skeletons, teeth, grave contents, coffin hardware, and surroundings to combine into 33,000 pages of information in all. Some 185,000 photographs were taken and catalogued. Researchers also combed through archives for written records. They were able to greatly narrow the time period for all of the excavated burials except one.

Of the 1,157 bodies exhumed, over three quarters were from the last major active period of Freedman's Cemetery – 1900 to 1907. Just 5.5% were prior to 1885. The National Register narrative reports that in 1987 only one stone was visible when the project got underway. It marked the grave of Emma McCune, emancipated at age 10 and dead at 48 from breast cancer. It carried the inscription "Gone from our homes but not from our hearts."

Only one other marker was uncovered intact. There were also pieces and shards from the stones of countless others, the markers which had been used as fill rubble. One piece still held a poem: "How much light, how much joy, is buried with a darling boy."

As TXDOT was wrapping up the excavation of graves, the City of Dallas commissioned Black sculptor David Newton to create a fitting memorial to the people who had lived and died in North Dallas. He imagined something that would serve as a collective headstone, but he also wanted more. He later told the *Texas Observer*: "My primary theme for the project was telling the whole African American genesis, from freedom in Africa to enslavement and then to emancipation here in the United States."

The end result of Newton's work includes a Warrior and Prophetess representing West African culture, two shackled figures in bronze bas-reliefs that are struggling through the Middle Passage of the slave ships, and beyond a large archway are a newly emancipated couple. Two headstones from the original cemetery configuration are embedded in a black granite slab. It brings some peaceful healing to the long forgotten neighborhood, though the relentless traffic noise that brought the community's demise is always there.

Nearby the Freedman's Cemetery Memorial are other historic Dallas graveyards – Greenwood, the Jewish cemetery Emanu-El, and Calvary, a Catholic burial ground. Today a person can take a tour that visits all of them and once again pay tribute to Dallas' forebears.

Chapter Nine

Red River Bridge War

"It's 4:57, and ou still sucks."

University of Texas alums have disliked their Oklahoma counterparts since their first game in October 1900. For the record, The Longhorns won that by a score of 28 to 2.

There is an episode in the history of the two states in which the animosity went beyond a fun-loving football rivalry, however. It contained all of the usual grandstanding and braggadocio connected to the gridiron, but this one came with armed men in uniforms.

At the start of July 1931, a new bridge across the Red River opened. The span, built jointly by the two states, was on the Jefferson Highway, one of the earliest designated national motorways. The Jefferson had opened 20 years prior with a motto of "Pine to Palm," and it allowed intrepid automobile enthusiasts to venture from New Orleans to the Minnesota-Alberta border. The $225,000 bridge connected the Texas town of Denison with the town of Colbert in Bryan County, Oklahoma.

Everyone was happy about the development: city fathers, state officials, and especially, the citizens who traveled the two-lane pavement.

The old system of highways was both antiquated and expensive. River crossings like bridges and ferries were privately owned. The proprietors of these crossings raked the income from both ends. They contracted with the state, built a station house at each end of the span, and charged tolls to the motorists. A state investigation out of Austin confirmed that the toll-collecting entities not only frequently bumped up their rates, it was highly likely that they had been "fudging numbers" about crossings in order to pocket more state money. State representative Jake Loy, who represented Grayson County, came close to accusing them of that fraud outright. Taxpayers badly wanted nationalized federal highways that included free access across rivers.

Even though Texas and the nation was mired in the lowest ebb of the Great Depression, people in the Red River Valley were getting what they wanted. The bridge at Denison was not the only one under construction, but it was about to be the one that got the first pushback from the private bridge owner.

That was the Red River Bridge Company, and they had watched the free bridge going up just parallel to their own old toll span. Clearly, it did not sit well. Just as the new bridge was done, the company filed in the federal court at Houston seeking an injunction to stop the Texas Highway Department from opening the new road. The toll company claimed that the highway commission had promised to pay $60,000 to buy out the old operation plus another ten grand a month if the new bridge opened within a specified window. The court granted the injunction, and Texas Governor Ross Sterling duly ordered barricades erected on the south end of the new bridge, and, for good measure, the south end of other new bridges – north of Ringgold on Highway 81 and on Highway 77 at Gainesville. He was in no mood to hand out the state's money so freely, and highway personnel stayed by the barricades to enforce the injunction.

In Oklahoma, however, their governor was not so inclined. William Murray, a native Texan who sported a big, bushy moustache and the magical nickname of Alfalfa Bill, issued an executive order on July 16 to open the bridge. Oklahoma had a geographic ace in the hole. Back in 1803, when the United States completed the massive Louisiana Purchase from France, the treaty granted the U.S. both sides of the Red River along that portion of the southern boundary of their new land. The Texas side was claimed by Spain, and no one asked the Spanish what they thought, but the boundary stood, as it still does today.

Alfalfa Bill announced that since his state owned both banks of the river, Oklahoma's half of the jointly owned bridge ran north and south. Furthermore, the State of Oklahoma was not named in the Texas injunction, so Murray had an Oklahoma Highway Department crew cross the bridge and demolish Ross Sterling's barricades. W.R. Ely, the Texas Highway Commission chair applauded Murray's action. Texas had already removed the barrier at the south end of the Highway 81 bridge, and the Gainesville one was allegedly delayed by construction trouble. But the Denison bridge was a serious point of contention.

Sterling responded to his northern neighbor's actions by ordering the barriers at Denison rebuilt, and he sent three Texas Rangers to prevent further hijinks. Accompanying the Rangers was William Warren Sterling, who the like-named governor had appointed as state adjutant general, the person who oversees both the Rangers and the Texas National Guard. W.W. Sterling had a background as an A&M dropout, South Texas cowboy, U.S. Cavalry "posseman," hired scout, and deputy sheriff. The Texans clearly meant business.

So, too, did Alfalfa Bill Murray. On July 17, the morning after the Rangers arrived, Murray ordered Oklahoma highway crews to destroy "the northern approaches" to the still operating toll bridge. That led to giant community meetings in Denison and Sherman. The public was several clicks north of outraged over the closure of all traffic across the Red, and they sent their demands to the legislature in Austin. The state lege, already meeting in special session, voted to allow the Red River Bridge Company to sue the state to collect damages. They were willing to do most anything to get rid of the injunction. The State of Texas and the toll bridge owners asked that the federal court in Houston dissolve its previous order.

Alfalfa Bill Murray and his guardsmen. Oklahoma Historical Society

William Henry Murray was a Farmer's Alliance populist and a born headline-seeker. He had failed in both the newspaper and law businesses in Texas, and that's what sent him north across the river to make his fortune in the Chickasaw nation of Indian Territory. He was involved in politics, and though he failed in his efforts to create an American State of Sequoyah for native Indians, he wrote a large chunk of the Oklahoma Constitution. Murray remained a progressive to his core.

At the same time that he was playing to reporters in the bridge controversy, he was also threatening to shut down every oil well in Oklahoma unless that industry raised prices to a minimum of a dollar a barrel. Oil companies promised to stand firm. Though the bridge issue offered a diversion, out of control oil drilling was a serious problem. The recent discovery of the East Texas Field and huge reserves in Oklahoma had glutted the market with petroleum.

Murray said "the state and schools are getting nothing in the way of taxes at the present price – a top of 50 cents a barrel. We can't let this go on. Depleting our resources and getting no taxes from them."

The Texas governor was wringing his hands about oil prices at the same exact moment, as well. Ross Sterling, a conservative Democrat, was one of the five founders of Humble Oil Company. Black gold had made him an extremely wealthy man. On the same day that Alfalfa Bill was making headlines even in Texas newspapers, Sterling walked down the Capitol hallway and testified at the invitation of the Texas Senate. As an old oilman, his perspective may have been slightly different than Murray's, nonetheless, he told the senators that rock bottom oil prices must be eliminated.

"I think the oil industry is suffering more than all others – more than agriculture. Oil should sell at a dollar a barrel; nevertheless it is selling at ten cents," the governor said. He admitted that he was generally against government oversight of business, but "we will have to forget what we used to believe improper. The great thing wrong with the oil business is overproduction. How to regulate that is up to you people."

Oklahoma had enjoyed a free hand that allowed as much
bridge-related grandstanding as Alfalfa Bill desired. That changed on
July 24, the day after the legislature down in Austin worked out their
deal with the toll bridge owners. Governor Murray got wind that the
federal district court at Muskogee was in the process of issuing an order
enjoining him from closing off the northern approaches to the old pay
bridge. He responded immediately.

A matter of hours before the injunction was officially issued, Alfalfa
Bill declared martial law in a thin strip of land that included the northern
ramps to both bridges – toll and free. He also ordered Oklahoma
National Guard troops to the area and announced that, as commander
in chief of the guard, his position superseded the court's order. The
governor had his aides drive him down to what reporters were dubbing
"the war zone" and appeared in front of photographers brandishing an
antique revolver.

The other federal court, the one in Houston, suspended their
injunction the next day thanks to the deal with the legislators in Austin,
and Ross Sterling called his three Texas Rangers home. A line of cheering
motorists stretched over a mile on the Texas side of the free bridge, and
as soon as the barriers were removed, they crossed into Oklahoma, made
U-turns, and came back to Denison. With the free bridge now open on
the Texas side, Governor Murray also reopened the northern approaches
to the toll bridge, but that was a short-lived reprieve.

A mere two days later, Murray told assembled reporters that he had
caught wind of rumors that the Houston injunction would be brought
back and the shiny new free bridge permanently closed. He extended his
martial law all the way to the Oklahoma boundary marker, which, of
course, stood on the Texas side of the Red. Now Oklahoma guardsmen

were stationed at both ends of the free bridge. Some Texas papers called it an "invasion."

The comically tense state of interstate affairs lasted just over another week. The Houston injunction was officially and permanently dissolved on August 6, 1931. Governor Murray moved his guardsmen to the Oklahoma oilfields to enforce martial law where he was carrying out his order regarding the price of crude.

The new, free highway bridges being enjoyed elsewhere in Texas at the start of the 1930s still had another controversy to endure. Just one month after the situation at Denison was resolved, another toll bridge company on the Red River threatened to cause trouble all over again. The Gainesville Red River Bridge Company operated a span at Sacra's Ferry, an historic crossing. Perhaps observing the public relations melee to their east, the Gainesville toll outfit filed an injunction "to stop traffic on the free bridge."

The angst in Gainesville was not over a potential closing as much as it was over the location of the new bridge and highway. While the toll bridge at the old Sacra's Ferry site connected to Grand Avenue in Gainesville, the new road, designated Highway 40, used the location of another old crossing – Brown's Ferry. That placed the new road three miles west of downtown, and worried the Gainesville merchants to no end.

In Oklahoma City, Alfalfa Bill saw another opportunity to tweak Texas noses. Claiming that the road bed on the Texas side of the Red River "had settled approximately five feet below the bridge roadway," Murray made the generous offer of road-building equipment and "Oklahoma talent to actually use it." The Texans demurred.

There was construction needed, but nothing to do with the
new bridge. The concerned citizens of Gainesville "raised funds by
contribution to build the three mile detour from Highway No. 77 to the
short, completed section of Highway No. 40." It solved the problem of
downtown being bypassed, and in September 1931, the old toll bridge
at Sacra's Ferry closed.

The two major players in the Red River Bridge War diverged to
different paths. Soon after the events of summer 1931, Ross Sterling
declared martial law in Texas oil fields to enforce the drilling regulation
issued by the Texas Railroad Commission. He lost reelection in favor of
the return of Miriam Ferguson and moved back to Houston. Sterling
sold his newspaper, the *Houston Post Dispatch*, started the Sterling Oil
& Refining Company, became chairman of a large bank, and soon
amassed another fortune. Alfalfa Bill Murray began believing his own
press clippings. He toured the nation as a Democratic candidate for
president with the slogan of "Bread, Butter, Bacon, and Beans." Murray
got only a single delegate outside of Oklahoma and made a permanent
enemy of the nominee, Franklin Roosevelt. He retired to his farm near
Tishimingo, Oklahoma and wrote pamphlets railing virulently against
the New Deal, Blacks, and Jews. As for the new, free highway bridge
at Denison, on December 6, 1995, it was dynamited and replaced by a
newer one.

Chapter Ten

Ripley Arnold

Ripley Arnold was not born in Texas. In fact, he never set foot in the great state until the final decade of his short life, but those years touch on several ingrained elements of the Lone Star legend.

Arnold was born on the Mississippi Gulf Coast and wrangled an appointment to the United States Military Academy at age 17. The Army certainly became aware of the red-headed young man during his tenure. He penned musical compositions that became favorites on the campus. Arnold also demonstrated a temper and a willingness to do violence. He fought a duel, his first of several in life, at an infamous West Point drinking den called Benny Havens'. The tavern sat outside the Academy gates and also supplied whiskey for smuggling back to the cadet barracks. It was the subject of the most celebrated and lasting song co-written by cadet Ripley Arnold.

Cadet Arnold graduated 33rd in a class of 45. It might be overstating that the class had a snakebitten reputation, but 14 of the young men were killed before the Civil War even started. Twenty-one officers from Arnold's class served in that conflict, half of them, including P.G.T. Beauregard and W.J. Hardee, for the Confederates.

Like many of the newly minted second lieutenants, Ripley Arnold was assigned to duty in Florida just in time for the Seminole War. It was an era when the U.S. Army still had regiments designated as dragoons, and it was as part of that outfit that Arnold earned two promotions for gallant conduct. One such act was charging the Seminole's line with only four men. There is a fine line between gallant and foolhardy.

Following his duty in Florida, Arnold returned to his hometown long enough to elope with his fourteen-year old girlfriend, Catherine Bryant. The wedding, in fact, took place on the birthday of Arnold's "blue-eyed, brown haired lass." They married in nearby Pass Christian and remained together until his death, having five children along the way.

The first time Arnold saw Texas soil was at the outset of the Mexican War. He fought with "promptness, coolness and courage" according to his immediate superior at the battles of Palo Alto and Resaca de la Palma near the Rio Grande. His actions earned him a brevet promotion to major. Arnold stayed under the overall command of General William Worth until after the Battle of Monterrey. He was transferred to Winfield Scott's army in time to fight at Molino del Rey and capture Mexico City in 1847. By then, he had the regular army rank of captain.

Rip Arnold's big post-war assignment was to lead Companies F and I of the Second U.S. Dragoons to northern Texas and establish a new military post "at or near the confluence of the West Fork and the Clear Fork of the Trinity River." He and his men set up at Fort Graham, a new outpost built atop the site of an Anadaca Indian camp on the western edge of present day Hill County. That spot is currently beneath the waters of Lake Whitney. Arnold's men were the first soldiers to occupy Fort Graham.

After barely two months at Fort Graham, Arnold took the 42 men of Company F and headed north to find a site for the next post. Lieutenant

Fowler Hamilton was left in charge at Fort Graham overseeing a skeleton crew of troopers. Arnold located what he believed to be the ideal location and named it in honor of his old commanding general, William Worth, who had only recently succumbed to cholera in San Antonio.

Camp Worth was built on a river bluff and was completed in mid-winter. The company constructed a barracks, mess hall, commissary, blacksmith's forge, infirmary, and stables. They also installed a horse-powered sawmill to aid in their efforts. Major Arnold and his troops stayed at the new Camp Worth for about two years, and relations with the native Indians was relatively quiet. Most of the indigenous Texans he saw were those who came into the camp to trade captured horses. It was a sad time for the major and his family who had joined him in North Texas, since two of the couple's daughters died of cholera there. They were buried near the fort. It was doubly difficult for Kate Arnold who, now at age 25, was the lone woman at the outpost. After a brief recall to duty in Washington, D.C., Arnold was returned to Texas to command Fort Graham, once again bringing his family with him.

Forts Worth and Graham were the northern end of the frontier defense line established by the army after Texas joined the United States. The southern end of the line of some eight military posts was anchored by Fort Inge at Uvalde and Fort Duncan near Eagle Pass. Prior to statehood, small bands of rangers patrolled the countryside, responding to reports of trouble on the edges of the Comancheria. Arnold launched at least one preemptive raid against the war parties of chiefs Jim Ned and Feathertail. The soldiers ran down the Comanches in what is now Palo Pinto County, killing Chief Jim Ned in the process. Comanches never raided as far east as Fort Worth after that action.

Depending on one's point of view, Arnold can be called either a strict disciplinarian or a bit of a sadist if he felt he had recalcitrant men under his command. When one soldier stole a hog from a neighboring farm, Arnold ordered the man tied up in front of the officers' quarters. He left him there for several hours in the unrelenting July sun with the entrails of the slaughtered animal adorning his neck.

Things came to a crashing end for Major Arnold on September 6, 1853. He had what was often known then as a rencontre with the post surgeon, Dr. Josephus Steiner. The two men had feuded for some time over matters both military and personal, specifically Steiner's criticism of Arnold's parenting. On the morning of the gunfight, Major Arnold sought to arrest Steiner for drunken rowdiness the previous night. Instead, the not-so-good doctor pumped four bullets into the major's body, and Arnold expired fifteen minutes later. Steiner, who fled after the killing, was acquitted by a civil jury and escaped an Army court-martial. His lawyers were future Texas governor Richard Coke and William H. Parsons, who later became a Confederate general. Like many murder defenses, their case attacked the victim. It was established to the jury's satisfaction that Arnold had been procuring Army horses under sketchy circumstances and then pocketing the money from their sale. The attorneys claimed that Steiner knew of the scheme and was in the process of exposing the major. One defense witness testified that Arnold promised "I will put him out of the way." The allegations brought forth at trial did nothing to dissuade generations of leaders in Fort Worth from honoring Ripley Arnold.

The major was buried at Fort Graham, not far from where he fell. A short time after, his remains were dug up and brought back to Pioneer's Rest Cemetery, less than a mile north of old Fort Worth. His resting place is marked by a large engraved boulder and is near the graves of his two infant daughters. Arnold's reburial came complete with full Masonic rites, allegedly the first such ceremony ever performed in Fort Worth.

The City of Fort Worth puts its birthday as June 6, 1849. The massive stockyards trace their beginnings to Major Ripley Arnold, though that may be a bit of a stretch. There is no doubt that the army had great need of cattle and horses.

Ripley Arnold Statue in Fort Worth.
Wikimedia Commons

Both Fort Worth and Fort Graham were abandoned by the Army in 1853. The latter moldered into oblivion, but the former is currently the fifth largest city in Texas. Though the two events were not related, the fort established on the Trinity lasted only eleven days longer than its founder.

Chapter Eleven

Pappy O'Daniel

For some, the name Pappy O'Daniel is a fictional character from the Coen Brothers classic *O, Brother, Where Art Thou*, but he was very much a real person who dominated Texas politics for over a decade despite a staggeringly ineffectual record. Virtually no one today would claim that the real O'Daniel, not the wonderful political caricature played by Charles Durning, possessed even an ounce of scruples.

W. Lee O'Daniel, the son of a Union Civil War veteran, was born in Ohio, raised in Kansas, and spent time in New Orleans before he moved to Fort Worth at age 35 as the local sales manager of the Burrus Mills flour company. Three years later, he took over the firm's radio advertising, writing songs and speaking about religion on the air. Higher ups at the mill also decided to hire a bunch of musicians to play on the radio and at live appearances under the name of the mills highest selling flour. They were called the Light Crust Doughboys.

From their first appearance, O'Daniel hated the Doughboys. In his opinion, they were too hillbilly sounding, and after the second week on air, he cancelled their deal. Letters poured into Burrus Mills, and O'Daniel relented. He was nothing if not adaptable to the moment.

The Light Crust Doughboys were soon back, and American music was forever changed.

The trio was an already existing group playing around the area under the name of their leader, fiddler Bob Wills. The other members were guitarist Herman Arnspiger and vocalist Milton Brown. They went out live over the airwaves at noon every weekday and developed such a following that O'Daniel expanded the company's radio presence across the state and into Oklahoma. In 1933, O'Daniel fired Bob Wills, the most famous band member, for drinking and missing broadcasts. Wills formed another band called the Texas Playboys. The flour mill hired new musicians to imitate the Wills sound, and they recorded top-selling records. O'Daniel remained their manager and radio announcer until he entered politics. In spite of initially dismissing the jazzy sound, his flip flop on western swing is easily his biggest contribution to Texas.

Lee O'Daniel was ambitious, but not especially smart. His radio appearances, however, made him exceedingly popular in North Texas. Around the time he was elected to a term as president of the Fort Worth Chamber of Commerce, he managed to finally alienate himself from his employers. Burrus Mills canned him. O'Daniel, now known to everyone as Pappy, started his own flour company and christened it Hillbilly Flour. The persona he detested just seven years earlier was one he now fully embraced. Almost needless to say, Hillbilly Flour had their own touring band. Pappy understood public relations.

After residing in Texas for fewer than a dozen years, loyal radio listeners bought into O'Daniel's questions about whether he should run for governor. With no legal prohibition against it, he laid out his platform on the airwaves. There was a great deal of Bible waving and talk about the Ten Commandments. His key policy goals were $30 old age pensions, industrialization, and tax cuts. There was no explanation as to how he would accomplish the first two in harmony with the latter. O'Daniel also never missed a chance to extol the great virtues of Hillbilly Flour. He employed PR men to direct his appearances as a hillbilly candidate not wise to the ways of politics or government, always holding his Bible aloft and always accompanied by the Hillbilly Boys band playing *Beautiful Texas*, a song he wrote. In rural Texas, his crowds were large and enthusiastic. He also sold 75,000 copies of the sheet music and 100,000 78rpm records.

Thirteen gubernatorial candidates made the race for the Democratic Primary in 1938. In a one-party state, it was the only election that counted. His two main opponents were the state's attorney general, William McCraw, and a sitting Railroad Commission member named Ernest Thompson. A darkhorse candidate named James A. Ferguson, no doubt looking to capitalize on the name similarity to former governor James E. Ferguson, was also among the field. Pappy O'Daniel proved the power of mass media. He won the primary election without a runoff, getting 51.4% of the vote. In the general election, Democrat O'Daniel won almost 97% of the total count. The Republican did manage to outpoll both the Socialist and the Communist candidates.

A minor early scandal was that O'Daniel had neglected to pay his poll tax and therefore could not even vote, but the bigger issue was his reneging on every campaign promise he had made. He wanted to abolish capital punishment, but that topic was not broached again. Vowing to block any attempt at a sales tax while he was a candidate, as governor, O'Daniel pushed a secret tax plan written entirely by manufacturing lobbyists that amounted to a double helping of sales tax. After the legislature voted the plan down, Pappy campaigned against his opponents in the House and Senate, and the majority of them lost in 1940. He also won a second two-year term as governor.

During that second campaign, O'Daniel announced that he had wired President Roosevelt to inform him of fifth column traitors operating in Texas. Like Joe McCarthy over a decade later, O'Daniel claimed he had a list of Communist and Nazi sympathizers in Texas factories. No names were ever produced and no saboteurs were ever found, but his constant harping on catchphrases worked.

Pappy O'Daniel campaigning in McAllen 1940s.
McAllen Public Library

O'Daniel was largely isolated as governor. He did not get along with legislators on any personal level, and proved unable to make deals to pass any agenda, diaphanous as it was. His main focuses by his second term were to curtail academic freedom at the University of Texas and to crush organized labor which was a powerful force in the Lone Star State. His big business backers demanded it. He developed a habit of vetoing bills that he did not fully comprehend, but 18 of his 57 vetoes were overridden by the legislature. It is a record that still stands.

In 1941, halfway through his second term, Pappy O'Daniel decided to switch offices and run for the United States Senate in a special election following the death of Senator Morris Sheppard. He was pitted against a total of 28 other candidates in the open election. Among them were a "goat gland doctor," a tin-can reclaimer, a former bootlegger, a homeless Dallas man, and a laxative maker. The four frontrunners were Governor O'Daniel, the sitting attorney general, Gerald Mann, Martin Dies, the East Texas congressman and head of the House Un-American Activities Committee, and a young, progressive congressman named Lyndon Johnson. LBJ was closest with the Roosevelt administration, and he campaigned tirelessly on that bond and gained great popularity with the large number of Texans who supported the New Deal. FDR stopped short of an endorsement, but when LBJ announced his candidacy from the White House steps, the president said that Lyndon was "a very old, old friend of mine." Johnson and O'Daniel seemed poised to move slightly away from the field. Last second points were scored when LBJ read a telegram from FDR calling O'Daniel's scheme for a separate Texas army and navy "preposterous."

On election night Johnson held a comfortable lead of more than 5,000 votes. The *New York Times* reported Johnson's victory, but as "corrected" returns from 17 East Texas counties came in over the following days, a few thousand votes moved from the other candidates into the column for Pappy O'Daniel. The final tally that included the manipulated ballots gave O'Daniel a thousand vote win. Former governor Jim "Pa" Ferguson took credit for the fraud because his cronies in the liquor business wanted O'Daniel out of the state and in a spot where he could not harm their profits. Lyndon Johnson vowed never to be blindsided in such a manner again.

Once in the Senate, O'Daniel's main focus was to attack organized labor, and he was repeatedly on the losing end of votes by huge margins. He drew serious opposition when the seat came up for a full term election in 1942. Not one but two former governors, Jimmy Allred and Dan Moody, challenged him. O'Daniel cried that there was a conspiracy between his two opponents and "communist labor leader racketeers." Many conservatives, fed up by their man's hijinks, backed Allred in the runoff. O'Daniel countered by falsely claiming to be a backer of President Roosevelt. Once again, his radio broadcasts rallied just enough rural votes to reelect him.

Back in the Senate, this time for six years, he opposed FDR more than any other Southern Democrat. In 1944, he joined the oil and business-backed Texas Regulars, a third party attempt to wrest the state's electoral votes from Roosevelt's total, with inflammatory radio chatter. One of their main concerns was the court decision that had ended the Whites-only Democratic Primary. Roosevelt won Texas and the general election easily. By the time the 1948 Senate election rolled around, Texans had sniffed out Pappy O'Daniel for the incompetent politician he had always been. With his pre-election poll standings at 7%, he declined to run for reelection.

There were two final gasps for O'Daniel as he put on desperate campaigns for governor in 1956 and 1958. His major theme both times was running against the "Communist-inspired" Supreme Court decision of Brown v. Board of Education which desegregated American schools.

Chapter Twelve

The Texas Airline War

The history of how Texans fly around the state is a tangled tale, and the case could be made that a good chunk of it starts in Oklahoma. Thomas Braniff, a very successful Oklahoma City insurance man, and four buddies put a down payment on a secondhand five-seat Stinson Detroiter airplane in 1928 and started flying between OKC and Tulsa with Braniff's little brother, Paul, at the controls. The shoestring operation was soon bought by one conglomerate and then another, but by 1936, rebranded as Braniff Airways, the company was flying Lockheed Vegas on routes that included Chicago, Kansas City, St. Louis, and Wichita Falls.

Still the airline was on the verge of insolvency in 1934 when Paul Braniff went to Washington, D.C. to complain in front of Congress about certain companies holding a monopoly on airmail routes. Just like in the days of the stagecoach, moving the mail was where the consistent money was. Paul returned home with a contract to fly the mail between Dallas and Chicago. Braniff Airways promptly moved its operations and maintenance facilities to Love Field. One year later, Braniff bought Long and Harmon Air Service, another Texas carrier. With the purchase came additional mail routes that included the Panhandle and Brownsville with connections to Mexico. The Braniff slogan became "From the Great Lakes to the Gulf."

Airmail was the very lifeblood for regional airlines. It started in 1918 with Army pilots then with ex-Army daredevils who carried mail through fog, snow, rain, sleet, and darkest night following riverbeds and railroads for navigation and sometimes using half-empty whiskey bottles as air level indicators. Of the first 200 government pilots hired to fly mail, 35 died in crashes. The Post Office led the way with navigational lights and beacons at landing fields. Then in 1925, the department passed on the routes to existing small carriers. At a time when few people traveled by "aeroplane," it was steady income for the airlines that got the contracts, and often corporate death for those who did not. Braniff was now among the haves.

There were other early airline entrants in the Lone Star skies. Texas Air Transports, underwritten by a who's who of Fort Worth investors, was awarded the first two Texas airmail routes just three months after Charles Lindbergh crossed the Atlantic. One of those twice daily flights ran between Dallas, Houston, and Galveston, and the other serviced Dallas, Waco, Austin, San Antonio, and Laredo. T.A.T. was doing so well off the mail that it was bought out by A.P. Barrett, a former Texas legislator who saw riches to be made in the transportation industry.

Bowen Airlines, started by a Fort Worth family who was successful with motor coaches, was another pioneering carrier. The Bowens had also been investors in T.A.T. Bowen's first plane was destroyed in a Houston hangar by a Gulf storm in the summer of 1930. Its replacement started flying a return route between Fort Worth and Houston that

October. The airline had a good run, five and a half years and more than four million miles flown, but its failure to ever secure the steady income from an air mail route led to its shut down in 1936.

When WWII arrived, Braniff gave more than half its fleet over to military use, and airline personnel trained pilots, mechanics, and radio operators. Most importantly for the long term, the airline acted on a notion Paul Braniff had begun exploring years earlier – they expanded into Latin America. First Mexico, then Ecuador, Panama, and Cuba. After Thomas Braniff died in a plane crash near Shreveport, Charles Beard took over as president and added more South American routes and even a maintenance facility in Peru. With 1.5 billion passenger miles by 1964 and a new ten-story headquarters at Love Field, it was one of the world's largest airlines.

Another airline came on the Texas scene in the 1940s, though it was no threat to Braniff. Earl McKaughan was a Houston oilfield hauler who had learned to fly in 1928. In 1940, he started an air service company, selling airplanes and training pilots. It was the latter capacity that won his Aviation Enterprises a government contract to teach more than 1,000 women to fly for vital war effort jobs with the Women's Airforce Service Pilots.

When the war ended, Aviation Enterprises changed its name to Trans-Texas Airways. The inaugural route went from its Houston home to Victoria and San Antonio. The aircraft was a Douglas DC-3 that held 21 passengers. Soon the airline added a second plane and service to Dallas, Fort Worth, Brownwood, San Angelo, and Palestine. Most of the pilots, like chief flyer A.J. High, and many of the mechanics were just out of the service. Majorie Post was hired as chief engineer for the carrier when women did not get such jobs, and Lamar Muse came aboard as treasurer.

Texans joked about "Tinker Toy Airways" or "Tree Top Airways," but they loved the carrier. The Little TTA prop planes shuttled them from Tyler to Lufkin for under ten bucks four times a day, or from Alpine to McCamey or Edinburg to Beeville, all for a similar price. Sometimes the planes seemed to fly as low as crop dusters, but a Lone Star graced the tail and flight attendants wore skirts, vests, cowboy boots, and hats. For almost two decades, Texans had two home state choices - Braniff with its expanding global footprint, and TTA which aimed to stay dependably Texan.

Nothing stays local and comfortable forever, though. In 1964, a Dallas insurance company called Greatamerica Corporation examined an internal study that showed Braniff to be one of the worst managed companies in the country. Greatamerica bought it. To run its new acquisition, they brought in a man who had started at Pioneer Airlines then worked his way up to being an Executive VP at Continental Airlines in his early 40s. He was Harding Lawrence, described by the *New York Times* as "a dark-haired Texan who looks as though an agency had sent him over to play the part of a dynamic airline president." *Texas Monthly* saw him as the "cold shark of the boardroom, charm and calculation mixed in his icy stares and fixed smiles."

Whatever Lawrence might have been personally, he wanted his airline to be flamboyant. He hired a New York marketing firm, and not long afterward left his wife to marry that firm's senior partner. Braniff planes were painted bright solid colors outside, redesigned inside, and flight attendants donned revealing Emilio Pucci-designed uniforms. Modern artist Alexander Calder was commissioned to paint one airplane that promoted South American vacation destinations. Using a new slogan of "If You've Got It, Flaunt It!" Braniff expanded to Europe and Hawaii to go with the mainland U.S. and the rest of the Americas.

While Harding Lawrence and his showboating was raising Braniff's profits to its highest levels ever, TTA was starting to have a little trouble servicing all of the small town Texas markets that were not paying for themselves. In the mid-60s, a bunch of Minnesota investors bought Trans-Texas and started a game of musical chairs among the airline's leadership. What had been modest profits disappeared, and the company, recently renamed Texas International, was $20 million in the hole when it was taken over by a 30-year old Harvard Business grad named Francisco Lorenzo.

Texas International Convair-600. Wikimedia Commons

Not long before Lorenzo came to Houston looking to be TI's white knight, another Harvard biz grad, Rollin King, and a corporate lawyer named Herb Kelleher were cooking up plans for a low-fare airline venture in Texas. By staying within the borders of the state, an airline could avoid compliance with stiff federal regulation. In 1968, the Air Southwest Company was awarded a certificate of "public convenience and necessity" by the Texas Aeronautics Commission. A joint injunction was filed the next day by Braniff, Trans-Texas, and Continental. It was the start of an ugly battle that would last for years.

The tales of an airline drawn up on a cocktail napkin notwithstanding, Southwest started with some heavy Texas hitters. Robert Strauss, Dolph Briscoe, and a member of the famous Murchison family were among them. Braniff and TI dragged the TAC certificate fight through a litany of courts until the Texas Supreme Court ruled unanimously for Southwest. The plaintiffs tried the U.S. Supreme Court, but that then-august body refused to hear the case. Southwest, by now with former Trans-Texas officer Lamar Muse as its CEO, made its first flights between Houston and Dallas in 1971.

On one important front, Southwest's timing could not have been better. The Civil Aeronautics Board, which oversees the nation's aviation industry, had ordered the cities of Dallas and Fort Worth to stop their petty feuding and get a deal done for a joint major airport. All of the commercial carriers serving the Great Southwest Airport and Love Field signed an ironclad agreement to use it. The shotgun wedding also chained the airlines to hefty landing fees that would retire the enormous bond issue. But upstart Southwest was not yet in business when the pact was inked, and therefore they were free to utilize close-in Love Field. As Kelleher put it, "The passenger has a right to travel from Dallas to Houston, and not from Grapevine to Conroe."

While Southwest was fighting to avoid a move to the new and mammoth DFW Airport, Braniff and TI were doing everything in their power to run their new competitor out of business entirely. That made sense for Texas International which had been squeaking by on a similar business model, but Braniff should have looked upon Southwest as more of a pesky little gnat. It looked personal for Harding Lawrence.

On the same June day that Southwest made its inaugural flight, both of the other carriers deeply discounted their fares. They worked to keep Southwest from using the fuel hydrant at what is now Hobby Airport and to "blackball" Southwest from the inter-airline credit card system used by all other carriers. When TI or Braniff had to cancel a flight, they sent the passengers to the other one, but if that didn't work, the public was loaded on a bus directly to another carrier's airplane rather than risk them wandering past the Southwest counter. Braniff threatened to pull a wad of money from a stock brokerage firm in Houston unless they removed their recommendation of Southwest Airlines as a good investment. The federal government finally indicted Braniff and TI on antitrust violations for trying to kill Southwest, but still the legal action went on seemingly ad infinitum. At one point a senior federal appeals court judge said, "This litigation should have been terminated long ago; it's prolongation approaches harassment."

There were also fare wares. For a brief period in 1973, a Braniff passenger from Hobby to DFW could fly for $13, but if they wanted a Braniff jet from Houston Intercontinental, where Southwest did not have a presence, the fare was $27. Lamar Muse called it "laughable" even though his Luv airline was spending $35 from the profits for each flight to pay lawyers. While Muse was off "fighting the suits," he was also quick to paint Braniff and TI as bullies, every chance he got.

Over the next few years, a few self-inflicted wounds dogged both Braniff and Texas International. At almost the same time the Thirteen Dollar War was being waged, Harding Lawrence pled guilty to making illegal contributions to Richard Nixon's campaign, specifically $40,000 given to the committee which bore the acronym CREEP. Punishment was a gentle tap on the wrist, but the feds also uncovered a much more sizable Braniff slush fund. The airline had sold several thousand tickets off the books with the cash dropping into a secret account that approached a million smackers. The pittance given to Nixon was nothing compared to under the table kickbacks and bribes passed to South American ticket agents and officials. The federal complaint in that case was a dire threat against Braniff operations, as long as "present management retains operational control."

TI's problems came not long after. In the winter of 1974-75, the Air Line Employees Union went on strike against the carrier. Mechanics soon followed. Southwest used the opportunity to go into the Rio Grande Valley. It began flying to Harlingen while TI flights were unavailable. TI filed yet another lawsuit against Southwest but also asked the CAB that they be allowed to move out of the Valley. They could not compete head-to-head. Southwest, non-union and not federally regulated at the time, had lower overhead. Their fares out of Harlingen were $25 compared to $40 for TI. The fifteen bucks made a difference. Whereas TI averaged just over 300 people a day out of the Valley before the strike, Southwest had 785 passengers a day in August 1975. Texas International left the Valley and other small Texas towns and looked to add Las Vegas, Mazatlan, and La Paz.

Harding Lawrence was still bringing in good money over at Braniff. In 1974, the airline set a record for profits and an 18.2 per cent return on equity. Unbeknownst in the happy board room was the fact that trouble was looming just ahead.

When President Jimmy Carter signed the Airline Deregulation Act of 1978, the industry dominoes immediately began to fall every which way. Braniff reacted with the largest expansion in its history, tacking on 31 new destinations, but the debt incurred was massive. There were huge layoffs and a loss of $131 million in 1980. Before the year was done, Harding Lawrence was gone, and soon thereafter, so was Braniff Airlines.

Southwest had already expanded to Austin, Corpus Christi, El Paso, Lubbock, and Midland-Odessa, but as soon as deregulation was announced, the airlines said it would add out-of-state destinations beginning with New Orleans. The CAB quickly signed off. That move panicked the other big airlines and every politician in Fort Worth. If Southwest brought its low fares nationwide, air traffic at DFW was bound to plummet. Powerful Fort Worth Congressman Jim Wright successfully tacked an amendment onto the International Air Transportation Act of 1979 that put the clamps on business at Dallas' Love Field. No passenger service would be allowed from that close-in airport except to Texas and its four neighboring states. Through service connections to other airlines was also prohibited.

Frank Lorenzo certainly landed on his feet. After deregulation and just as TI was in its final flounder, Lorenzo formed Texas Air Corporation and bought the once proud Continental Airlines, rolling TI into that carrier in 1982. Continental had started in El Paso as Varney Speed Lines in 1934 hauling passengers and airmail. After a move to Denver, Continental operated interchange routes with American, United, and Braniff. In 1955, they bought out Pioneer and inherited

Harding Lawrence, the same young executive who later ran off to Braniff.

With the tectonic shift in the deregulated airline landscape, Continental attempted to merge with Western Airlines, but the deal failed, and Lorenzo engineered a hostile takeover by Texas Air. The Proud Bird with the Golden Tail moved to Houston. Lorenzo added Eastern Airlines, New York Air, and Peoples Express before he was through and just missed out on buying National and TWA. He finally sold off all his airline interests in 1990 to start Savoy Capital in Houston.

One statement from Lorenzo in the mid-1970s was especially prescient. "What you'll see... is two types of airlines. You'll see United Airlines, and you'll see some lines like Southwest." Braniff, TI, and the other mid-sized airlines would all be gone, he prophesied, and the flying public would pay the price.

Before the Wright Amendment was completely repealed, Fort Worth was suing Dallas, Dallas was suing Fort Worth, American Airlines was suing Dallas, and both cities were suing Continental Express. Still the Wright Amendment held firm. Then in 2006, a Missouri senator wanted an exemption so Southwest could fly to St. Louis and Kansas City, and the erosion was underway. New states got added for Southwest until a stake was finally driven through the Wright Amendment's heart in 2014. Though Southwest may have its troubles, today, it serves well over 100 airports in 11 countries, while the biggest remnants of its two early nemeses is through nostalgic talk in airport lounges and curated collections of memorabilia.

Central Texas

Texas Calves. USDA

Chapter Thirteen

Washington County Election of 1886

The Voting Rights Act passed in 1965 for very good reasons. The 15th Amendment extended the right to vote to African American men in February of 1870, but abuses preceded the amendment. As the United States Constitution goes, the 15th is an amendment that is short and to the point. Section one says: "The right of citizens of the United States to vote shall not be denied or abridged by the United States or by any State on account of race, color, or previous condition of servitude." There is a second section which is even more brief: "The Congress shall have the power to enforce this article by appropriate legislation." For freedmen in Texas and other states that were "unrestored" to the Union, the Reconstruction Acts of 1867 had already authorized the Army to register Black voters. It also unleashed White efforts to stop them.

Elections under early American democracy had been rustic, contentious, overly convivial and more. Since the days of George

Washington, kegs of beer or whiskey were supplied at polling places by one candidate or the other, and voters were expected to drain a few drams courtesy of the politician who carried their interests. New York City's Tammany Hall allied itself with thousands of Irish immigrants fleeing the Potato Famine by openly supplying needed help and services in return for loyal votes. For all of the regular hijinks, though, outright violence in the runup to election days was relatively rare. That changed completely following the Civil War.

Men who served in the Confederate military were required to swear an oath renouncing their treason to the United States and accepting the emancipation of the enslaved before their citizenship could be restored. The majority did so quickly, therefore regaining their right to vote, but with the enfranchisement of Black men and newly arrived or recently returned Union men came formidable competition at the ballot box. Since chattel slavery had been so pervasive in heavy cotton and sugar growing regions, several Texas counties had a majority Black population. That demographic brought a wave of former slaves into elected posts across the South, and with that, came a prolonged and brutal campaign waged by unreconstructed rebels to prevent such results.

There were hundreds of cases in Texas and other formerly rebellious states that could have warranted a federal investigation, but it was the "Washington County Election Outrage" of 1886 that finally made it to the halls of Congress.

In the Census of 1860, the last done prior to Emancipation, the four Texas sugar counties of Brazoria, Fort Bend, Matagorda, and Wharton, held the largest percentage of enslaved Africans among their population. Several other counties, including Washington, either had a slight majority of slaves over Whites or were virtually equal. When the war ended and Union soldiers occupied the state, those newly freed people had a modicum of protection, though official records show that many hundreds of Texas Blacks were murdered by Whites in the four years following Emancipation. Some were waylaid on dark roads. Others were murdered for having the unmitigated gall of trying to leave the plantation and go work for pay elsewhere. Some stories were more brutal still. Once the Freedmen's Bureau and the U.S. Army troops left the state in the early 1870s, all bets were off.

The Republican Party had never had a presence in Texas before the Civil War, but suddenly, with a mass of freedmen and loyal Union men ready to utilize their vote, the former Confederate conservatives found themselves in the minority. In Washington County, the numbers were with the Republicans in the late 1860s and throughout the 1870s. Those voters propelled fiery Black politicians such as Matthew Gaines to the Texas Senate and a dozen freedmen held elective office in the county. The Union League, an organization to serve the interests of the Republican coalition was strong. In Washington County, it was headed by Benjamin Watrous, a freedman who was attacked and wounded while registering voters in 1867. Some of the League's meetings drew crowds of 2,000 supporters in a county of only 12,000 people overall. The effects of winning elections were real, especially notable in Black schoolhouses and the inclusion of freedmen on county juries beginning in 1877.

In 1884, the conservative former Confederates who then made up the Democratic Party won most every race in the county. They benefitted from focused racism that congealed amidst outcries against "corrupt Negroes" in power. The electoral landscape had also been muddied by the rise of the mostly agrarian People's Party who opposed the very wealth and privilege which the Democrats represented, and a group of "Lily White" Republicans who were for the Union but increasingly against having their party dominated by freedmen. To ensure their return to power, the Washington County Democrats also employed violence, murder, and intimidation to lower Black turnout.

There was another element amplified in Washington County. There was a large and growing German immigrant population. Though some of the immigrants had followed the local flow, most had been strongly opposed to secession and slavery. They also brought with them a distrust and dislike of planter elites in Germany which they readily applied to the same group in Texas. The Germans in the county's rural areas tended to be more politically liberal than their Anglo neighbors. Most supported either Republicans or the burgeoning socialist Farmer's Alliance movements, but the Democrats actively wooed that voting bloc in 1884 with a good measure of success.

Two years later, the Republicans fielded a full slate of candidates for local, state, and Congressional elections. By all accounts, their efforts were well-organized and both sides expected a close tally. The Democrats had no intention of letting that happen. County Judge Lafayette Kirk, who was standing for reelection, notified local men, including by telegraph, that "Things look doubtful here. Do your work." They followed Kirk's orders.

In Graball, where Blacks outnumbered Whites five to one, the precinct returns were being tallied in a house when a group of disguised and armed White men broke in. Polk Hill, a Black sharecropper, opened fire with his shotgun, killing one of the attackers with a shot to the head. The dead man was a White named Dewees Bolton, the son of a Democratic county commissioner candidate. Eight Blacks were arrested for the killing and three were hauled from the Brenham jail and lynched without a trial. Not surprisingly, the Texas press defended Bolton as "inoffensive" and called the lynchings simple hangings.

Other armed men took the paper ballots from the Graball precinct and burned them. Seven miles away at Lott's Store, Republicans tallied 156 votes for their ticket out of 189 cast. The tally sheets were sent to the county seat at Brenham, but armed men intercepted and destroyed them. Local officials could not locate the attackers.

In Chappell Hill, where three Republican election officials had been cold-bloodedly murdered during the campaign of 1884, the precinct judge closed the polls and allowed no one to vote at all. He claimed that he could not find enough competent election judges. At Independence, the election judge refused to count special diamond shaped ballots the Republicans were using for illiterate voters even though the Texas Supreme Court had upheld their legality only one year earlier. County Judge Kirk backed the decision to discard all of the Republican votes at that town.

Three effected parties, knowing they could find no satisfaction through state or local channels, filed a request for an investigation by Congress. One was Carl Shutze, the Republican's German immigrant candidate for county judge who was running against Lafayette Kirk. The hearings were convened at Washington, D.C.

Sitting Texas Senator Richard Coke and former governor John Ireland both testified that the complainants were "propertyless... troublemakers" and swore that no such violence had taken place and no Klan-like organization existed. Coke's testimony ignored the obvious fact that the three who filed the federal complaint were only without property because they had been forced to flee the county at the hands of White terrorists. Coke tried to blame the Republicans for attacking their own polling places. Others blamed "northern agitators." Furthermore, the avowedly racist Coke said the federal government had no standing to interfere in a Texas election.

Several dozen Washington County residents went to the nation's capital to testify, and the resulting report topped 700 pages. Yet when Senate Democrats, led by the two Texans, filibustered against reform, the Republicans in Washington failed to pass a bill to ensure fair elections.

Richard Coke, Texas governor & US Senator. Library of Congress

The U.S. Attorney in the Western District of Texas brought
Washington County's Democratic judge Lafayette Kirk and several of
his cohorts to trial in Austin's federal court, but with White juries, there
was first a mistrial and then an acquittal. Ex-governor Ireland was among
the defense lawyers, and Senator Coke sat at the defense table, laughing
with the defendants. Several Republican office holders, Black and White,
in Washington and other Texas counties were forced to move away after
intimidation, and the party ceased to be a force in the vast majority of
Texas for the better part of a century. For decades after the middle 1880s,
in most statewide or national elections, Republicans never made it out
of single digits, a spot they shared with the Socialists.

Chapter Fourteen

John Holland Jenkins

Memoirs are a fascinating phenomenon. By definition, they are written years after given events took place, and are often penned by the elderly. Both of those things makes them vulnerable to great lapses of memory. In Texas history, there are several which were later assembled with help from younger relatives, and one of those belongs to John Holland Jenkins who sat down in 1884 with his daughter-in-law, Emma Holmes Jenkins. The resulting stories ran in his hometown newspaper – the *Bastrop Advertiser*. While he was at it, Jenkins collected and ran tales from other early Texans who were still alive and kicking at the time – Old Rufe Perry and John Day Morgan – and one from Samuel Highsmith who had been gone three and a half decades. Like Jenkins' own life stories, they were rollicking adventures lived by Texas Rangers, Indian fighters, expeditionary explorers, and volunteer soldiers of the Republic.

Jenkins came from Marengo County, Alabama with his family at the age of six or seven. They were allied with the Barton family and lived with them before settling on their own league on the west bank of the

Colorado River just south of what is now the heart of Bastrop. When they arrived in Texas at the end of the 1820s, the family's frontier location gave them a front row seat for the comings and goings of several tribes of Texas Indians, often as the bands sought to make war on one another. It did not take long until the interactions with the newly arrived Whites grew more aggressive.

What the boy Jenkins felt at the time is impossible to discern, but when he set his memories to paper in his early 60s, he recollected his first meeting with Comanche warriors. He wrote that they were "large, fine-looking men...erect, graceful." They wore only a small cloth "apron attached to a belt or girdle," and, combined with their long black hair and their array of "bows, arrows, lances, and carbines, made a rare picture of wild untamed beauty which could not be viewed without interest, and once seen could not be forgotten."

If life on the unhoned edge of Texas was not enough, John Jenkins was forced to grow up even faster when his father, Edward, was found murdered and scalped in his field at a time when the family was just putting a firm imprint on their land. The boy called it "the most bitter experience of my life." No one was charged and no pursuit sent out for retribution. John Holland Jenkins, only ten years of age, went to live with Edward "Ned" Burleson, arguably the most formidable frontier Texan of all at the time. It was Burleson who later told his ward that he believed a mixed race slave of Moses Rousseau murdered the senior Jenkins in retribution. Edward Jenkins had killed his neighbor, Rousseau, in a knife fight a year prior and never faced trial.

Jenkins was the oldest boy in the family, and when he went to live with Burleson, his three younger siblings remained with their pregnant mother. She remarried to James Northcross, a Methodist minister in

Bastrop, but that relationship also ended in tragedy. Northcross left to fight in the Texas Revolution and died at the Alamo.

John Holland Jenkins himself, a boy of just 13, joined the Mina Volunteers, a company within Ned Burleson's First Regiment of Texas Volunteers. They were under overall command of General Sam Houston as he moved east, stretching the supply lines of Santa Anna's Centralist Mexican armies. Historians believe Jenkins to be the youngest member of the San Jacinto campaign, and he lapped up the experience.

"I found myself among old friends and acquaintances, with all of a growing boy's appetite for good beef, bread, and adventure, I thought there had never been such fun as serving as a Texas soldier marching against Mexico," he wrote in his memoirs.

Jenkins did not make the battle at San Jacinto. After he learned of the boy's stepfather's death in Bexar, Burleson dispatched young Jenkins to help his own family and neighbors flee eastward in the Runaway Scrape. The Jenkins party, with hundreds of others, were awaiting a small ferry boat to cross the flooded Trinity River when they heard news of the Texian victory.

Though many Texas settlers returned to the United States, the Jenkins family went back to Bastrop and tried to start anew in country that had been stripped of a great deal by the passing armies and outright opportunists. Just four years later, his mother, Sarah Jenkins, died, leaving John to care for the rest of the children. Despite that responsibility, he developed a reputation as an Indian fighter, and those tales make up the lion's share of his memoir. That includes tales of raiding Comanches coming after their cabin only to be dispersed by John, his younger brother, and their dog named General Cos.

The more Americans settled on the Texas frontier, at the edge of Comancheria, the more ruthlessly the Comanche and Kiowa fought to keep them at bay. Jenkins chronicles many murders committed in ambush, and tells of two men slain at Hornsby's Bend by Comanche warriors carrying a white flag of peace. His neighbor Joe Rogers was killed with a lance within site of his house. Tending to the cattle or working the fields often meant placing one's life into the hands of fate.

There are also many accounts of captives being taken. While the Comanche did not hesitate to murder adult Whites, they preferred to assimilate certain child captives of both genders into their ranks. It was a practice that had been even more prevalent toward the Tejanos to the point that estimates are that by 1870 some 45% of the Comanche Nation was of Hispanic blood. The young captives usually bought into the native life completely, and several prominent people who were recaptured by the Whites died soon after their reintroduction to "civilized" society.

For all of the depredations Jenkins laid out, he did not shirk telling the other side of the story. He included an anecdote about Colonel James C. Neill, the man who Jenkins stated fired the famous "Come and Take It" cannon at Gonzales and who was in charge of the Alamo garrison before Travis and Bowie. During a summer raid by White Texans against the Comanches, Neill "adopted a singular, if not barbarous, method of sending destruction upon the Indians. Having procured some smallpox virus, he vaccinated one of the captive warriors, and then released him to carry the infection into his tribe!"

He also told of a participant at the Battle of Plum Creek gleefully running an injured Indian woman through with a lance. Jenkins rode to that fight with a large group of Bastrop area men under the command of Ned Burleson. It was in response to the Great Comanche Raid of August 1840 during which a party of 600 to 700 Comanche and Kiowa warriors, seeking revenge for the January murder of twelve of their chiefs during a negotiation in San Antonio, sacked the towns of Victoria and Linnville all the way down on Lavaca Bay. Leaving the coast with hundreds of captured horses and the contents of plundered warehouses, the Indians retreated back the way they had stealthily come.

Jenkins was one of the lead riders for the Bastrop contingent when they fell in close behind the warriors as they traversed an open prairie alongside Plum Creek south of today's Lockhart. He spoke of the "wild and fantastic band" before them. Red ribbons festooned the tails of all the mounted horses, and warriors were decked out in captured stovepipe hats or a "fine pigeon-tailed cloth coat, buttoned up behind."

Seventy to eighty Indian warriors were killed at Plum Creek, and the remainder escaped to their Hill Country homeland. Both sides believed their efforts to be a victory, but the Great Raid of 1840 was the last major raid into the Central Texas area.

Next came the Mexican Army. Twice in 1842, forays across the Rio Grande resulted in the capture of San Antonio, and John Holland Jenkins chased both invading forces as part of Captain James Gillespie's company.

Using tales he heard firsthand, Jenkins wrote of the Santa Fe and Somervell Expeditions and the disastrous trip on to Mier which ended in captivity and death for many of the Texans involved.

Jenkins finally settled down in the fall of 1845 when he married Mary Jane Foster. They had seven children together, but it was not the end of his adventures. Though he was roughly 40 years old, John Jenkins joined Malcijah Highsmith's Bastrop cavalry company at the start of the Civil War. They were part of the Texas State Troops, but the company was mustered into official Confederate service as part of the Twelfth Texas

Cavalry. Most of his service was with the rank of private, and he fought at Palmito Ranch under Colonel Rip Ford. Coming a month after Lee's surrender in Virginia, it was the last large action of the Civil War.

John H. & Mary Jane Jenkins

At the war's close, John Holland Jenkins returned to farming and hunting in Bastrop County but did serve as a Texas Ranger captain in Major John B. Jones' Frontier Battalion.

Jenkins had a final adventure when he was involved in a gunfight in Bastrop on November 11, 1890. He was 68 years old. It is commonly told as an attempt to save his son, Holland Jenkins, a deputy sheriff, from an alleged ambush. Two other sons, Sid and Bob, were also part of what became a general gun battle. Holland Jenkins killed Sam Smith, but both he and his father were shot. News reports in the following days called

John H. Jenkins' injury a "painful flesh wound" but not serious. The reports were wrong as Jenkins died on November 30th.

In 1958, John Holland Jenkins' life story got another life. His great-great grandson took on the task to collect and contextualize his forebear's writings. The youngster, like his frontier sire, began his work at a tender age. He was only 15 when he started his research and editing process and was still a Bastrop high school senior when *Recollections of Early Texas* was published by University of Texas Press.

J. Frank Dobie complimented "Johnny" Jenkins on a job done "ably," and the *New York Times* review called the story "a fascinating one – clear, frank, terse." It also proved that many earlier writers of Texas history had lifted the reminiscences of John Holland Jenkins whole and without attribution.

Chapter Fifteen

Doris Miller

A popular theme among certain observers of our past is to sneer at what they term "revisionist history." Generally, they are hand wringing over legitimate work that incorporates a fuller telling, one that moves beyond one-dimensional hero worship to be inclusive of various viewpoints and context. There are, however, real instances when our past has been wholly revised. Hollywood has made a habit of something that American Studies lecturer Robert K. Chester calls "retroactive multiculturalism," and one of the professor's most used examples is that of Texan Doris Miller.

Until President Harry Truman signed Executive Order 9981 in 1948, the United States military was, like most of American society overall, rigidly segregated. Less than a decade before Truman's act, Blacks in the armed service were primarily assigned to support roles as opposed to combat, and no branch of service was more hidebound in its segregation than the Navy.

When it came to race relations, the Navy had actually taken major steps backwards following the First World War. Going back to the War of 1812, the U.S. Navy had included Black sailors, 15 to 20%, though some of the enslaved sailors defected to the British in return for promised freedom. By the Civil War, the Union Navy held roughly twice the percentage of African-descended men as the Army. Some 18,000 Black men and 11 women served in the Union Navy with many crews being entirely integrated. Distinctions were made between free Blacks and those escaping slavery when it came to pay and promotion. Some enlisted crewmen in support and fireman units remained integrated on Navy ships through WWI, though any advancement was shut off at the rank of petty officer.

The administration of Woodrow Wilson, though, was one of the most racist in U.S. history, and his Secretary of the Navy, Josephus Daniels, was perhaps the most virulent cabinet member. It was Daniels who stopped the enlistment of Blacks altogether in 1919. No new Blacks were allowed into the branch between that order and 1932. In that year, enlistment was reopened, but only for service as stewards and mess attendants. That was the United States Navy that Doris Miller joined in 1939.

Miller's mother later admitted to reporters that she had been hoping for a girl, and had selected the name Doris after the midwife who delivered the baby. The boy was stuck with it over his father's best objections. His friends took to calling him Dorie. After attending the small school at Willow Grove, a Freedom Colony just west of Waco, Doris Miller went to segregated A.J. Moore High School in the nearby city. By then, he was one of the largest kids in his class, and the football coach signed him on as a fullback. Miller also supplemented his family's income by working in a restaurant kitchen. With employment options limited for a young Black man just out of a Texas high school,

Miller weighed his choices. He considered the Army or the Civilian Conservation Corps, but neither panned out. Instead, just a few weeks before his 20th birthday, Doris Miller went to Dallas and signed on with the Navy as a Mess Attendant Third Class. His enlistment was for six years.

After basic training in Norfolk, Virginia, Miller was assigned for about a month to the ammunition ship *USS Pyro* in anticipation of his first posting. That came on the second day of 1940 when he was received aboard the Battleship *West Virginia*. She was a "super dreadnaught" of the Colorado Class and was then assigned to the Pacific Fleet based in Hawaii, the group considered a rather foolproof deterrent to Japanese imperialism. Twice Miller was temporarily moved to the *USS Nevada* for temporary duty at Secondary Battery Gunner School, though his Navy records do not make clear what, if any, training he may have received on real guns. Back aboard *West Virginia*, he fit in well with shipmates and even won the title of the battleship's heavyweight boxing champion. Miller received promotion to Mess Attendant, Second Class in February 1941.

Early on the morning of Sunday, December 7 of that year, just before eight in the morning, Dorie Miller was collecting dirty laundry. The first bombs blasted the ship while it was anchored in a great row of seven battleships off the naval air station at Ford Island. *West Virginia* was alongside the *USS Tennessee* and just astern of the *USS Arizona*. Before the surprise attack ended, she would take two large bombs through her main deck and at least seven aircraft torpedoes into her port side. Quick counter-flooding orders by her junior officers saved the ship from capsizing.

With the first explosions, Dorie Miller ran topside to the main deck. The action reports were written by the officers, and there were some conflicting statements, but many details are consistent. Ship's Captain Mervyn Bennion was seriously wounded early in the attack when a large bomb fragment pierced his abdomen making a wound "about three by four inches, with part of his intestines protruding." Lt. Commander D.C. Johnson took credit for racing to the signal bridge and bringing a "colored mess attendant with me--a very powerfully built individual, having in mind that he might pick the Captain up and carry him below." An oil fire had started in the galley, and thick, black smoke blew in on the men. Lowering him to the boat deck was out of the question because of fire. That blaze had also spread to the flag bridge. In the absence of a proper stretcher, Lt. C.V. Ricketts and others had the mortally wounded captain lashed to a wooden ladder, and Miller was one of four men who eventually took him higher to the navigation bridge on the starboard side of the ship where there was air to breathe. The captain, still inquiring about his ship, died soon after.

The *Tennessee* lay between the *West Virginia* and Ford Island, and therefore could not be reached by torpedoes, and with the help of the ship's crane, firehoses were run across *Tennessee's* decks in a vain attempt to combat the many blazes. In the midst of this, with the ship listing 25 degrees and decks either ablaze or covered in oil, Lt. F.H. White and Mess Attendant Miller moved other wounded sailors through the smoke and furious fires amidships.

Finally, before the order to abandon ship was given, Dorie Miller grabbed an unattended .50-caliber Browning deck gun and fired at the attacking planes. It was Miller's first experience firing such a weapon, but as he said later, "It wasn't hard. I just pulled the trigger and she worked fine. I had watched the others with these guns. I guess I fired her for about fifteen minutes. I think I got one of those Jap planes. They were diving pretty close to us."

Of the 1,541 men on *West Virginia* during the attack, 130 were killed and 52 wounded. Most were evacuated or swam to the *Tennessee* or the island.

Though the *West Virginia* would be salvaged from the harbor bottom, that was almost three years coming. Dorie Miller was reassigned to the *USS Indianapolis*, a ship that would earn its own disastrous reputation before the war was over.

American newspapers were filled with stories about the sneak attack in the weeks after December 7th. Among the first reports came mention of an "unnamed Negro messman" having jumped in to man an anti-aircraft gun and shoot down a Japanese plane. The lack of specific mention was completely by design. Secretary of the Navy Frank Knox, a Bostonian, was also a strident segregationist opposed to Blacks in combat roles, and he was loathe to name a Black sailor as one of the first heroes of the war.

Outside of the Navy, Miller's identity was kept secret. It was not until March 1942 that the *Pittsburgh Courier*, one of the country's top Black newspapers, published the name of Doris Miller. He soon became a hero among his fellow African Americans and was promoted as a symbol of the Double V campaign urging victory against fascism overseas and victory over Jim Crow at home. The Congressman for the 11th District was Waco's own Bob Poage who was serving the third of what would eventually be 21 terms. Throughout Poage's long tenure in D.C., he proved himself an enemy of civil rights, and his response was no different when some constituents demanded an appropriate honor for local war hero Miller. At the same time as his own representative turned his back, a Michigan Congressman and a New York Senator recommended Miller for the Medal of Honor.

The Navy was against it, but they finally gave in to pressure and awarded Dorie Miller the Navy Cross in May 1942. He was the first Black so honored. The commander-in-chief of the Pacific Fleet happened to be a fellow Texan, and Adm. Chester Nimitz personally presented the Navy Cross to Miller on board the carrier *Enterprise* noting, "This marks the first time in this conflict that such high tribute has been made in the Pacific Fleet to a member of his race and I'm sure that the future will see others similarly honored for brave acts."

A few days after the ceremony, Dorie was promoted to Mess Attendant, first class. While the White sailor who received the same medal for actions on December 7th was brought back to the United States on a publicity tour, that was not immediately offered to Miller. He finally toured the States that December pushing for Blacks to buy war bonds.

Miller speaking at Great Lake Naval Training Station. US Navy

After his appearance tour, Miller was sent to Bremerton, Washington where he was part of the commissioning crew of the escort carrier *Liscome Bay*. It was a ship intended for the British Royal Navy, but the Americans changed their mind. That June, Miller was promoted to Cook, third class.

By the fall of 1943, Nimitz and Fleet Commander Admiral Ray Spruance were leading the charge north through the islands of Oceania. The goal was to take the Solomons, the Marianas, the Philippines, and continue to Japan itself. The *Liscome Bay* was part of Operation Galvanic to capture the Makin and Tarawa atolls. Horrible fighting on the latter cost the lives of more than 1,000 Marines. The small carriers handled planes to support operations ashore. Cruising near Butaritari Island just before dawn on November 24, the *Liscome Bay* took a lone torpedo hit from Japanese submarine *I-175* near the stern. Moments later, the bomb magazine exploded, sinking the ship within minutes. Only 272 sailors survived. Dorie Miller was among the 646 missing and presumed dead. That was made official a year and a day later.

Not surprisingly, the honors for Miller were slow in coming. San Antonio named a segregated elementary school for him in 1952, and Houston followed suit not long after. Other recognition took some time. In 1973, the Navy commissioned a Knox class frigate the *USS Miller* and on MLK Day in 2020, they announced that the *USS Doris Miller*, a Gerald Ford class carrier, would be launched near or after the end of the decade. He was the first enlisted man so honored. His name now lives on through parks in Waco, an auditorium in Austin, a plaque at Pearl Harbor, and a postage stamp.

Yet the cultural memory of the harsh racism of WWII often continues to be glossed over. The 2001 *Pearl Harbor* movie includes Miller surrounded by White characters who see no prejudice at all. A quarter century earlier, then presidential candidate Ronald Reagan mistakenly told audiences that the "great segregation in the military forces" was "corrected" in World War II. As proof he offered a scene a few seconds long from the 1970 movie *Tora! Tora! Tora!*. "I remember the scene," Reagan said. A "Negro sailor...cradling a machine gun in his arms."

As for the official government racism aimed at stories like Dorie Miller's, after decades of decency and truth on their part, however tardy they may have been, the Department of Defense, following Donald Trump's orders, cleansed all official Navy websites of Miller's story in 2025. In the same purge of history, hundreds, if not thousands of other sailors and soldiers of color were also cleansed from the record. The mass deletions included the military histories of such famous Americans as Jackie Robinson, the Tuskegee Airmen, and the Navajo Code talkers. Portions of those biographies, all chronicled in popular movies, were returned, but the vast majority of the removed heroes were not. One page about Miller was eventually restored after public outcry – under a red banner saying "revised to meet presidential guidelines." In August 2025, the Department of Defense issued a statement that the planned carrier *USS Doris Miller* would not be renamed.

Chapter Sixteen

Friedrich Ernst

Friedrich Ernst was a clever man. He had moved his young family, a wife and five children, to a scenic but bitterly difficult part of a foreign country where he did not understand the customs or the language. Though deer, bison, and small game were abundant, Ernst was an inept hunter. Native Indians were kind right up until they were not. He had acquired 4,400 acres of wilderness, his children were disgruntled, and the entire family survived largely on cornbread made from kernels they ground in a hollowed out log. Ernst's solution was not to pack it in and sail away with his tail between his legs. It was to write an almost absurdly optimistic series of letters and send them back across the ocean asking that his fellow Germans join him in Texas. His efforts brought Friedrich Ernst the title "Father of German Texas."

There were a handful of German-born Texans as early as the mid-1700s and some German soldiers of fortune were among filibustering expeditions several decades later, but by the time the Republic was established in 1836, barely 200 Germans lived within her borders. Most of those arrived in response to Ernst's printed letters. A decade later there were thousands more.

Though he was Johann Friedrich Ernst when he arrived in America, he was born Christian Friedrich Diercks near the village of Neustadtgödens, just north of Oldenburg in Lower Saxony. His father worked at the castle there, but after the older man's death, now using the name Ernst, Friedrich and his mother moved to Oldenburg. After five years in the duchy's regiment of soldiers, Ernst gained an appointment as a postal clerk. It no doubt went well for a while, but in September 1829, the duke charged Ernst with embezzling a large sum of money. The family "escaped by way of Bremen, Osnabrück, Münster, and Brussels," and then quickly sailed for New York.

There was a thriving German neighborhood on the city's Upper West Side, and the Ernst family started a boarding house there. Among the fellow Germans he met was an adventurous native of Westphalia named Charles Fordtran, a surname unquestionably morphed over generations from its French origins. Fordtran was advised to invest in farmland on the northern edge of the growing city of New York. Decades later, Ernst's wife, Louisa, misremembered that Ernst had a chance to buy property on Wall Street.

Instead, Ernst and Fordtran, by then good friends, set out for Missouri, another popular destination for immigrants from the German states. That land on the Mississippi River would put even more distance between Friedrich Ernst and potential imprisonment in Oldenburg. On board the ship from Manhattan to New Orleans, though, the pair read about opportunities for almost free land in Mexican Texas. They decided to see for themselves and took the schooner *Saltillo* for Harrisburg in early 1831. Fordtran was traveling alone, but Friderich and Louisa Ernst and their children were the first German family to settle in Mexican Texas.

Fordtran waited in Harrisburg while Ernst traveled to San Felipe de Austin to see if the land rumors were true. They were. By mid-April, Friedrich Ernst owned a league of land on the west bank of the west fork of Mill Creek in what is today the west end of Austin County. The family was not part of the Old Three Hundred, but rather a portion of Stephen F. Austin's second batch of land grants. Charles Fordtran worked as a surveyor for other grantees in the area in return for property of his own.

The Ernst Family stayed in Fordtran's hastily assembled house before building something for themselves. What they came up with left a good deal to be desired. There were no doors or windows, just openings. The second-oldest daughter Caroline later described their home for the first three years as a "miserable little hut, covered with straw and having six sides, which were made out of moss. The roof was by no means water-proof, and we often held an umbrella over our bed when it rained at night, while the cows came and ate the moss."

Friedrich tried to build a chimney from clay-covered logs, but the family was so afraid that it would catch fire and destroy their abode that they opted to shiver through the coldest winter nights instead. They arrived with few clothes and no spinning wheel. There was no fabric to make anything new. The shoe situation was even worse – when those wore out, they went barefoot.

Despite all of these hardships, Friedrich Ernst penned his letters back to Oldenburg where they enjoyed wide circulation. On the first day of February 1832, in the midst of his inaugural Texas winter, Ernst composed his first long and uplifting report.

"Climate like that of Sicily," he wrote. "Soil needs no fertilizer... no winter, almost like March in Germany. Bees, birds, and butterflies the whole winter through." He listed the primary crops: "Tobacco, rice, indigo grow wild; sweet potatoes, melons of an especial goodness,

watermelons, wheat, rye, vegetables of all kinds; peaches in great
quantity grow wild in the woods, mulberries, many kinds of walnuts,
wild plums, persimmons sweet as honey." Ernst exaggerated the average
number of cattle, and spoke of "birds of all kinds, from pelicans to
hummingbirds. Wild prey such as deer, bears, racoons, wild turkeys,
geese, partridges as large as domestic fowl."

He had little negativity to offer. In passing, he mentioned panthers
and wolves, "but of a feeble kind." He wrote of "many snakes, including
rattlesnakes, (but) each planter knows the safe means against them." And
fessing up to at least one experience of his family, Ernst said that "clothing
and shoes are very dear."

But it was the amount of land that got the most attention - 4,440 acres
that could be had with no money down, to be paid for later out of profits
from cattle. He called this "a small kingdom." Lest anyone was afraid
of the labor, Ernst spoke of cattle feeding freely on the copious grasses
leaving the planter with "hardly three months of real work."

Though Louisa Ernst and daughter Caroline spoke of those first years
more in terms of misery when they shared their recollection forty years
later, Friedrich was aglow with rhapsodic praise: "Working regularly in
the open has made me healthier and stronger than I ever was in Germany,
and my wife is blooming like a rose, as are the children,"

For an unlanded German to acquire property was exceedingly
difficult, and the news of an almost free league of land was nothing
short of mind-boggling. Though their wives and children may have
been more hesitant to leave the home they knew, German men thought
Texas sounded like a once-in-a-lifetime opportunity. As a final note,
Friedrich made a personal plea that in hindsight is quite transparent:
"Next summer I will be building a house for prospective arrivals and will

grow some fruit. May I soon have the pleasure of both being used quite shortly by friends; how happy that would make me."

At the time Ernst's letters were being read, the many states that make up modern Germany were experiencing horrific income disparity, stiff competition for jobs, and building agitation for social justice. The tales of a beautiful country, cheap land, and high wages fired the Teutonic imaginations of hundreds, and they took up the offer to join Ernst in paradise. Most of those first Texas German families, largely from Oldenburg, Westphalia, and Holstein, settled in the fertile land between the Brazos and Colorado Rivers.

Having growing numbers of his fellow Germans nearby brought out the best for Friedrich Ernst and his family. The boarding house was a success, and he sold lots from his league to several of the newcomers. While he was at it, Ernst offered the sage advice of one with two or three years seniority in the wild lands of Texas. The settlement around the Ernst farm grew into Industry, the first German town in Texas. Cat Spring followed shortly thereafter.

The Texas Revolution was an interruption. The Ernsts and other early Germans fled as part of the Runaway Scrape, going just a little way north and riding out the panic not far past what later became Brenham. Friedrich was away serving with the Texian Army. The native Karankawa who had been mostly peaceful when the Ernsts and Fordtran first arrived turned hostile and raided near Industry amidst the confusion of the Runaway Scrape. A family named Juergens had stayed behind, and the native Indians kidnapped pregnant wife Mary Therese Juergens and her children. She and her daughter, born in captivity, were later ransomed, but the tribe refused to return the two boys.

When the Ernst family came home to Industry, they found that the fleeing Mexican Army had "butchered our best milk cow" and made a general hash of their property. The Mexicans did not, however, find any of the family valuables which had been buried in the expansive garden.

With the Revolution behind them and the Republic period underway, several other German hamlets rose in Austin County. Friedrich Ernst was elected as a justice of the peace and became nominally involved in the Republic's politics. He advocated for formal encouragement of immigration from the German states, and his friend Charles Fordtran went so far as to secure a contract to bring in 800 families. After luring only two, Fordtran abandoned that scheme. For a brief while, President Lamar toyed with the notion of naming Friedrich Ernst as envoy to the Netherlands.

In addition to gardening, a skill he was said to know well, Friedrich Ernst was known for two things during the 1840s. He diligently recorded the rainfall and temperature at his farm and maintained records which he sometimes shared with the newspaper in Houston. He also concentrated on growing tobacco and made and sold cigars, some of the earliest in Texas.

When Prince Carl of Solms Braunfels and his Adelsverein group first looked to set up German settlements in Texas, the Ernst family was a source of advice. In so many ways, the German nobles were inept when it came to the needed skill set for Texas. Ernst son Fritz served as their guide and sometimes savior. That included killing a deer when the "professional hunter" the group brought from Germany was unable to accomplish the task.

After Ernst's glowing reports of Texas were published, more Texas-German travel books by the likes of Detlef Jordt, Hermann Ehrenberg, Ferdinand von Roemer, and Gustav Dresel followed. It was a formula that filled the boats from Bremen to the Gulf Coast. Ernst's countrymen kept coming. Around 10,000 Germans immigrated to Texas in the 1840s. A number significant enough that the state published a variety of official documents in their language. Lutheran churches were almost exclusively German, and several Methodist congregations had immigrant founders, as well. Some families were prominent merchants and saddlers. The majority of the new German-Texans, though, dug into the rich soil and became farmers who were soon known for hard work and tidy, prosperous homesteads.

Eventually, Texas gained an entire "German Belt" running from Houston and Galveston to the Hill Country near Fredericksburg, Kerrville, Mason, and Hondo. By the 1880s, San Antonio was a third German-descended. Even today, those with German heritage make up more than 17% of Texans, the third largest ethnic group in the state.

Chapter Seventeen

George Sessions Perry

To this day, it is still thought of as the best novel about Texas farming. The never-ending hardships and the simple rewards of working the soil are beautifully laid out in *Hold Autumn in Your Hand*. The hardscrabble life of tenant farmers was not a new subject to George Sessions Perry, but this novel, his second, was a home run in the publishing world. It garnered a prize from the Texas Institute of Letters, and a year later, it became the first Texas book to win the National Book Award.

If his real life was novelized, a modern editor might reject it as a story that has been told for it was filled with struggles, a flash of success, and a painful ending. Perry was an only child who grew up in Rockdale. By age twelve, he was an orphan who had watched his sensitive and artistic mother commit suicide not long after his father's death from kidney disease and a hasty and horrible second marriage. He spent his adolescence living with his maternal grandmother, a woman who rarely knew doubt. She often served as a model for characters in his fiction including in *Autumn* and as the titular character of his later non-fiction book *Granny Van*. His biggest recurring character was Rockdale itself. His relationship with the town went from adversarial in Perry's mind to an appreciative embrace, and the area was the setting for most every fictional paragraph Perry crafted. It remained part of his soul for as long as he lived.

His childhood was not a deprived one. His parents had owned two drugstores, and there was a modest inherited income. Following some academic struggles borne of disinterest in high school, Perry was packed off to Allen Academy in Bryan to get a diploma. From there, he went off to college, first at Southwestern in Georgetown, then at Purdue, and finally at the University of Houston. Along the way, he managed to avoid ever getting a degree. He ended up selling lampshades in Chicago for six months. On the campus in Georgetown, however, he met a girl named Claire Hodges. In 1931, while most Americans were struggling against the Great Depression, George Perry traveled overseas to France, Spain, and Algeria. When he returned, he married Claire and moved her back to Rockdale to help him pursue his dream of being a writer.

Perry started out scribbling with pencil and tablet. With his wife serving as typist, proofreader, and all around sounding board, George Sessions Perry cranked out over fifty short stories and six of what Perry later called "unpublishable novels" in six years. He wrote about what he knew – small town and rural Texas. Though his output was impressive, his diligence brought only an admirable stack of rejection letters, and the young couple scraped by on George's $100 a month inheritance income. Through it all, Claire supported him and unflinchingly stood up to the autocratic grandma.

The first big break came in 1937 when one of his short stories, a piece called "Edgar and the Dark Morass" that was atypical of his other more somber contemporary works, sold for $500 to the *Saturday Evening*

Post. It served as a bit of an epiphany that if he wrote marketable stories, they might actually sell. Congratulations poured in from his family, and the author wrote that the citizens of Rockdale ceased to regard him as "that big guy who don't do nothin' but hunt and fish."

Quick on the heels of his article, his novel *Walls Rise Up*, a funny and on point story of three Brazos River vagrants, was purchased by Doubleday. Shortly thereafter, Perry sold his masterpiece *Autumn*.

Perry during WWII. Harry Ransom Center, University of Texas

The years before WWII were a time when rural life was still understood and appreciated in America, even in literary circles, and *Hold Autumn in Your Hand* drew high praise. The lofty *New Yorker* called it "a miniature 'Grapes of Wrath' seen through optimistic glasses." Decades later Don Graham wrote in *Texas Monthly* that the book offered "the best picture we have of a vanished way of life—a world of subsistence farming and the yearlong ritual of planting and picking cotton ... He crafted a book chock-full of colorful rural idioms, scraps of songs, and the mores of a rawboned American peasantry."

Film director Jean Renoir bought the rights and made it into a movie called *The Southerner* starring Zachary Scott, an actor born and raised in Austin. Perry went to Hollywood to work on a movie script.

Perry spent some of his earnings to buy a horse, one which had never been ridden. Claire wrote a friend that "he stayed with the cayuse seven jumps, but the eighth got him." The fractured left arm and elbow bothered him the rest of his life.

Within the next two years, George Perry sold another dozen short stories to East Coast magazines, and in 1942, there was a book about his home state's history, traditions, and folklore called *Texas: A World in Itself.*

Perry was a large burly man, 6 foot 3 and generally north of 230 pounds, but the horse accident had left him with an arm that healed poorly, and, to his everlasting shame, he was ruled medically unfit for service during the Second World War. It was a self-imposed stigma he would never outrun.

Instead, he managed to score an assignment as a war correspondent. He traveled to several hotspots, but the worst was in July 1943 when he volunteered to go ashore with the Allied landing in Sicily. The close up horrors of war that he witnessed on the beaches permanently changed the arc of his career. He later said it "defictionized" him for life. After seeing death firsthand, he was done with lighthearted Texas tales. His final book of fiction, a short story collection called *Hackberry Cavalier,* hit the stores in 1944. He testily wrote a friend, fellow writer Truman McMahan who made the error of asking when George would return to writing novels that "I am going to write a novel just as soon as I have something to say... having written one or two by accident, it seems at least possible that such accidents might reoccur."

Commercially, however, George Sessions Perry, the winner of the National Book Award, was still a hot commodity. He and Claire bought a home in Guilford, Connecticut to be close to the eastern publishers. George was now a well-paid feature writer who cranked out 57 articles over the first five postwar years. Most of them were for either the *Saturday Evening Post* or its sister periodical *Country Gentleman*, both owned by the company which had given him his success. A major assignment was to tour the country, writing a popular series entitled "Cities of America."

The prose was good. Writing of Houston floods, Perry said within "its flat, bayou-striped acres... the sight of barefooted big shots, their limousines drowned out and their britches rolled high, wading down a flooded street, is a recurrent Houston phenomenon when the sky opens up and lets drive."

With monetary success came an increasing restlessness and unhappiness. Perry felt that somehow he had abandoned his rural Texas roots and forsaken fiction, which he likened to black land farming, for the easier and more lucrative field of journalism. He may have also realized that the high flying success of *Autumn* would never be repeated. Unpublished writings from the period show strong signs of a growing depression. His magazine pace dropped to six or seven articles a year, and there was but one book, a for hire history done for Texas A&M's 75th anniversary.

Perry was also in ever increasing pain from arthritis of the spine. He put off doctor visits and opted for self-medication via large amounts of bourbon whiskey. By 1954, he was frequently succumbing to hallucinations and voices in his head. He told a friend that "The best thing I can do in this depressed state is either jump into the river and swim to the north pole or run into the woods until I drop."

On December 13, 1956, George Sessions Perry chose the first option. While Claire was out of the house one day, he walked out into the frigid Connecticut River next to his home and disappeared. It was front page news across much of Texas. It was two months before his body was found and identified by the same friend in whom he had confided. The local coroner called it accidental death by drowning, though he neglected to posit as to why anyone would go swimming in an icy river in December.

Perry wrote most of an autobiographical novel called *After Many Days*, but it was never published. One passage late in the book calls out: "Though he understood his mood, he knew no way to escape it. He was so filled with shame and disgust that he had very little desire to feel any other way... for having betrayed the youth that he had once been."

Chapter Eighteen

Bill Pickett

Right or wrong, the cowboy, and by extension rodeos, have been an enduring Texas image for over a century and a half. According to the most knowledgeable experts, during that entire time only one event can have its origins traced to a single individual. The sport is steer wrestling, and the man is Bill Pickett. Don Reeves, the retired curator at the National Cowboy and Western Heritage Museum said Pickett "is venerated, not just legendary."

But how does one go about creating a rodeo event all by his lonesome? For starters, it seems at least some of Bill Pickett's brothers also mastered steer wrestling soon after their older sibling, and they learned their technique from watching herding dogs. That gave the original name to the task – bulldogging. The canines, quite literally bull dogs, worked in pairs to chase stray cattle out of the brush and mesquite. One, called the heel-dog, nipped at the cow's back legs while the other caught and held her by the lip until a cowboy could get a rope around her. Jumping from a running horse, twisting its head up, then taking the cow's lip or nose between their teeth became the Pickett technique.

There are multiple versions of the bulldogging creation story. One romantic tale has Pickett "wrassling" down a runaway steer to save his fellow cowboys. Another has him winning a bet when he caught a roped calf by the lip and held it still for branding. In the town of Rockdale, there is a version that "in 1903, Pickett, frustrated with an unruly Longhorn steer, rode alongside it, jumped from his horse onto the steer's back, and grabbed its horns." What is certain is that Bill's bulldogging style caused enough of a stir that he was soon doing exhibitions at county fairs and passing the hat to supplement his income.

Bill Pickett was born in the Jenks Branch community in southwestern Williamson County near the end of 1870. His formerly enslaved parents were a mix of African, White, Cherokee, and possibly Choctaw who were part of the post-Civil War Freedom Colony there. While Bill was still a child, the family moved to Taylor. He was the second of 12 children, and about age 10, after finishing the fifth grade, which may have been the highest level on offer to a Black child at that time and place, Bill Pickett left schooling in favor of work in the horse business.

Pickett, who went by Will at first, served in a local militia company and was a church deacon. He married Maggie Turner, and the couple would go on to have nine children, but his domesticity changed when Pickett competed in the fair rodeo in Taylor in 1888. His stunts and style proved popular, and around the turn of the century, Bill and four of his brothers including Benny, Charlie, and Jesse Pickett, were traveling and performing throughout Texas and the Southwest as The Pickett Brothers Bronco Busters and Rough Riders Association.

Bill with his bulldogging prowess was the headline attraction. In 1903, the *San Antonio Light* reported on a multi-day engagement featuring "the Colored Titan" who "throws a wild steer with his teeth and exhibits a courage and skill that is remarkable." The term "Titan" was bandied about in spite of the fact that Bill Pickett was, like many rodeo cowboys, quite diminutive. "It reminds one of ancient Greek heroes," the writer glowed. "Yesterday he downed two bulls. With one he had the most severe struggle, and it seemed for a time he would fail, but he eventually forced the brute on its side."

That same year, Pickett appears to have gained a professional promoter who dubbed him the "Dusky Deamon." In 1904, his steer exploits set the Cheyenne Frontier Days on its ear. The following year, Bill contracted with the Miller Brothers of Ponca City, Oklahoma and their 101 Ranch and Wild West Show. The outfit's first performance brought national newspaper editors to northern Oklahoma where among other feats they saw Geronimo shoot a bison from the front seat of a car. Two year later, when the Millers mounted their first major tour back East, Bill Pickett was one of their stars.

Wild West shows had reached their zenith with the worldwide fame of Buffalo Bill Cody. Cody was made famous by western dime novels following the Civil War, and a Chicago stage show morphed into a touring extravaganza by the early 1880s. There were sharpshooting demonstrations, wild animals unknown outside the American West, and, less than a decade after the real thing, battle recreations of Little Bighorn featuring Native Indians who were actual participants. With Cody's success came knockoff shows. An Oklahoma neighbor of the Millers, Gordon Lillie, had sporadic success as Pawnee Bill, and even combined forces with an aging Buffalo Bill in 1908, a grand venture that was foreclosed on in Denver.

The Miller's timing and luck was not great. They entered the world of Wild West shows just as the proliferation of motion pictures was undercutting their audience. There was a major railroad accident in their first year on the circuit, and later a typhoid outbreak among the cast. Still the list of performing cowboys connected to the 101 Ranch Shows was a veritable who's who, and they were all friends with Bill Pickett. Tom Mix, the first superstar movie cowboy, and Will Rogers, who drawled jokes while he performed rope tricks, were by far the most famous, but there were many others just as well-known at the time - Lucille Mulhall was known as the first cowgirl. Lillian Smith, who had once been Annie Oakley's flirtatious rival, Bessie Herberg and her Educated Horse Happy, trick roper "Mexican Joe" Barrera, Jack Hoxie, who became a film star like Mix, and Bee Ho Gray, a trick roping, knife throwing comic often compared to Rogers.

Bill Pickett's bailiwick remained bulldogging, and during times when the 101 was not out on tour, he still hit the rodeo circuit on his Texas-style saddle with square skirts and double rigging. Pickett's ethnicity, though, like athletes in other professional sports, was an issue. Many small town rodeos forbade Black cowboys, but so did some large ones. Madison Square Garden in New York refused to allow Pickett to appear. On several occasions, Bill Pickett swore that he was Comanche in order to get a ride against his White peers. In one of the great condescending racist statements of the day, Pickett's 101 boss Zack Miller eulogized him by saying, "Bill's hide was black, but his heart was white."

With the exception of the show's long hiatus during WWI, the bulk of Pickett's reach was still with the touring 101 Ranch Show where he headlined for 26 years. He did the usual rodeo events, but was also known to bulldog from the running board of a moving car, or there was a time at the El Paso Fair where Pickett wrestled an elk, but things did not always go swimmingly. In England in 1914, Pickett was jailed on charges of cruelty to animals. For the rest of the run in Britain, the show paid a weekly fine that allowed Bill to continue. Eventually, biting steers was banned in the United States, as well.

The show suffered bigger difficulties during European tours. The British confiscated most of the horses and some of the vehicles during the military buildup prior to the First World War. In Germany on that same tour, several Oglala Sioux performers were jailed on suspicion of being Serbian spies. Zack Miller was forced to spirit the entire cast out to England via Norway. Once in Britain, Miller had trouble finding sufficient passage back to America. When they finally returned to Oklahoma, the Miller Brothers refused to pay overtime to their Indian performers. All of them quit the show.

Bill Pickett and the 101 Ranch Wild West Show traveled across Europe and North and South America reaching spectators who numbered in the millions. Movie footage of the show toured nickelodeons across Texas and the West, often with one of the 101 cow punchers appearing live to narrate the scenes. Most of the audiences were thrilled with the entertainment, but one large crowd in Mexico City in 1910 turned so violent that Bill feared for his very existence. The magazine insert of the *New York Herald* featured the story, and it became the widest circulated tale of Pickett's colorful life.

The spectacle was the result of a challenge and/or bet over whether a steer wrestler like Pickett could subdue a Mexican fighting bull. The matadors and toreadors are said to have "laughed uproariously" at the mere notion. A crowd of 25,000 packed the new steel and concrete El Toreo bull ring. The impresario of the arena selected "a coal black bull" named Bonito who had allegedly killed two bull fighters and

five picador's horses. Afraid of losing face, the governor of the Federal
District intervened to deny Pickett's test of Bonito, but Americans
prevailed with a substitute bull – Frijole Chiquita, "fully as wild, wary,
and wicked."

After a dozen Mexican vaqueros had aggravated the bull into "a
man-hating frenzy," Frijole Chiquita was released into the arena where
Bill Pickett was mounted on his favorite horse, Spradley. Immediately,
the enraged bull charged and gored Spradley in the shoulder. Pickett had
no choice but to leap onto the shoulders of Frijole Chiquita. The hostile
crowd raised its voice in a collective bloodlust, but "down in the arena,
the unexpected – no, the supposedly impossible – was happening. The
dreaded bull was frantically turning his head with all his great strength,
bellowing his rage and bewilderment, pirouetting in dizzy circles, and
there still dangled Pickett, his bearlike hug unshaken, clinging like a
burr."

The lovers of Spanish bullfighting were horrified at the prospect of the
American shaming their beloved pastime. First a canvas chair cushion
flew from the stands and hit Bill Pickett full in the face. More cushions,
then stones, fruit, cerveza bottles, and even open bladed knives followed,
raining down on the besieged cowboy in a shameless torrent. One glass
bottle broke two of Bill's ribs. At that point he had held onto the huge,
angry bull for seven and a half minutes. Vester Pegg, another of the
101 cowboys, jumped over the boards and began waving his red shirt
at Frijole Chiquita. The confused bull hesitated just long enough for a
groaning Bill Pickett to rise from under the animal's head and be hauled
over the rail by friendly American spectators.

Those Americans, many covered in the spittle of the Mexican crowd,
were forced to conceal themselves behind iron gates for more than two
hours before being escorted to safety. Three days later, the show sailed for

home. Joe Miller, one of the brothers, offered $10,000 for any Mexican willing to even attempt Bill Pickett's feat, but there were no takers. It took over a month for Bill to recover from his injuries. Though Pickett always insisted that he would have wrestled Frijole Chiquita to the ground if left alone, the only lasting result of the contest was "a great scar" in Spradley's shoulder.

Bill Pickett on a movie poster. Library of Congress

At the age of 50, Pickett finally got his personal piece of movie cowboy fame. *The Crimson Skull* and *The Bull-Dogger* brought his exploits to even wider audiences. The Richard Norman Studios of Jacksonville, Florida came to Oklahoma to film both silents. Bill's smiling face graced the poster for the second film. Those ads billed him as "World's Colored Champion" and promised "Death Defying Feats of Courage and Skill." Surviving scenes from *The Bull-Dogger* show close-ups of Pickett and plenty of footage of him jumping from his well-trained horse to wrestle big steers to the ground before tying them off and raising his hands in best rodeo fashion. That movie, which ran to five reels in its full length version, was especially thrilling to African American audiences who had never seen a Black cowboy film star.

As goes the everlasting hope of all cowboys, Bill Pickett died with his boots on. On April 2, 1932, the 61-year-old was kicked in the head while trying to break a wild horse at the 101 Ranch. The official statement from the ranch said, "The accident occurred while Pickett was working with horses. After roping a horse and tying the rope to his saddle-horn, Pickett dismounted. He became entangled in the rope and was thrown to the ground and under the feet of the broncho."

He lingered in a coma for the better part of two weeks before succumbing. The ranch held a funeral and buried him near the White Eagle Monument. Will Rogers talked about his old buddy on the nation's most popular radio show, saying, "Bill Pickett never had an enemy, even the steers wouldn't hurt old Bill."

In spite of the obstacles presented by his dark skin, Bill Pickett was easily the most famous Black cowboy in America, and his "theatrical savvy and skill in the saddle" earned accolades from audiences of all stripes. Decades after his death, Pickett was honored with place names in Taylor and Georgetown and numerous spots in Oklahoma. He was the first African American elected to the Cowboy Hall of Fame. In 1994 the U.S. Postal Service placed Pickett among its Legends of the West series. One year later, the USPS was forced to admit they mistakenly used a picture of his younger brother, Benny. A new Bill Pickett stamp was issued using the movie poster from *The Bull-Dogger*.

Edwards Aquifer

Jacobs Well Natural Area. Larry D Moore via Wikimedia Commons

Chapter Nineteen

Chili Queens

The Aztecs and their descendants made a popular dish called carne con chile, and other indigenous people were cooking meat and seasoning it with hot peppers. A Spanish conquistador even wrote that some of his luckless countrymen were captured and stewed with tomatoes and chiles. But here's the thing: that cuisine of Southern Mexico, noted by Europeans as far back as the 1500s, was made with tasajo – dried strips of beef that were salt cured in the sun like jerky. Some of the early 19th century British visitors liked the dish, others said they only wanted their meat boiled. Mathieu de Fossey, a French visitor to Veracruz in 1831, said despite the efforts to "prevent putrefaction" in the curing, the meat "always retains an unpleasant smell and taste." In other words, that "meat with chiles" sounds very different than the chili con carne that is the official state food of Texas.

Our proud and meaty ambrosia infused with garlic, chile peppers, and comino, the dish we love and nitpick over, is a native product of Texas. It came about thanks to the Canary Islanders who were encouraged by the Spanish crown to move to San Antonio de Bexar in 1731. Joining an earlier population of Franciscan clergy, Spanish soldiers, and mission

Indians, the Islenos, as they were known, quickly became the town's business elite. Like migrants everywhere, they brought along the flavors of home. In the case of the Canary Islands, a place strongly influenced by centuries of North African Berbers, that meant copious amounts of comino molido – the dried cumin that separates Texas chili from heathen concoctions in places like Cincinnati.

Texas food historian Robb Walsh wrote about the first public purveyors of real Texas chili in 2008: "Chili con carne was introduced to America by the "Chili Queens," women who served food in San Antonio's Military Plaza as early as the 1860s. Chili stands were also common in Galveston and Houston; they were the taco trucks of the 1800s. Tamales with chili was the most common order."

Walsh also noted that frequently frijoles were served as a side dish. Let's reiterate that. There were no beans in the chili because they were already a ubiquitous part of the plate.

My great friend, the late John Nova Lomax, was fascinated by the origins of Tex-Mex, and wrote several lengthy articles about it for magazines including *Texas Monthly*. Lomax found evidence that Walsh, and a number of other historians, missed the mark by about half a century. Not that people could fully blame them since the Anglo writers, from spots other than Texas, were facing both a language and culture barrier. Add to that the relative difficulty of even getting to San Antonio before the railroad connected it to the world in 1877.

That was the same year that the first English mention of chili con carne appeared in print. An anonymous reporter from Fort Scott, Kansas filed this dispatch from his Texas trip: "Speaking of hot things, at San Antonio they have a dish called chili con carne. It is of Mexican origin, and is composed of beef, peas, gravy and red pepper. It is awful seductive looking, and gives a fellow the idea that he has a soft thing on hash. They always have enough to go around, for no stranger, no matter how terrific a durned fool he is, ever calls for a second dish. He almost always calls for a big cistern full of water, and you can't put the water in him fast enough with a steam engine hose."

Ah, Yankees.

Five years later a pamphlet was published, though extant copies may well be lost. *Gould's Guide to San Antonio* referred to chili con carne being sold around the plaza.

"Those who delight in the Mexican luxuries of tamales, chili con came, and enchiladas, can find them here cooked in the open air in the rear of the tables."

It was quite clear, however, that Mexican food was already abundantly known to people elsewhere in Texas. The *Brenham Weekly Banner* reported in 1878 on a Denison man who was opening "a Mexican restaurant. Chile con carne, tomales [sic], and other 'hot' dishes will be served to order." Brenham itself already had a fellow from deep South Texas who ran a stand suppling Mexican food to drinkers at one of the town's largest German-owned bars. That is the same true Texas fusion that also influenced Tejano and Norteno music.

In the late 1870s, a former Texas Ranger, Confederate captain, and San Antonio city marshal named W.G. Tobin was canning chili con carne and even secured a substantial contract with the United States Army and Navy. The Army believed it would prevent scurvy. When a train car load of his stuff arrived back in the Alamo City, the paper said "It sounds like bringing coals to Newcastle, but it is just the thing for pic-nics and for travelers, and it is easily prepared for family use." The *San Antonio Light* also suggested spooning it over eggs.

The largest part of the story is that a majority of English-speaking people just may not have been calling it chili con carne. Lomax pointed out that New Orleanian landmark Café du Monde did not use the word beignet for almost 100 years after they opened. They were simply "French doughnuts." So it was with numerous descriptions of meaty stews being sold in San Antonio.

There is substantial evidence, much of it run down by Lomax, that places chili con carne for sale on San Antonio's plazas as far back as the Gutierrez-Magee Expedition and the subsequent pillaging by the Spanish Royalist Army. If I might be permitted a personal reminiscence, I recall well the breathless phone call from my buddy, John, when he discovered two stories that named Jesusita de la Torre as the first Chili Queen, cooking out of necessity after an ill-advised but irresistible love affair with a Frenchman who rode among the rebels. Bexar's supporters of the Spanish Crown turned their backs on the rebels after some of their officers gathered up the town's royal governors, marched them to a live oak motte outside the city, stripped the captives naked, and slit their throats with machetes. You can read John's detailed TM story online.

Personally, I put more faith in the notion that the lavanderas, the camp followers who accompanied most all decent sized armies in the 19th century and before, were forced to cook the meat stew for the occupying Spanish Army in 1813. These women, the wives and girlfriends of the soldados, washed clothes in tubs during the day and often used the same vessels to cook pots of food by night.

A Houston-area colonist named J.C Clopper visited San Antonio in 1828, well before the Texas Revolution, and observed that "When they have to pay for their meat in the market, a very little is made to suffice for the family; it is generally cut into a kind of hash with nearly as many peppers as there are pieces of meat—this is all stewed together." One

century later, Frank Bushick, a San Antonio tax commissioner wrote
that women were cooking chili "away back there when the Spanish Army
was camping in Military Plaza."

Vendors were to be found in downtowns the world over, but San
Antonio's Chili Queens flourished at night, serving well into the wee
hours of the morning. It is easy to imagine them catering to tipsy bar
patrons in much the way revelers in New Orleans seek out a Lucky Dog
cart.

Lit only by the moon, stars, and a kerosene lamp, they served
everyone. As a later *San Antonio Express* article recalled: "Their tables
were patronized by people of all walks of life. The banker touched elbows
with the newsboy. The doctor sat by the farmer, the lawyer, judge and
Sheriff sat next to the barber, the policeman and the porter."

Julian Onderdonk painting of chili queens circa 1912.
Witte Museum

Visitors to the Alamo City were positively entranced by the
Queens. An 1882 reporter from Alabama's *Greenville Advocate*, a
man who spelled it "chille cancarne," was overcome by the allure.

He found an art-worthy tableau in the mesquite fired braziers tended by sarape-wearing hombres "with their broad-brimmed sombreros, their melancholy countenances, and piercing black eyes." The food was pushed into the plazas on "primitive hand carts" and tended by "swarthy señoritas with long black hair that falls loosely over well-formed shoulders, often reaching below the waist."

Other scribes spoke of the flirtatiousness of the Chili Queens, wiles that were used to entice healthy tips and sell an extra bowl to a starry-eyed, lingering stranger. Professor Marci McMahon of UT-Rio Grande Valley commented in Robb Walsh's *The Chili Cookbook* that the flirting belied good business tactics. "Their proud representation of Latino culture and their cuisine flew in the face of the era's anti-immigrant rhetoric and the 'Americanization' that attempted to rapidly assimilate Mexican Americans into the mainstream," McMahon wrote.

Not every Chili Queen was a Tejana according to another San Antonio newspaper article of the late 1880s. That reporter mentioned that one was German and one Irish.

Nor did every non-Texas writer enjoy the food. Famed newsman and novelist Stephen Crane was in San Antonio in 1895. His purple prose described "the soft atmosphere of the southern night, the cheap glass bottles upon the stands shine like crystal and lamps glow with a tender radiance. A hum of conversation ascends from the strolling visitors who are at their social shrine." As for the menu – "They sell food that tastes exactly like pounded fire-brick from Hades—chili con carne, tamales, enchiladas, chili verde, frijoles."

The chili tables of San Antonio were not static over the years. Every time city leaders decided to promote or gentrify one plaza, the Queens were relocated, thus they traveled from Military Plaza to Alamo Plaza to Market Square to Milam Park and back over the decades. The only painting of the state's greatest shrine that Texas virtuoso Julian Onderdonk ever produced came in the early 1910s and is titled "Dusk at the Alamo with the Chili Queens."

Of course, the dish was also available indoors. Hundreds of Chili Parlors dotted the Lone Star in the years before WWII. Most worth their salt, and comino, claimed to have a secret family recipe. Those "parlors" likely trace their origin to literal parlors in homes.

A writer named Edward King contributed a Texas travel story to *Scribner's* magazine in 1874. He spoke of private homes in the slum of Laredito where a hungry visitor could enter and demand supper at a dimly lit "long, rough table." All levels of San Antonio society dined at these sketchy establishments where a "fat, tawny Mexican materfamilias will place before you various savory compounds, swimming in fiery pepper which biteth [sic] like a serpent; and the tortilla, a smoking hot cake, thin as a shaving, and about as eatable, is the substitute for bread."

In 1893, chili was a popular sensation at the Chicago World's Fair courtesy of a vendor operating the San Antonio Chili Stand. Thanks to jars of dried chili powder manufactured in Texas and Tobin's canned version, entrepreneurs began exporting the notion of chili parlors to far flung cities such as Nashville and Midwestern states like Illinois and Wisconsin. Like every other Texas export that catches on, it was not long before chili was adulterated with things like sugar and turkey and, Lord help us, beans.

The demise of the Chili Queens came in the 1940s when the San Antonio health department finally decided that they were unsanitary. Perhaps, in a time when food trucks are thicker than fleas on a camel, there might be a way for the Queens to return and bring that old-school charm and romance to some spot near the Riverwalk. It was a scene that enthralled scores of authors over a century ago including the Texan William Sidney Porter, better known as O'Henry.

In his ghoulish short story "The Enchanted Kiss," he described the scene like this: "Drawn by the coquettish *señoritas*, the music of the weird Spanish minstrels, and the strange piquant Mexican dishes served at a hundred competing tables, crowds thronged the Alamo Plaza all night." O'Henry also loved the fare, the "delectable chili-con-carne...composed of delicate meats minced with aromatic herbs and the poignant chili Colorado, a compound full of singular savor and a fiery zest."

If you close your eyes, maybe you can still see it and smell it.

Chapter Twenty

Eugene Barker

It must be a relatively few historians who become the subject of a book-length biography as opposed to writing one, but Eugene Barker is among them. William C. Pool took one of Barker's classes in 1939 and stayed his friend until Barker's death in 1956. Pool wrote the biography of his mentor, remembering him as an "excellent classroom teacher" and noting that Barker "stood for honesty and integrity above all else." Pool also called Barker the most important historian of Texas that we have had.

Other top historians agree. Stephen L. Hardin, an Emeritus Professor from McMurry University, said in 2025: "Precision, gravity, and grace distinguished his scholarship. This year marks the centenary of his seminal Stephen F. Austin biography. A century later, Texas historians still consider it indispensable to an understanding of the man and his times--a tribute both to the book and its author."

Barker was born at Riverside in Walker County, near where Harmon Creek flows into the Trinity. It was in the pine forests and close to the Big

Thicket. Small farms with sandy loam soil. Barker walked the railroad ties two and a half miles to school and read by the light of burning pine knots or kerosene lamps. He carried water from the creek in buckets.

When his father died, Eugene was only 14, and the family moved up to Palestine. He started as a waterboy at the International & Great Northern Railroad and moved up to being a railroad blacksmith, working during the day and going to evening school in a local woman's home. But he yearned to do better. At the age of 20, he went to Austin to take the entrance exams for the state university. He failed the English portion. He studied and tried again the following year. This time he passed, starting school in the fall of 1895.

Eugene Barker circa 1899. Briscoe Center for
American History, University of Texas

He had to work a night job as a railroad mail clerk, but he got his bachelor's and master's degrees before the century turned. After a few years as a tutor to undergraduates, Barker went to Penn and earned his doctorate before coming back to Texas as a professor. By then he was married to Matilda Weeden.

Barker's arrival on the academic scene coincided with a growing professionalism of historical research and writing that had been building through the last decades of 19th century. The University of Texas history department was separated from the English department in 1888 and given to George Garrison. It was part of a major change in how history worked at American universities.

Garrison brought in Barker in 1899 in close proximity to Lester Bugbee and Herbert Bolton. All had great interest in Texas history, and the university established a graduate level course in the subject. Bolton developed the field of Latin American Studies, an effort Barker would fully embrace. Just two years prior to Barker's hiring, UT became the founding partner of the Texas State Historical Association and with it the *Southwestern Historical Quarterly*. That publication was destined to become the very Bible of academic papers on Texas.

When George Garrison died in 1910, the history department needed a new head. The initial frontrunner was Herbert Bolton who had resigned the previous year to take a better paying job at Stanford. There was speculation that Barker would get the position in an interim capacity, but it turned out to be quite permanent. He also inherited the post as director of the TSHA and editor of the *Quarterly*.

At the same time Barker took the helm, there was also an awakening of historical scholarship in and of the South. The 1890s had seen a flurry of manuscript collecting across the U.S., and Eugene Barker thought the UT history department should be a part of it. He found a financial champion in one of the newest members of the Texas Board of Regents.

George Washington Littlefield, who had fought with Terry's Texas Rangers during the Civil War, made a fortune in cotton, cattle, real estate, and banks. He joined the Regents in 1911. The post gave him a pulpit to air a personal complaint. Littlefield believed there was a "complete misrepresentation of the Southern cause in published histories of the U.S." History was written by Yankees, and Littlefield wanted a "fair and impartial" representation.

Barker's answer was that Littlefield should not be blaming historians. He said the South was making no effort to preserve source materials. Many records had been deliberately burned during the war, but others were simply neglected. Barker asked Littlefield for money to acquire manuscripts. In 1914, Littlefield gave $25,000 in securities and upon his death, there was another $100,000. It established the Littlefield Fund for Southern History, the starting point for UT's collecting.

As the best known historian on Texas, Barker was soon being quoted in newspapers across the state, including a big story in 1912 about where the ashes of the Alamo defenders resided. He gave speeches, sometimes with the not-so-subtle goal of adding to the Texas Collections such as when he talked to the Daughters of the Confederacy about donating old family papers and letters.

On the personal front, the Barkers became prominent in UT faculty circles. Matilda was frequently written up in the Austin paper for her social activities. The couple took time to go camping at Lake Medina and entertained important visiting professors. Eugene gained popularity with his peers, even doing a stint as acting dean while the top administrators went hunting and fishing at Marble Falls.

Jim Ferguson came on the Texas political scene as a champion of the downtrodden and the tenant farmer, but he quickly proved to be "petty, vindictive and arbitrary." One of the first people to run afoul of the governor was UT President William J. Battle, and Barker was not far behind him. It was the beginning of what would become "Farmer Jim" Ferguson's effort to destroy the university, and it led to the end of his time as governor. Somewhat.

Ferguson's beef first started over a misunderstanding of the way UT handled their annual appropriation. The school wanted flexibility, so they expected the money to go on the state books without enormous detail as to specific targets of spending. That kerfuffle put Battle in the crosshairs, and next came Barker.

When he took over the history department upon the death of Garrison, Barker automatically joined the State Library Commission and was elected chair not long after. The commission was run by Ernest W. Winkler, a former student of Barker who had become a friend. The governor wanted to fire Winkler so he could appoint a Presbyterian minister who had done him a solid during the campaign. Barker responded first with a flat no then with a rather strident and likely insulting letter to the prospective candidate. After the livid Ferguson got his way, Barker wrote to a friend that the "governor is as devoid of general education as he is historical appreciation." Things went downhill from there.

The Texas Board of Regents elected a new school president in R.E. Vinson. This time Ferguson was mad that he was not consulted. At their first official meeting, the governor told Vinson that he disliked him and promptly demanded that six specific faculty members be fired. When asked the reason, Ferguson replied, "I am the Governor of Texas; I don't have to give reasons."

When the United States had been part of WWI for only a handful of weeks, another small war broke out in Austin. The Regents refused to dismiss the teachers. Summoned to the capitol, the board were given additional names to be let go or Ferguson would veto the entire university appropriation. One hundred faculty members met at the University YMCA and declared they would rather shutter for two years than hand over their independence. Students marched the next day with signs that read "Kaiserism is a menace abroad & Kaiserism is a menace at home!"

As restraining orders flew through the Travis County courts, Eugene Barker publicly proclaimed that, "The governor is entirely without conscience or scruple." Barker also urged President Vinson not to resign. At the same time, he wrote letters to professors back East inquiring about Ivy League jobs for a "possibly unemployed historian."

Ferguson, now stumping around the state for a second two-year term, called the UT faculty "day dreamers and butterfly chasers," and ranted that Texas did not need "an army of educated fools to run the government." He kept talking throughout the summer of 1917, and the Regents fired several of the targeted faculty members without effect. Finally, powerful Texas alumni led by Will Hogg and Chester H. Terrell rallied legislators to seek impeachment.

Hogg was particularly eloquent. He leased a floor at the Driskill Hotel to conduct his lobbying efforts, and his rhetoric may have hit its pinnacle with this comment during an interview: "To call our thimblerigging, swashbuckling, swaggering governor a common garden liar would be the grossest flattery... Farmer Jim is a farce, and my prediction is that he is riding to the biggest fall, personally, and politically, in the short and simple annals of the misguided politicians of Texas."

Barker, in a letter to fellow historian Alex Dienst, was less glib when referring to Ferguson: "I merely wish to say that if your friend is not dead, he ought to be and I wish he were."

One personal tragedy followed closely behind the Ferguson troubles. In August 1918, Barker's brother, Paul, was burned to death in a gas explosion at Harrington near Silsbee. For the most part, though, things went well for Eugene.

With the dangers of an out-of-control, anti-intellectual governor behind them, the Forty Acres returned to the business of education, and the "tall and angular" head of the history department was a prominent figure. He began releasing important books on Texas.

It was Lester Bugbee who had gotten a first peek at the Moses and Stephen Austin papers over Christmas holiday 1896-97. They were at the house of Guy M. Bryan, SFA's nephew. Bryan died in 1901, and the collection eventually went to UT, but by then, Bugbee had died of tuberculosis. Eugene Barker inherited the Austin project. He first collected and edited *The Austin Papers*, volumes still utilized today, and he followed that up with *The Life of Stephen F. Austin* in 1925. His next book, *Mexico and Texas, 1821–1835*, was another classic of American history. He worked on the writings of Sam Houston and authored or co-authored multiple school textbooks in Texas history.

In addition to editing the *Quarterly*, Barker contributed many articles. He helped cement the importance of Texas and the Southwest in American history overall. He tackled some Lone Star myths, particularly debunking the notion that the Mexicans were solely at fault for the Texas Revolution and the Mexican War.

A few years after Jim Ferguson removed Ernest Winkler as state librarian, Winkler came to UT. While there he acquired the Genaro Garcia Collection and justified it to his boss Barker as an addition to Texas history, not the start of something else, but that is where it led. Under Carlos Castaneda and Nettie Lee Benson, the Latin American Collection became internationally regarded. Controversy arose among some small minded folks in the early 1930s when the Latin Collection was placed on the floor "literally above" the Texas Collection, but Barker said he did not care where they put it "as long as he can find what he needed."

When the title of distinguished professor was inaugurated at Texas in 1937, Barker was among the first three distinguished professors chosen. As Pool wrote "he had about him an unconscious austerity, the sort found in generals and Indian chiefs"

"Chief" was precisely what everyone in the history department called Barker. Light Cummins, a future Texas State Historian who served as one of Bill Pool's research assistants while he was a Master's student, said that Barker "was quiet, reserved, and most often had a serious expression on his face. Most people who did not know him well found him somewhat taciturn." Barker walked the campus daily, "always dressed formally in a suit with a Knox hat no matter how hot the weather."

When Homer Rainey was named university president in 1939, trouble over academic freedom and support for the New Deal started brewing almost immediately. Eugene Barker played golf with Rainey regularly. The men were friends, and, when the conservative faction of the Board of Regents quickly turned on the new university president, Barker was even instrumental in a faculty resolution supporting Homer Rainey.

That changed when Barker's son, David, brought home a book that was on the reading list of English 312Q. The professor read it and was "scandalized" by sexual content that he found "obscene and wholly objectionable." *The Big Money* was the third part of John dos Passos' U.S.A. trilogy. Barker rather publicly complained to a university vice president. His comments drew the ire of Ralph Long, chair of the committee which had selected the text. Long defended the choice but admitted that it would probably be dropped at the end of the semester.

Barker replied, again disparaging the book but stressing that he was probably more tolerant than "at least two million other adults in Texas." In short, this book could blow back on President Rainey, so "why, then, invite disaster." Barker was correct. The Regents became aware of *The Big Money*, and it became another nail in Rainey's eventual coffin.

An inflection point for the professor came after someone from the English Department wrote him "a rather dirty anonymous letter and sent a copy to the" student newspaper the *Daily Texan*. Barker said he allowed the letter to be published "partly to show just what sort of skunks we sometimes unfortunately get in university faculties." Though Barker claimed that he never told the Regents about the "pornographic" book, but rather was trying to head off controversy, the rift between him and many others on the faculty was complete. Soon, the Regents fired Rainey.

Don Carleton and Katherine J. Adams wrote in the *Quarterly* that Barker "came forward with great reluctance as a supporter of the board's decision." He tried to maintain a peacemaker role, asking for "an attitude of helpful cooperation with the Regents." It did not work. Light

Cummins said that "many UT faculty members ostracized Barker" for supporting the Regents and approving of the hiring of Theo Painter. Carleton went a step further saying that Barker was "actively opposed by the pro-Rainey faction among the faculty."

A key player in the post-Rainey world at UT was J. Evetts Haley, an old student of Barker's and the lead acquisitions man for the Texas Collection until he was fired for his anti-New Deal politics. Haley was a Panhandle rancher, historian, and hard core right-winger. Haley rekindled his association with Barker at the same time he was courting the most conservative of the Regents to create a dedicated and top tier place for the growing Texas & Southwest Collection. He was especially close to Regent Orville Bullington. The target location was the old library, a building which Rainey had devoted to the Fine Arts Department. When the Regents first agreed to the idea, Haley said "it will be sometime before... the Board (does) a better day's work than memorializing that great, rugged and gentle Texan Eugene C. Barker."

The continuing hostility of a large part of the faculty toward Barker plus Rainey's campaign for governor put the concept of the Barker Center in peril. Modesty be damned, Barker was lobbying for it, too. In January 1946, he wrote Haley "If we do not keep after the administration, nothing will be done."

Bullington ordered acting president Theophilus Painter to get to work on the history center, and he cared not what happened to the Fine Arts folks. It had no business at UT anyway. "If the dirt and paint dobbers (sic)" want to study art, "they should go to a girl's school or to Paris or some other 'furrin' seaport,'" Bullington railed. He blamed "certain faculty bleeding hearts" for the controversy.

The resolution to evict the Fine Arts Department passed the board in March 1946, less than a year before Bullington was scheduled to roll off the Board of Regents. A second resolution, this one to build a nice Barker History Center, was unanimously approved that September. The center opened in April 1950. *The Alcalde*, UT's alumni magazine, called the large Barker portrait by Houston artist Robert Joy that looked down on the main entrance "half sabre-toothed tiger and half St. Francis of Assisi."

The center outgrew the Old Library and was moved to Sid Richardson Hall on the eastern edge of campus in 1971. The Old Library building, built in 1910 according to a design by Cass Gilbert, is now Battle Hall, named for one of the casualties in Jim Ferguson's war against the university.

In 1991, the Barker Center became part of the Center for American History. It sits next to the Latin American History Collection, and the Littlefield Southern History Collection is still a component. The entire place was given the umbrella of Briscoe Center for American History in 2008 after former governor Dolph Briscoe gave $15 million. In a statement that may well have made "Farmer Jim" Ferguson flip in his casket, Briscoe declined to direct any particulars on how the money would be spent. "Their judgment would be better than mine on how to use it." History News Network called it "a donation for which every Texan should be grateful." It tripled the endowment at CAH.

The Barker Texas Collection includes original and early newspapers from almost every county in Texas along with some 750,000 photographs, 30,000 maps, 30,000 phonograph records by Texas artists, and 3,500 separate collections of personal and family papers related to Texas.

Barker's influence flowed forward through his direct students like Walter Prescott Webb and Carlos Castañeda, and the generations they taught and the books they wrote. The Texas History Department family tree keeps growing, and UT Austin remains a center for scholarship on the American Southwest.

Chapter Twenty-One

Frederick Law Olmsted

From the creation of the Republic until the years before the Civil War, there was no shortage of travel diaries about wild and wooly Texas. Germans, Brits, Frenchmen, and Yankees passed through the state and published their impressions. Among the most famous was *A Journey Through Texas* which recounted the lengthy trip by Frederick Law Olmsted and his brother, John. They made the trip in 1853, and, by agreement, sent 15 letters back for the *New York Times*. The paper wanted a correspondent to personally observe the institution of slavery and send back a firsthand account. Those reports provided the framework for the book, a tome that sold out its first printing in a single month.

Their route wended from Natchitoches, Louisiana, through East Texas to Austin, then south through San Marcos and New Braunfels to San Antonio and all the way to Indianola on the coast. There were side trips to Sisterdale and Boerne. The Olmsteds ventured west to Eagle Pass and crossed the Rio Grande for a spell before returning to San Antonio and back to the Sabine via LaGrange, Houston, Beaumont, and finally Turner's Ferry.

In addition to the job for the *Times*, Frederick Olmsted may have undertaken the trip to outrun a bit of social embarrassment. The Olmsteds were a well off family in Connecticut, and though he did not get a degree from Yale, Fred did attend many scientific lectures there. He studied surveying for two years, traveled extensively through the rest of New England then on to Canada, China, and Europe. He tried life at sea and despised it. He wrote a book about his strolls through England. His father bought Fred a farm on Staten Island where he dabbled in scientific agriculture. Frederick also played the field of available women throughout most of his twenties.

In 1851, with his brother John engaged and his friends all married, Fred settled on Emily Baldwin Perkins of Hartford, the granddaughter of the famous preacher Lyman Beecher and niece of Harriet Beecher Stowe. The two had courted on and off for years, and both sets of parents pushed the match.

Olmsted said the right things. He wrote that Emily had an "incomparably fine face" and that she was a "lovely and loveable girl." Tellingly, he also described her with the oh-so-unromantic word of "sensible." They were engaged in the summer of 1851, but Olmsted delayed setting a date because he had to tend to his crops on Staten Island. Shortly afterwards, Emily's mother wrote to Olmsted asking him to break off the engagement "because of a revulsion of feeling in E." When Fred went to Hartford in person, his once betrothed refused to see him. Fred's father believed his spurned son to be secretly pleased and wrote a family friend that Frederick "seems like a man who has thrown off a tremendous weight. Can it be that he brot it about purposely?" As for Emily, she soon met and married preacher and author Edward Everett Hale, a man who cheated on her with a long-running mistress.

Whether Frederick was disappointed or not is open to debate. His brother John soon married a woman named Mary Perkins, who was not related to Emily. John had also begun coughing up blood. That was the state of the two Olmsteds when they headed southwest toward Texas.

Accompanied by Nack and Fanny, horses they bought in Louisiana, and a pack mule named Mr. Brown, the brothers crossed into Texas just before Christmas 1853, slowly making their way through the Piney Woods toward Nacogdoches. There were only two ways into Texas for Americans – by sea into Galveston or Indianola, or on roads from Natchitoches, Shreveport, or Fulton in Louisiana.

The New England-bred Frederick was already a strong opponent of slavery in the abstract, but the travels through East Texas, seeing the practice up close, cemented his hatred of the cruel institution. He branded the White citizens of the region ignorant and lazy. Olmsted observed housing and clothing that was woefully inadequate for the enslaved people in winter, heard locals speak of torture and whippings, and while he had moral objections, he felt that pragmatic arguments were more effective. He wrote of the greater efficiency and prosperity that paid labor and crop diversity could bring.

From Nacogdoches, the brothers and their paid guide crossed the Trinity. At a drafty log cabin dubbed the hotel in Centerville, the Olmsteds added a "sturdy bull terrier" named Judy who wore her pads raw throughout the journey until they fashioned moccasins for her. She remained a companion all the way back to Staten Island where she lived out her final days.

The small party bought food at private houses - venison haunches, pone, and corn by the bushel. In western Leon County, they came upon their first Texas prairie, land with "swells like the ocean after a great storm," edged by woods, dotted with single trees, populated with contentedly grazing cattle and deer." It was a sultry forenoon, but that changed with a puff of wind at the next summit. The Olmsteds were about to experience their first norther. The temperature dropped 12 degrees in as many minutes. The north wind forced them into their overcoats, and they bent "against it in our saddles," and still the gale rose. From the morning high of 67, they faced a nighttime low of 25. The weather kept at them through Caldwell and on to Bastrop where the newspaper owner skipped an edition because the "printing office was on the north side of the house."

The Olmsted Brothers, temporarily without a guide, spent a "pleasant week" in Austin but hated the food. The "hostler in his frock, smelling strongly of the stables" served them "a succession of burnt flesh of swine and bulls, decaying vegetables, and sour and mouldy farinaceous glues, all pervaded with rancid butter." He also observed the legislature in session and was most taken by their "trustworthiness" and "manly dignity."

A Journey Through Texas is filled with eloquent observations, both pro and con. Olmsted "did not see one of the inhabitants look into a newspaper or book" from the Sabine until past Austin. His opinion of the people changed dramatically, though, as they moved south from the capital.

Crossing the blue-green Colorado, stopping at Manchac Springs, seeing large cranes that baffled them, and being enamored with live oaks, the brothers began to fall in love with Texas. They raved about the neat, prosperous, and civilized town of Neu Branfels where the food was good and a tame doe licked their hands. The river in San Antonio left Fred "so struck by its beauty. It is of a rich blue and pure as crystal, flowing rapidly but noiselessly over pebbles and between reedy banks." The drunken gunfights on the city's plazas happened almost daily and impressed the brothers much less, but they found the town's "odd and antiquated foreignness" unlike anything else in the United States.

Frederick Law Olmsted in 1857

What the Olmsteds called "Western Texas" is the Hill Country to us, and it charmed them so thoroughly that they briefly discussed settling amongst the "free-thinking, cultivated, brave men" at the small community of Sisterdale. Fred Olmsted wrote that he had "rarely seen any resort of woodnymphs more perfect than the bower of cypress branches that overhang the mouth of the Sister creek... You want a silent canoe to penetrate it; yet would be loth to desecrate its deep beauty."

They did not end up buying land, but advice was given "To any friend of mine who has faith in pure air and pure water, and is obliged to run from a northern winter, I cannot recommend a pleasanter spot to pass his exile than this."

Rejoined by their guide at San Antonio, the journey took them out to Fredericksburg, then backtracking until they turned south toward the coast. Seguin proved to be "the prettiest town in Texas." The Olmsteds saw Gonzales, Victoria, Indianola, Goliad, Mexican ranchos in Medina County, and then headed toward the frontier. They met Lipan and Mescalero Apaches and some Tonkawa out past Castroville. They joined a company of cavalry to lead them to the Rio Grande. Along the way, Fred killed a six-foot rattlesnake and picked up some horned toads to keep as pets.

The trip wound its way back east where they stopped at Houston, the busiest town they'd seen and with well-supplied shops. In addition to commenting on the unfamiliar pronunciation of the place and the cock fights with a $100 stake, Olmsted noted the magnolias, "in full glory of bloom, perfuming delicately the whole atmosphere."

Up to Liberty, past the mineral baths at Sour Lake, battling insects through bogs, they finally reached Beaumont where they sold the "flesh and blood companions" who had taken them on their great trip. Mr. Brown would lead travelers in the Neches bottoms, Fanny was to become a brood mare, and saying farewell to "poor Nack," sold for only 26 dollars, left Fred with tears in his eyes. Only Judy the bull terrier was destined to continue with the Olmsteds.

John, "a pulmonary invalid" was slightly better, but the "hot, soggy breath of the approaching summer was extremely depressing." The months of "pure air and stimulating travel" was largely cancelled out by a

largely "abominable diet" and "two thousands miles of active exposure."
The great Texas saddle trip had come to a close.

Just a few years after the Olmsted Brothers returned to the Northeast,
Fred leveraged connections made during his literary career to secure the
job as superintendent of Central Park in New York City. During his time
in England, Olmsted had become enamored with Birkenhead Park in
Liverpool. It was one of the few truly public parks. Grand European
park spaces were generally attached to the sprawling estates of major or
minor royals. In the U.S., aside from overgrown village greens, there was
nothing that opened the doors for city dwellers to enjoy nature. Olmsted
felt that was most undemocratic.

Only a few months after he took the job at Central Park, a young
English architect named Calvert Vaux asked Olmsted to join him for a
design competition to greatly expand the park into the centerpiece of
Manhattan. They got the job, of course. For the next 15 years, some "50
million cubic yards of stone, earth and topsoil" were manipulated by
3,000 workers. Thirty-six bridges and arches were constructed, and half
a million trees, shrubs, and vines went into the ground.

The screaming success of Central Park made Frederick Law Olmsted
the world's first landscape architect, a job title he made for himself. Over
the next four decades, Olmsted and his partners designed 20 major urban
parks including the famed Emerald Necklace in Boston and park systems
for Buffalo, Louisville, and Rochester. There were dozens of college
campuses including Stanford. He did the grounds at the U.S. Capitol
and the White House. There were cemeteries and parkways, and he was
certainly not above doing private gigs for the ultra-rich. Olmsted did

a couple hundred of those including the elaborate gardens at Biltmore near Asheville, North Carolina.

Did his months in Texas influence his work? Do the famous community playgrounds of the East contain any hidden pieces of the Hill Country? Certainly, there were many other places that impacted Olmsted's thinking. Even after he started the Central Park project, he had a Civil War-era job in Northern California where he fell in love with Yosemite. Clayton Maxwell of *Texas Monthly* believed that Olmsted carried some Texas hidden there in his heart. The man himself dropped references to his saddle journey through Texas when he spoke about Prospect Park, a project he did in Brooklyn. He said the same "governing circumstances" that brought the water features and open meadows in his designs were what he and his brother looked for in a campsite back in 1853.

For all of his success, Frederick Olmsted could not avoid the winding paths thrown up by life. In 1857, the same year he got the Central Park job, John Olmsted died of tuberculosis. Though Fred was a busy man, he moved his widowed sister-in-law and her three orphaned children to his Staten Island farm, and later brought them nearer his home in New York City. In 1859, when he was 37, Fred married his brother's widow. They had three children of their own, and two of the brood followed Fred into landscape architecture.

There are many places across the nation where someone may visit the gentle paths and contoured terrain that Olmsted designed for the purpose of giving the common American an escape from the "bustle and jar" of city life. He was, as one contemporary put it, an artist who "paints with lakes and wooded slopes; with lawns and banks and forest-covered hills; with mountainsides and ocean views."

Frederick Law Olmsted was also an artist who deeply appreciated other works of natural art. Reading *A Journey Through Texas*, it is impossible to miss that he found such genial grace and grandeur at most every turn in Central Texas. It offered "bewildering beauty." The sky felt closer, and fields of wildflowers were "radiant and delicious." He told us that he and his brother did not miss a chance to drink it all in: "We made it a point to secure as much beauty as possible in the view from our tent door."

Chapter Twenty-Two

Gutierrez-Magee Expedition

The Gutierrez-Magee Expedition may be the most important missing piece of the Texas Revolutionary puzzle. Even those who endured the sanitized Texas history of 4th and 7th grade classrooms likely recall only vagaries about filibuster expeditions that came into Texas in the years before legal foreign settlement in Mexican Texas. Of those who preceded Moses and Stephen Austin, schoolchildren were probably told about the Long Expedition in a way that was heavily weighted toward the wife that James Long left stranded and pregnant on the Bolivar Peninsula for a bitter winter spent with only an enslaved girl and a small child while she waited for the husband who would never return.

The story of Jane Long, as interesting as it is, perfectly underscores two major issues about historiography. One, common in all parts of the globe, is that people who live longest get to tell the tale. Those who survive into their eighties or nineties and bury their contemporaries leave memoirs that are either purposely embellished, exaggerate their roles, are plagued by faulty memories, or all of the above. The other difficulty for Texas history specifically is that almost as soon as Anglo-Americans from the United States became a majority they began to write Tejanos out of the script, both in history texts and real life. That is what makes the notion that Jane Long was in any way the "Mother of Texas" so laughable.

The vital tale of Gutierrez-Magee suffers from both historical maladies. Very few people among what modern Texans will consider the good guys survived to tell the tale, and when Anglos wrote about the influences of the Texas Revolution, they were not inclined to include much Mexican history, no matter how important it was to the story.

The first battles for freedom and the first declaration of independence written on Texas soil happened not in the 1830s but from 1811 through 1813. They were part of the Enlightenment movement to free Mexico from Spain. A year earlier, a popular 50-year old priest in the State of Guanajuato had gotten fed up with mercantile interests in Spain hurting poor people in Mexico just to put more money into their pockets. His cry from the pulpit started an uprising. In San Fernando de Bexar, known today as San Antonio, Juan Bautista de las Casas was inspired enough by Father Hidalgo's efforts that he captured the governor and his military staff. De las Casas' efforts were short lived since he was in turn captured by royalists and executed, but they inspired one of his fellow revolutionaries to head to Washington, D.C. and seek assistance from the United States.

Jose Bernardo Gutierrez de Lara met with Secretary of State James Monroe and with representatives of Britain, Denmark, and Russia. At each stop he explained plans to establish a republican government in Texas and use it as a base to expand that democracy across New

Spain. Though he did not leave with an American army in tow, he was convinced that the United States would not interfere. Gutierrez de Lara also made new friends. At New Orleans on his way home, he met with Governor William Claiborne and William Shaler, a United States special agent who was eager to come to Texas as an observer for President James Madison. At Natchitoches, Louisiana, they enlisted a disgruntled U.S. Army lieutenant named Augustus Magee, a frontier veteran who was recently passed over for promotion.

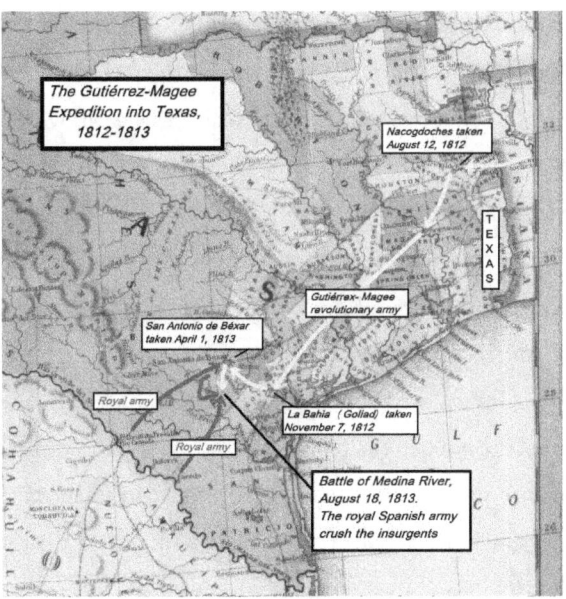

A map of the expedition. Wikimedia Commons

The band of men they assembled was a motley one – Mexican exiles who were true believers in independence, former supporters of Aaron Burr who had already bitten at western adventure, and American frontiersmen who saw visions of free land and unknown booty. They crossed the Sabine on August 8, 1812 with 130 men, and left Nacogdoches a short time later with 300. They styled themselves the Republican Army of the North and marched under a solid green flag. The Boston-born Magee was their military commander.

Their first successful target was a small fort and barracks on the Trinity River near present-day Madisonville. Governor Manuel Maria de Salcedo, the one who had been held captive by de las Casas, moved out of San Antonio to meet the insurgents on the Guadalupe River, but Magee turned south and captured La Bahia, or Goliad, instead. The small garrison there promptly switched sides. Salcedo, reinforced to 800 Spanish troops, laid siege. Overwhelmed, Magee requested surrender terms, but the offer contained no pardon for their Mexican compadres, so the revolutionaries stayed put. Meanwhile, Magee grew deathly ill, passing away in February while the presidio was still under siege and subjected to artillery fire.

Magee was replaced as military commander by Samuel Kempner, an American tavern keeper. Kempner proved to be the best leader the rebels had, surprising the Spaniards in a ravine and killing more than 100 of them. Governor Salcedo and Colonel Simon Herrera retreated back to San Antonio. After slowly resupplying, the Republican Army, reinforced with more Spanish Army deserters, won a major victory at Rosillo, just southeast of San Antonio. They soon took the town.

It was supposed to be Gutierrez de Lara's moment to shine, but he raised some eyebrows when he declared himself President Protector of the State of Texas. He also oversaw the writing of a declaration of independence from Spain and, one week later, a Constitution for the State of Texas within the still rather mythical Mexican Republic. It was exactly the triumph of republican government that he wanted, but the treatment of his high profile prisoners brought about his downfall. Gutierrez ordered that Salcedo, Herrera, and the other royalist officers be marched to the battle site near Rosillo Creek. There they were stripped of their clothes then stabbed and mutilated. The garments were kept intact for later sale. When the carnage ended, Kempner led more than 100 thoroughly disgusted Americans back to Louisiana. Gutierrez was found guilty of murder at a court martial convened among his troops.

The replacement for Gutierrez de Lara was Jose Alvarez de Toledo, a Spanish-born politician Gutierrez had met in Washington. Alvarez and William Shaler, still reporting back to the American government, had a hand in fomenting the discontent with Gutierrez through printed broadsides circulated through Texas.

Alvarez pulled his Republican Army together and waited to meet the next retaliatory thrust from the Spanish royalists. It came near the banks of the Medina River, south southwest of San Antonio. Over 1,800 royalist soldiers were led by General Joaquin de Arredondo. The plan of Alvarez de Toledo was to catch Arredondo in an ambush, but it was the Republicans who were lured into the trap. The 1,400 fighters under the green flag battled for four hours against infantry, cavalry, and artillery before they broke and ran, leaving hundreds of their comrades dead among the oaks and mesquite scrub. Most of those who fled were caught and killed on their way back to San Antonio. Some solid accounts say that only about 100 survived. Arredondo lost but 55 soldados. It remains the deadliest battle ever fought in Texas.

What came next changed the course of not only the brief First Texas Republic but the trajectory of Mexico, the United States, and even European politics. Arredondo, not satisfied with the one-sided victory on the battlefield came into San Antonio and began his ironically named "pacification" through wholesale executions. From the battle site, which is still not definitively pinpointed, all the way to San Antonio, exhausted revolutionaries were run down, killed, and hung from trees by their heels. Roughly 50 made it all the way back to Bexar, but they were also killed and their bodies displayed publicly. As many as 327 suspected Texas republican supporters were either forced into labor or executed on the Military Plaza. Five hundred local women, many undoubtedly recent widows, were imprisoned in the Curbelo house which the royalists jokingly called La Quinta. There the women were repeatedly beaten and raped all while being forced to provide thousands of tortillas for the soldiers' daily diet. During the three or four months that the women were held, their children remained on their own, fending for themselves.

Arredondo sent Lt. Colonel Ignacio Elizando and 500 men all the way to Nacogdoches, the second largest settlement in Spanish Texas, to carry out the same purges there and "clear eastern Texas of enemy combatants, revolutionary sympathizers, foreigners" and anyone who had helped the Republican Army of the North in any way. Some historians estimate that by 1814 the population of Texas had been reduced by 40%. The hundreds of republican corpses - Tejano, American, and free Black - rotted on the battlefield of Medina for nine years. It was not until 1822 when Chihuahuan Jose Felix Trespalacios, named the first governor of Texas for the Mexican monarchist Agustin de Iturbide, brought men to the site and had the bones of the revolutionaries buried together under a large live oak tree.

Though Texas remained a trouble spot throughout the remainder of the Mexican Revolution against Spain, every Tejano remembered the brutal lessons. When Antonio Lopez de Santa Anna returned to Texas with his own army, he already knew the landscape since he had been among Arredondo's officers in 1813. Even as the Alamo was being bombarded in early 1836, a majority of the citizens of San Antonio, with the events of two decades earlier still seared in their memories, chose to remain neutral or side with the Mexican Centralists.

Chapter Twenty-Three

Harvey Penick

Golf done right is a beautiful game played amidst quiet nature, capable of yielding great satisfaction. For most who've ever shouldered a bag, though, it provides a few fleeting glimpses of joy and a boatload of frustration. It is player versus course, player versus self. The simple act of hitting a golf ball well is routinely called the single most difficult action in sports, but one soft-spoken Texan spent a lifetime teaching the game as well as anyone ever has.

Harvey Morrison Penick was born in Austin and grew up in Hyde Park, just north of the University of Texas campus. At the age of eight, he got a job as a caddie at the Austin Country Club. Those golf links, bisected by Red River Street, were just a few blocks east of the Penick home. He worked weekends and summers, and advanced to shop assistant. Golf held infinitely more interest for the boy than did school work. By the age of 13, he was assistant club pro. A few years later the country club offered him the top job, but his parents demanded their son finish at Austin High. The club held the job open. In May 1923, as soon as Harvey Penick graduated, he took over as head golf professional.

Harvey Penick played some on the Texas professional golf tour with men including Jack Burke, Sr. and Lighthorse Harry Cooper. It was a far cry from the modern Professional Golfer's Association, and most of those players quickly figured out there was better money and more stability in being the head pro at a nice country club. With his seniority at one of the two oldest golf courses in Texas, Penick served for a time as president of the Texas PGA. He was in that post "when two youngsters named Ben Hogan and Byron Nelson applied for membership."

Penick working on clubs at ACC. Austin History Center, Austin Public Library

For decades, the bulk of Penick's personal and professional life stayed within a good driver shot of the UT campus. He continued his work at Austin Country Club, and in 1931, he took over as golf coach for the Longhorns. His team did not win the Southwest Conference golf title in his first year, but he won the following year, then the next eight in a row, or for those who like a longer view, 20 out of the next 23. He finally hung it up as the Horns coach after the 1963 season.

Penick was almost 60 years old, and many people might be looking toward retirement, but Harvey Penick, in his quiet and simple way, kept teaching golf. He was already the local guru of the links, but professionals from around the country began coming to Austin for lessons, too. Penick established a sterling reputation among women's golfers. At least five of the top LPGA pros during the 1960s and 70s were Harvey's students, among them Kathy Whitworth and Mickey Wright who won 88 and 82 LPGA tournaments respectively. Those numbers are still first and second highest of all time. His pupils from that era won 10 U.S. Women's Opens.

The University of Texas has produced more winners of golf's four "major" tournaments than any other college, and the first two were students of Harvey Penick long after he was through being the official coach of the program. Tom Kite and Ben Crenshaw started coming to Penick years before they became national collegiate champions. They started heeding Penick's carefully honed wisdom as boys, and they kept doing so.

In 1971, after 43 years as the head pro at Austin Country Club, the board pushed Penick into a role called "Professional Emeritus." It was a very nice way of saying that his time had perhaps passed. Penick's son, Tinsley, was given the top job. Harvey may have misunderstood the inference, however. One of his frequent sayings was, "When I quit learning, I'll quit teaching," and he was far from done learning.

Penick continued giving swing advice to Crenshaw and Kite, and they did all right for themselves. The pair led the Longhorns to two NCAA championships, and Crenshaw won the individual college crown three times in a row, the only person ever to accomplish that feat. Between them, they also account for two Masters green jackets, one U.S. Open trophy, and 37 PGA tour wins.

Despite that slate of results, Harvey Penick should not be thought of as a teacher to the stars. He improved the swing of hundreds of amateur golfers for five bucks a lesson, and they were just as important to Harvey. He was not a man who over-analyzed a player. He let the golfer retain their individuality. Sometimes he stayed behind a bush to observe them hitting balls so they did not even know he was there. His advice was sometimes nothing more than nudging the ball back two inches in a player's stance or telling them to "swing like you're cutting weeds." That was the entire point of Penick's success – carefully chosen words that were straightforward and uncomplicated. He was also effective because he was confident, and imparted to the student just how important their confidence was to shaving strokes off their game. As his words were paraphrased, "Each golf shot is new life, new hope."

By 1989, time had caught up with the gentle golf coach. He was in St. David's Hospital with a fractured spine, prostate cancer, and general disorientation. Not surprisingly, all of these ailments were giving the 85-year-old severe depression. His son Tinsley expected the worst. But when get well wishes began to pour in from golf professionals, club members, and even a note from Jack Nicklaus saying "we need you," Harvey Penick rallied. Donations from ACC members allowed the family to hire a private nurse. Penick went home, and soon he was back at the club handing out advice. That in itself would have been a nice last act to the life of a beloved golf professional. He had been around the game since it was only two decades old in this country. He knew Bobby Jones personally, and could comment on a backswing by dropping a matter of fact word that "Walter Hagen had that same problem." But amazingly, the best was yet to come.

Two years later, Harvey asked Bud Shrake to stop by the club and see him. Bud was a writer, a Fort Worth contemporary of Dan Jenkins who

had spent formative years at *Sports Illustrated* and penned articles for top
magazines and a dozen books including the wonderful *Blessed McGill*.
He was dating Ann Richards, he was buddies with Willie Nelson and
Darrell Royal, and since he had to give up drinking in 1984, Shrake
was obsessed with golf. Not that he was especially brilliant at it, but he
was known to play multiple rounds most every day of the week. Harvey
wanted to show Bud Shrake his private notebook.

The nurse stepped out of the golf cart to let Shrake sit and peruse the
pages that Penick had been filling with golf thoughts for decades. Only
Tinsley had seen it before that moment. Some of it was simplicity itself
– "Take dead aim." Harvey was big about aim, and the mental aspects of
golf - "Once you address the ball, hitting it to the desired target must be
the only thing in your life." He asked Shrake if it might be possible to get
the notebook published and how much that might cost him. The writer
said he "would see what (he) could do."

The book went to Shrake's agent and soon wound up with the
sports acquisitions editor at Simon & Schuster. It took only a few
hours before they offered a $90,000 advance. Because Penick was almost
deaf, the offer was relayed through his wife Helen. When Harvey spoke
with Shrake the following day, he was worried. "With all my medical
bills and everything," Harvey said, "I'm not sure I can afford to pay
ninety thousand dollars." The misunderstanding was addressed, and
Bud Shrake began the work of expanding the dog-eared notebook into
a real book. There were slow interviews as Penick lip read Shrake's
questions, then the organization of thoughts, and by 1992, there was a
book. Though the publisher had ponied up a decent advance, they only
committed to an initial print run of 17,500 copies.

*Harvey Penick's Little Red Book: Lessons and Teachings from a
Lifetime in Golf* became a sensation, the top selling sports book of all

time at that moment. Shrake had a successful career as an author, but nothing had come close to the *New York Times* Best Sellers list, let alone staying there for 54 weeks. Accolades came from around the world. The *London Daily Express* wrote, "The *Little Red Book*... is only a manual of golf if *Moby Dick* is about angling and *The Merchant of Venice* is a guide to investment." It sold 1.3 million copies and four more golf books with Shrake followed. At age 87, the "mystical holy man" of golf was suddenly an international celebrity. The attention grew so overwhelming that Tinsley Penick had to escape Austin for an extended vacation in Ireland. In a pub there, he was buttonholed to talk about his dad.

The straight golf advice was valuable. Penick routinely came back to suggesting that any golfer, no matter the skill level, should spend most of their time concentrating on the chip shots. That was the recipe for success, he wrote in several forms. As *Texas Monthly* put it, "What Harvey has done is remind us that the object of this game is to hit a ball with a stick."

There are thousands of golf books and videos to improve the swing, but likely nobody was ever better at communicating the mental requirements of golfing success. Though it is a tired sports cliché, much of Penick's advice transcends sports if one reads it as a metaphor extended to other aspects of life.

- "Like chess, golf is a game that is forever challenging but can never be conquered."

- "The woods are full of long drivers."

- "Most mistakes are made before the club is swung."

- "The golf swing is one swing, but it is made up of little things all working together."

- "There is nothing guaranteed to be fair in either golf or life, you must accept your disappointments and your triumphs equally."

To the end, Harvey Penick went to Austin Country Club on days when his health allowed it. His association with the club spanned 82 years. He sat in his golf cart with his nurse, barely able to speak audibly, taking several minutes to sign an autograph, but with a razor sharp memory for names and even recognizing specific golf clubs he had handcrafted 70 years before.

The week before he died, his two star pupils were both in contact, asking for advice. Ben Crenshaw visited Harvey at home, and the frail teacher gave a short putting lesson from his sickbed. Even though the Masters began the following day in Augusta, Georgia, Crenshaw and Tom Kite, who had given Penick his 1992 U.S. Open trophy, were in Austin to act as pallbearers. Ben Crenshaw, in fact, won the tournament that week by one stroke over Davis Love III, another professional who had sought lessons from Harvey Penick. When his final putt dropped on the 18th hole, Crenshaw's raw emotions came pouring out, and he fell to his knees and cried.

We should all be lucky enough to have a teacher in life who said, "My greatest reward has always been the look of pleasure in the eyes of pupils who have just made a perfect shot."

Chapter Twenty-Four

John Coffee Hays

The list of young men 19 or 20 years of age who sought adventure in the Texas Revolution is a long one, but few came with the pedigree of Tennessean John Coffee Hays. He was the great nephew of President Andrew Jackson, named for one of Old Hickory's closest lieutenants, and his father was a friend of Sam Houston. Arriving too late for the primary fighting, Hays joined Thomas Rusk's company in time to bury the remains of the massacre victims at Goliad.

With victory in hand after San Jacinto, General Houston set young Hays up with a Texas Ranger company under the command of Henry Karnes. Those Rangers fought a Mexican cavalry unit near Laredo and patrolled between the Rio Grande and San Antonio. Hays, known to all as Jack, split his time between Ranger work and surveying, and that latter occupation required him to learn the tricks of frontier self-defense or die. The Comanche and other tribes quickly figured out that when the two or three-person surveying crews came, unwanted settlement followed, so any man carrying a transit and chain was subjected to the harshest treatment.

Hays stood only five foot nine, and one of his Rangers described his thusly: "a slim, slight, smooth-faced boy, not over twenty years of age, and looking younger than he was in fact. In his manners he was unassuming in the extreme, a stripling of few words, whose quiet demeanor stretched quite to the verge of modesty. Nevertheless, it was this youngster whom the tall, huge-framed brawny-armed campaigners hailed unanimously as their chief and leader."

His Ranger troops had no set uniform; they supplied their own clothes. To outsiders, they appeared undisciplined and rough, but Hays trained them well. His company often rode with a band of Lipan Apache, allies to the Texans against their Comanche and Kiowa enemies. The Lipan chief Flacco rode with Hays and called him "Bravo-Too-Much." At the Battle of Plum Creek, fighting the hundreds of warriors who were returning from the Great Raid of 1840, Hays took part along with Chief Placido and Tonkawa scouts.

Jack Hays was the pioneer of a technology that changed the American West. Texas Anglo settlers who first encountered Comanche warriors found the Indians to be uncannily expert horsemen. The Comanche could ride with no hands and use a short bow that could very rapidly fire an accurate arrow, up to 18 in a quiver, by drawing a string back no further than their ear. Anglo Texans arrived from the United States with rifles that were far superior to the Spanish and Mexican muskets, but though they had a range that might hold a Comanche or Kiowa warrior at bay, the Whites could still not match the Texas Indians on horseback.

That changed when Hays adopted the use of the new five shot Paterson Colt revolvers for his Rangers. Trained to fire from horseback, the Rangers suddenly had multiple shots from a weapon as opposed to a single shot, muzzle-loaded gun. The number doubled with a second revolver, and increased even more with an added rifle. They tested their kit in a fight at Walker's Creek in 1844 where Hays and fourteen Rangers charged and routed some 80 mounted warriors. By matching the Comanches in the area of rapid fire weaponry, the frontier was forever changed, and the fate of the indigenous people was sealed.

Hays was an amazing tracker, even when riding at a good pace. One of his men said "he could dismount and observe the small pebbles, and by noticing the slightest displacement made by the horses, could, in a moment, tell in what direction they had gone." There were famous gun battles for Hays' Rangers at Canyon de Ugalde and on the Pedernales River.

One day at Enchanted Rock lives on in legend even if the facts of the encounter are in question. Hays and 15 or 20 of his company were scouting in the vicinity of the famous granite hill north of Fredericksburg when they were surprised by a large band of Comanches. The Indians came at a moment when Hays was alone near the top of the rock. The captain set himself into a hollow spot at the summit and decided that he would make each advancing warrior pay dearly for as long as he could hold out. The other men fought their own skirmish down below. Accounts differ as to how long Hays kept up his solo battle, with some stretching it as long as three hours. There is no doubt, though, that Hays used his ammunition sparingly and his rocky battlement well. He held off his attackers, killing at least five, until his company could get to him. Three other rangers were wounded in the fight, but none fatally.

Jack Hays rose to the rank of major in the Rangers, but at the outset of the Mexican War, he was mustered into federal service and became a colonel in charge of the First Regiment of Texas Mounted Riflemen. He led roughly a thousand men, a far cry from his Ranger companies that numbered in the teens. Under the overall command of General Zachary Taylor, their first large action came in scouting and fighting at Monterrey. The following year, Hays formed another regiment under General Winfield Scott and managed supply and communication lines between Mexico City and the coast at Veracruz. Just as with the Comanches, Hays' Rangers defeated Mexican cavalry even when outnumbered at Galaxara Pass. They fought guerillas at Teotihuacán and Sequalteplán. Under the Mexican War's two biggest commanders, Jack Hays and his Rangers did all that was asked of them and perhaps more.

Jack Hays

Their reputation among the Mexican people was that of efficient ruthlessness, and that view lingers south of the Rio Grande, also thanks to Jack Hays' men. Mexican citizens referred to them as Los Diablos Tejanos, the Texas devils. Ranger units, though not necessarily with Hays present, are known to have robbed and killed Mexicans off the battlefield, and had the same done to them. The Rangers in Mexico often used tactics they had learned from the Comanches. One of the lowest episodes was the Ranger killing of unarmed civilians, including women, children and elderly men, at Saltillo.

In the United States, their wartime exploits made them legends of American folklore. By war's end, the Texas Rangers were nationally known through stories and ballads, and Jack Hays was a hero.

In 1848, after the Mexican War had ended, most Ranger companies were disbanded since the U.S. Army had taken over frontier defense in the new State of Texas. Hays, still in demand, was picked to lead a trailblazing expedition from San Antonio to El Paso. The group struggled through uncharted desert. When their supplies were exhausted, they ate their mules. The expedition made it as far as Presidio before turning back. A year later, Jack Hays received an appointment from the federal government as Indian agent for the Gila River country of Arizona. He then pushed even further west, to California on the front edge of the Gold Rush, and was elected sheriff of San Francisco County in 1850. Hays was also one of the founders of the city of Oakland and built up a substantial fortune through ranching and real estate.

Even away on the Pacific, Hays was not forgotten in Texas. The Comanche respected bravery, and remembered Ranger Jack Hays after he moved away to California. Upon the birth of his first son, Hays received an engraved silver cup from Chief Buffalo Hump.

In 1870, Jack Hays made a final visit back to Texas. He was celebrated as a hero at each stop, and the *San Antonio Herald* declared that "the name of Jack Hays will almost wake the dead." The Alamo City gave a grand ball for the old Ranger at the Menger Hotel. A few weeks later, accompanied by his brother, a former Confederate Army general, Hays returned to the Bay Area of California. His resting place is in Mountain View there.

Hays County, Texas, is named in his honor.

South Texas

White Winged Dove. cricketsblog via Wikimedia Commons

Chapter Twenty-Five

The Bracero Program

There are certain undeniable truths when looking at the history of United States immigration policy. It is always complicated. It is often unfair. It was frequently built on anecdotal evidence, stereotypes, and pure racism. Above all, it has never, ever been consistent.

Despite any shrill hyperbole to the contrary, the U.S. has not had anything close to "open borders" in the past 100 years. In spite of that fact, the nation has relied on immigrant labor since the beginning. Even our revolution was fought with imported Germans on the side of the British Crown and loaned Frenchmen fighting alongside the rebels.

Though there have long been restrictions on who could become a citizen, for the first century of this nation, people could come as they pleased. The first restrictions on immigration did not arrive until 1875, and they were focused on prohibiting undesirable groups - criminals, people with contagious diseases, polygamists, anarchists, "beggars and importers of prostitutes."

The Chinese were the first national group singled out for bans, and soon after, so were most other Asians. It was not until the 1920s that true crackdowns came. Instead of the fair-skinned Irish, British, Germans, and Scandinavians who had arrived in great numbers during the 19th century, the flow had shifted to southern and eastern Europe. Specifically, huge numbers of Italians and Jews. Congress responded with two sweeping laws that set specific quotas by country of origin. Most Americans did not want the darker-skinned Europeans.

What the big 1924 law did not do was cut down on immigration from south of the Rio Grande. It was the perfect push-pull situation. At the same time that the Mexican Revolution was driving people from their homeland, several growing industries in the U.S. were in dire need of cheap labor. So many workers left Northern Mexico in the 1920s and 30s that employers there were left scrambling. In many cases, Mexican crops rotted in the fields from lack of pickers. Every year during the 1920s more than 150,000 Mexican workers entered the United States with Texas as the prime destination. There was virtually no attempt to stop them, and there was plenty of work north of the Rio Grande to go around. What could reasonably be considered exploitation by American standards was a monetary paradise to the impoverished Mexican newcomers.

That influx into the U.S. reversed itself during the Depression Era with large-scale deportations that sent both Mexicans and Mexican Americans back across the border. That was despite Franklin Roosevelt's "Good Neighbor Policy," and Mexico retaliated by seizing millions in American-owned property.

The event that again disrupted that pattern was WWII. With 16 million American men in uniform, the labor shortage fast became a crisis.

Young men from the immigrant families who came north to work also joined the fight. Almost half a million Mexican Americans and 15,000 Mexican nationals joined the United States military.

Famously, American women filled many roles in manufacturing, but agriculture was another matter. Certain ranch operations were deemed vital enough that draft-age men were ordered to stay at home and raise sheep or cattle. Less than a year into the conflict, however, it became clear that if Americans were to eat and clothe themselves, more workers were needed. German POWS were hired out to farmers, especially in Texas, but something bigger was required.

The answer was more labor from Mexico. That nation declared war against the Axis Powers on July 23, 1942, and just two weeks later, the U.S. started the Mexican Farm Labor Program by executive order. It was commonly known as the Bracero Program. That Spanish word translated to one who works using their arms, and that is precisely what American farms needed – helping hands and arms. It would become the largest guest worker program in U.S. history.

To make it happen, diplomatic accords were reached between the Mexican government and multiple American agencies. The program called for adequate living conditions, meaning shelter, food, and sanitation. It meant protection from the military draft, and a minimum wage of 30 cents per hour. There was also a requirement that a portion of the bracero's wages be saved in accounts in Mexico, money that many of the migrant workers never got back. Finally, the agreement said that these guest workers were legally protected against discrimination and could not be barred from Whites-only areas. Modern Americans might guess how that last provision turned out.

Selection of who got to come north was handled by officials at all levels of the Mexican government. The largest number of workers came from the states of Guanajuato, Jalisco, and Michoacán. Where local officials were able to exercise control, the system was often rife with political favoritism, bribery, and corruption.

During the war years, the number of braceros admitted was relatively small – less than 10% of U.S hired laborers. They were spread across 24 states, primarily in the South and West. Though most worked in the fields, only eight months into the program, the Southern Pacific and other railroads began using braceros, too. The early success of the program also brought increased numbers of Mexican workers being hired outside the official parameters.

Abuses in pay began popping up right from the start, especially in the Northwest states of Washington, Oregon, and Idaho. Almost immediately, the guest workers discovered that their wages were less than Whites got for the same jobs. The promise of an hourly wage was switched on some vegetable farms to an amount as low as eight cents a box, instead. The first grumbles that led to small work stoppages came at the start of 1943, but the biggest early issues were in Texas.

Life along the Rio Grande had been fluidly trans-border for decades, despite some efforts by Johnny-come-lately White leaders in El Paso and Brownsville as early as the 1850s. Over the century that followed, those moves succeeded in relegating the "Mexicans" to lower economic and social status, but did not actually seek to stop cross-border life. In fact, many South Texas farmers boycotted the Bracero Program because they liked paying much lower wages to the illegal workers.

Where Texas had proved itself different than the other states receiving braceros was in the amount of violence inflicted on Mexicans and Mexican Americans. That murderous tendency likely peaked with massacres performed by Texas Rangers and some local law enforcement in the years just prior to WWI, but at the start of the Bracero program, discrimination was still bad enough that Mexico refused to let its citizens come to work in the state. Texans might have been more aware than anyone that they needed laborers from south of the border, but they also had a tendency to place little value on those lives.

When the Mexican government cut off the Braceros coming into the Texas, Governor Coke Stevenson pleaded to no avail. It had been Texans at the forefront of asking for the imported labor in the first place. In 1943, the state legislature passed the Caucasian Race Resolution affirming that people of Mexican descent were indeed viewed as White and could not be discriminated against in Texas accommodations. The thing was that Mexico could look at a century of history that showed otherwise. Their skepticism was validated only a few months later when the owner of a restricted swimming pool in San Antonio won a court case that supported his exclusions because the legislature's resolution did not "have the effect of a statute."

Mexican Foreign Minister Ezequiel Padilla made a secret deal at one point to allow 5,000 braceros to transfer from other states to Texas farms, but he changed his mind after reading the hostile Mexican press. Governor Stevenson even traveled to Mexico City for Dies y Seiz celebrations, but nothing worked. Texans were reluctant to end Jim Crow lest it open the door for advancement by Black Americans, and officials in Mexico and groups like the League of United Latin American Citizens in Texas saw that ambivalence plainly. The braceros were officially kept from Texas until four years after the war ended.

There were periods, even during the shutdown, that U.S. immigration opened the border for a few hours at a time to appease Texas farmers. In October 1948, several thousand undocumented workers were not only let into Texas near El Paso, they were escorted by Border Patrol agents directly to the cotton fields. The American government later apologized for violating the Bracero Agreements. Of course, by then, the Texas cotton had been picked.

During the war, the number of Braceros peaked at 66,000 in 1944, but once the agreement's renewals began, the number climbed exponentially. Well over 400,000 Mexicans a year received work permits in the latter half of the 1950s. There had been multiple extensions, but the most sweeping was the Migrant Labor Agreement of 1951. Among other provisions, it stipulated that braceros could not be used as scab replacement workers for Americans on strike; however, the braceros themselves were not allowed to go on strike or renegotiate wages.

Mexico, still needing workers of their own in some regions, called for penalties on U.S. employers who hired workers illegally, but that provision did not make the final bill. A year later, thanks to objections from President Truman, another bill passed making it a federal felony to knowingly conceal, harbor, or shield a foreign national, however there was a "Texas proviso" that specified that simply employing undocumented workers did not constitute "harboring or concealing" them.

The United States set up reception centers both in Mexico and along the border. One of the largest was at El Paso. Once they had passed the selection process at home, the newly arrived braceros were inspected by American health officers and then stripped and sprayed with DDT to eliminate lice.

Despite the growing use of the Bracero program, American growers, including the increasing numbers of large corporate-owned farms, recruited and hired even more Mexicans illegally. For their part, the workers from south of the river wanted better pay and opportunity than they found at home. The Mexican government was interfering with mechanization of agriculture, and so much produce was being exported to the north that food shortages were common in Mexico. The flood of workers kept coming.

Braceros harvesting tomatoes. Library of Congress

The Catholic Church in Mexico was very much opposed to the Bracero Program. They believed that separating husbands and wives and exposing the migrant workers to the evils of alcohol, prostitution, and gambling in the United States would destroy family life. They were equally concerned about Protestant missionaries in the north.

The braceros themselves missed their wives, girlfriends, and children, so they found ways to bring them to the U.S. They learned the American system and saved money for homes. When American officials figured this out, they began inspecting and censoring letters that asked for families to join the braceros in the U.S. Though some workers were left wondering why they received no response from home, many others found alternate ways to reunite with their loved ones in American border towns.

Another strike against the program was a raft of complaints from American labor. Attempts to unionize agricultural workers after WWII were unsuccessful in part because of braceros. It was not just upsetting farmworkers. The AFL-CIO was also making a squawk on behalf of other American workers. Moreover, as the success of the legal immigration rose, so did the volume of illegal immigration. There were many known cases of undocumented crossings in which immigration agents simply handed people the paperwork to become legal.

During 1942, the first full year of WWII and the start of the Bracero program, the United States undertook some 12,400 returns and removals. That number gradually ticked upward from there. By the election year of 1952, there were well over 700,000 deportations. The Eisenhower Administration ultimately decided that was not enough. In June 1954, they launched Operation Wetback, a military-style program to repatriate more undocumented workers back to Mexico.

There were some actions in Los Angeles, Chicago, and San Francisco, but the bulk of it was carried out near the Texas and California borders. The first mobile task force in the operation was set up in McAllen and focused on the Rio Grande Valley. It was the start of inspection stations that still remain well inside the border to this day. It was also the beginning of a permanent Border Control presence along the Mexican border.

During the first year of the operation, the number of Mexicans and Mexican Americans sent back across the Rio Grande shot up to 1.1 million. At the exact same time, legal immigration under the Bracero program was also rising to new heights, and by that time, the lion's share of the immigrants were coming to Texas.

One major issue with the deportations under Eisenhower was that the people rounded up were not necessarily sent to anywhere remotely near their homes. If they were dropped near the border, they quickly returned. Some Border Patrol agents began shaving the heads of the deportees to make the repeat offenders easier to identify. So, the United States started taking them farther south. A quarter of the Operation Wetback returnees went by cargo ship to Veracruz and others were moved to the interior by land. They were given no food, money, or employment, nor had they been allowed to retrieve belongings in the United States. Many struggled to make their way home. In July 1955, 88 deported workers died in Mexican heat that topped 112 degrees.

Outcries in the United States led to the end of the mass deportation program after only one year. Two years after the giant spike, fewer than 90,000 Mexican nationals were returned to their homeland. And there the number stayed for the rest of the 1950s. In reality, it did nothing to stop illegal immigration, and the paradox of an American nation that wanted cheap labor from Latin America but maintained a widespread distaste for immigrants persisted.

As the civil rights and farmworkers movements gained steam at the start of the 1960s, many of the braceros' supporters began to fall away. It came at a time when increasing mechanization of farms was also reducing the overall need for manual labor.

The Bracero Program finally came to an end when Congress allowed it to expire at the end of the calendar in 1964. Some government spokespeople claimed that cross-border labor "slowed to a trickle." That was definitely less than true in the Rio Grande Valley and immediately up river. Across the country, temporary agricultural workers continued working under H-2 and H-2A visas, but the Hart-Cellar Act passed Congress in 1965. That law, for the first time in U.S. history, placed caps on the number of visas granted to residents of the Western Hemisphere.

There was still a need for laborers, of course. In 1965, a program dubbed the A-TEAM recruited over 18,000 high school students in Texas and California to work on farms as their summer jobs. Only about 3,300 ever entered the fields, and almost all of them quickly quit or staged strikes because of poor working conditions, oppressive heat, and horrible housing. The program did not make it to 1966.

Mostly, the labor gap was filled by much the same people who had been there before. Without a legal means to earn a living in the United States, workers did it illegally. Records show that the overall number of migrants entering the U.S. after 1965 remained about the same as during the Bracero program.

Chapter Twenty-Six

The Cart War

Historian James Crisp said that "It was a very tough time to be of Mexican descent in Texas from 1842 to 1845, 46."

In the first decade after the Texas Revolution, there were still enough longtime Texans who remembered colonial days, had lived under Mexico, and knew that many Tejanos took part in the successful rebellion against Santa Anna and the Mexican Centralists. As more Anglos from the United States came into the Republic, a tipping point was reached. It coincided with horrible economic times and two incursions that saw Mexican army units overtake San Antonio. Hundreds of Tejanos, including Revolutionary hero Juan Seguin, were uprooted from the homes their families had known for generations and forced across the river into Mexico.

To the arriving Americans, race and ethnicity was a completely binary world. Despite ubiquitous miscegenation on and around most every plantation in the South, Americans saw only White and Black. The "settled" portions of Texas, however, had been tri-racial ever since Austin's colonists started bringing a trickle of enslaved workers with them from the United States, and that is not even counting the indigenous tribes which controlled half the Texas land mass. The newcomer Americans saw only people with darker skin who fit into the category of other. To the new Americans there were no Tejanos, only Mexicans.

Just a dozen years after the end of the Texas Republic, the context of the times once again lined up profoundly against the Tejanos. The first was the peak of popularity for the Know Nothing Party, so called because they began as a secret society whose members were instructed to say "I know nothing." The Know Nothings were virulently anti-Catholic and anti-immigrant which meant being against the Irish and Germans in most of the United States, but many of the members in Texas used the doctrine against people of Mexican descent, as well. When Sam Houston associated with the Know Nothings during his run for governor in 1857, he was defeated. The newly arrived Germans overwhelmingly opposed him.

The other strike for those out to tar all Latinos with one broad brush was the internal politics of Mexico, a subject that was closely watched in Texas. The country had been embroiled in conflict after the conservative serial president Antonio Lopez de Santa Anna sold off parts of Sonora and Chihuahua to the U.S. in the Gadsden Purchase. It opened the door for Mexican liberals under Benito Juarez to seize control, and in February 1857, they ratified a new liberal constitution. Among many other reforms, it reaffirmed the nation's abolition of slavery, but it also went one further. The document specified that any enslaved person making it to Mexican soil was henceforth free. It also prohibited the extradition of political offenders.

Many Texans, always concerned about slave uprisings and escapes, were just short of apoplectic, and that was reflected in the press. The editor of the *Galveston Herald* wrote of American states potentially having to "take matters in their own hands," but also declared that the worst of it was that the enslaved in the South might "rob, pillage, massacre and commit the most horrible offences" then find safe harbor beyond the Rio Grande. Once again, there was a renewal of hatred among many Texas for everything "Mexican."

There had been one deadly attack on a Tejano carter in 1855, but that had stood as a seemingly isolated event for a time. In the summer of 1857, such depredations became an epidemic. Anglos, often wearing masks or with their faces blacked, attacked the Tejano and Mexican cart drivers, killed their animal, stole their freight, and wounded or killed the carreteros. Local authorities did not lift a finger to find or punish the culprits. Goliad County was a particular hotspot since it was on the lucrative route between the port at Indianola and San Antonio, but all of South Texas became treacherous to travel.

People taking the side of the attackers claimed that the "Mexicans" or "greaser wagoners" were thieves, some claimed that their livestock had been poisoned. Editorials from even two years prior had railed against "peon Mexicans" saying, "It is a most troublesome class in the community — one far more mischievous than free negroes, and they are doubtless all of them fugitives from service and labor in Mexico. .. It is a bad element of society, and sooner or later will be entirely extinguished."

Not everyone felt the same. An editorial in the *Goliad Express* near the start of September 1857 wrote that the truth had been "acknowledged by candid men." That being "that it is a war upon cheaper and more expeditious labor, and the effort to drive out this class, in order that business and high prices may be obtained by those who cannot or will not afford to work for small profits."

Reports made the papers that a wealthy trader crossed the river into Eagle Pass, but upon hearing of the rampant murders of "Mexican" carters, decided to spend his money in Monterrey rather than San Antonio. The loss of business and the potential for higher prices were especially worrisome to merchants in the Alamo City.

Still the attacks continued. Some killings were reported in the news, and others became no more than legend. The name of "Cart War Oak" is still ascribed to a large tree in Goliad where several men were allegedly lynched. Thirty years after the Cart War, the *Palo Pinto Star* spoke of an "old-fashioned wooden wheel" that was forever embedded in an Atascosa County mesquite after American teamsters hung it while attacking their Tejano competitors. The same article recollected that businessmen preferred the Tejano carreteros because "They did not extract whisky from the barrels and fill them up with water, and help themselves generally to the goods entrusted to them" like the Americans.

By September, the attacks were growing more brazen. Outside of Helena in Karnes County, 30 to 40 Anglo men with hidden faces made an unprovoked attack on the lead carts in a caravan of 17. The Tejanos defended themselves, but the Whites murdered one and wounded three others. Some reports suggested that two of the attackers were shot. When the main body of the train came up, under the command of an Anglo named Tobin, the attackers drew back only far enough to keep the rest under observation throughout the night.

The dead man was Jose Antonio Delgado, a prominent citizen of San Antonio. Some reports claimed that he had been shot 14 times. Delgado and his brother had fought with the independence movement at the Battle of Medina, and, after that defeat, fled to Louisiana where they fought with Andrew Jackson at New Orleans. Returning to Texas, he carried dispatches during the Siege of Bexar at the start of the Texas Revolution.

Governor Elisha Pease issued a $500 reward for the arrest of any member of the attacking gang, and he urged local law enforcement to do their jobs. No apprehensions were forthcoming.

San Antonians were outraged by the killing of Delgado. The *San Antonio Texan* wrote:

"These Mexicans are citizens of Texas, they were born here, and they or their fathers fought against Mexico for that liberty they now enjoy — 'liberty,' did we say — rather a poor show for liberty when they are not allowed to pursue their daily labor without being shot down like dogs!"

Theodore Gentilz's "Carreta Mexicana." Daughters of the Republic of Texas

Truth was that citizenship meant little to the newly arrived Americans. They had been using the term "Mexicans" to describe Tejanos even back into the 1830s. While many Tejano families had been in Texas for over a century, there were also newer arrivals from south of the border. Following the end of the Mexican War in 1848, in the ensuing Treaty of Guadalupe Hidalgo, citizenship for those Mexicans residing in Texas and all of the ceded territories to the west was specifically addressed. They were classified as White under the law and were promised "free enjoyment of their liberty and property, and secured in the free exercise of their religion without restriction." Clearly, things did not work out that way in real life.

In October, Mexico's minister to Washington, Manuel Robles y Pezuela, formally protested the murders to American Secretary of State Lewis Cass who in turn called upon Governor Pease to do something. He asked the legislature for a special appropriation to have Captain Nelson's company of soldiers provide armed escort. Some of the cart trains under the command of Americans were given assurances of safe passage by "parties in Goliad and Karnes Counties." Those promises were bogus. Again, in late November, there was another assault on an encampment of "Mexican" carters along Yates Creek north of Goliad and two were killed. The term of service for the militia was set to expire in early December, and Pease asked for another $14,500 to renew their service. This time the vote for money was a squeaker, but it was approved.

In his request to the legislature, Pease wrote, "It is painful to have to record such acts of violence, and a subject of deep mortification that the law places no means in my power to prevent them. Such outrages cannot occur and pass unpunished in a country where the Officers and the mass of the people entertain a proper respect for the laws."

Texas newspapers in 1857 widely used the phrase "Mexican Cart War," but the toll made it a very one-sided conflict. Estimates are that between 50 and 70 Tejano and Mexican carreteros were murdered. In fact, the press coverage around the state was a much more even battle than what occurred on the ground, and proverbial shots were fired throughout the last half of 1857.

Several of the editors relied on the tired trope that while some "Mexicans" were fine people, something needed to be done about the "depredations" of all the others. No specific or verified offenses were ever outlined. Such was the tone of the *Belton Weekly Independent* when the editor wrote "but a large portion of them, and most particularly among them are the Carretaros (sic), are the very worst possible race of mankind."

Aeneas MacLeod, editor of the *San Antonio Ledger*, was a Scotsman in his mid-20s who had arrived in the United States at New York only three years earlier. He was specifically called out by the editor of the *Goliad Express*, one of the apologists for murder. MacLeod responded by saying he had expressed his opinion "Frankly and freely...and without displaying unnecessary warmth," but he again deplored "high-handed outrages committed upon lives and property of citizens of this place."

Austin's *Southern Intelligencer* was unyielding in calling a racist a racist as they did with the authors of the report agreed upon by a citizens meeting in Goliad County at the end of November. "There is one marked feature in the whole report which stands out and characterizes its authors: They see room for distinguishing between 'white people and Mexicans.' It would not do to say 'Americans.'" The editor went on to say that "as soon as the Mexicans are expelled" these same Whites would be coming for the Germans, and that it eventually leads to "a war between the poor and the rich."

Upon the approval of Pease's appropriation to extend the armed escorts, the Cart War began to wind down by the middle of December 1857. That did not mean that the instigators of the murders were happy, and that included the newsmen who backed them.

In Columbus, the *Colorado Citizen* was still complaining about Pease's actions in the first month of 1858: "That the citizens of Goliad and Karnes have been harassed to death by contemptible Mexican greasers or peons, we have not a doubt. We respect a decent Mexican citizen, but for these low, thieving Mexican peons, we have no sympathy — they are not deserving of it." The paper's editor then accused the Tejanos of "interfering" with enslaved people, adding that "Some of these Mexicans had negro wives and placed themselves on an equality with the negroes." The editorial concluded by suggesting the governor "leave things alone."

The *Belton Weekly Independent* was blunt in their bloodthirsty hatred: "That there were some Mexicans killed no one denies, but that as many were killed as ought to be, we believe no one will admit."

One other interesting item arose in the legislature as the money was being approved for armed militia escorts for the embattled carters. Jose Angel Navarro of San Antonio, a member of the Texas House and the son of the famed Jose Antonio Navarro, offered a resolution to print Governor Pease's message in Spanish so that the carreteros and others affected might read the words. Navarro, like his father had been, was the only Latino in the legislature. He reminded his peers that they represented these people, "the majority of them are native born citizens, the original owners of this soil." Jacob Waelder, another House member from Bexar, backed him. T.J. Jennings from Cherokee County reminded the members that all of the early Texans had arrived "upon the invitation of Mexican colonization laws" and that many of those Tejanos had "united with us... in achieving independence."

The primary speaker against the idea, A.B. Norton representing Kaufman and Henderson Counties, bandied about the notion that if Norwegians could not get state business printed in their language why should Mexicans or Germans, ignoring the fact that those two groups made up a significant portion of Texans. "No, sir," Norton said. It must be "the American language."

Chapter Twenty-Seven

Dr. James Grant

The years leading up to the Texas Revolution were filled with complexities, intrigue, and international machinations that were omitted from the grade school lessons of most Texas children. The conflicts were not nearly as simple as Anglos fighting Mexicans. There was a civil war raging in Mexico between Centralists and Federalists, and that constitutional republic hung in the balance. Meanwhile, the European powers could read a North American map as well as anyone. The British and others were hungry for Texas-grown cotton and Mexican minerals, and those nations were willing to go through major diplomatic contortions to prevent the land hungry United States from expanding to the southwest.

Few stories underscore the twists more than that of Dr. James Grant, and even his tale requires wading through some confusion. There were three separate James Grants in Mexican Texas. One in Matamoros corresponded with Stephen F. Austin as early as 1824 and 1825 about establishing an overland mercantile route to Austin's Colony. He was sometimes referred to as Santiago Grant in order to distinguish him from Dr. Diego Grant. That James "Santiago" Grant was still residing in Matamoros in 1839 and was appointed an Indian agent in 1842, not long before he was murdered by banditos. The second non-doctor James Grant lived in Nacogdoches beginning about 1833. He was in his mid-twenties at the time when Doctor Grant was already 40. The younger James Grant associated with James Bowie and served in Thomas Rusk's company at the siege of Bexar. After 1835, that man disappears from Texas records.

Thanks to letters kept by a descendant of the doctor, handwriting can be combined with an examination of actions and circumstances to separate the story of the Scotsman Dr. James Grant from the others. This Grant, born in 1793, studied medicine at Edinburgh University and entered the service of the East India Company as a ship's surgeon. Between 1812 and 1819, Grant made three trips to India and China on company ships. He practiced medicine in the West Indies for a time, but by 1825, he had a less than satisfying position at a London children's hospital. That was the year his fortunes turned.

Dr. Grant wrote his Aunt Ann that an opportunity had arisen with him having only hours to make his decision. It was for a dual position in Mexico, and though other London physicians had applied, Grant's experience with medicine in tropical climes did the trick. He would be "Senior physician and medical superintendent of the large concerns of the Real del Monte Mining Company – and in medical charge of the Embassy." He told his aunt that "Mrs. Grant remains behind for the present with the children – and is provided for by the company."

Dr. Grant's descendant, Stuart Reid, laid out the rest of the story in a book containing his copious family research into the man. The most important point is that Grant also came to North America as an agent of the British Crown. Grant arrived in Mexico that same year that the British established formal diplomatic relations with the new republic there. Under the guidance of His Majesty's Mexican charge d'affaires, author and spymaster Henry George Ward, Dr. Grant made clandestine visits to Texas over the next two years. The British made large loans to a Mexico left destitute by an eleven year rebellion against Spain, and in return, they were looking for a share of the nation's wealth. At the same time, the last thing the Brits wanted was to see the U.S. gain part of that loot. The King's government believed their primary duty was the support of British commercial interests and bondholders. One of the first things Britain did was try to undermine American attempts to buy Texas outright.

Henry George Ward, British spymaster

Another move covered with British fingerprints was the Fredonian Rebellion of 1826 and '27. There were a tangle of reasons behind the uprising in the Nacogdoches area in which empresario brothers Haden and Benjamin Edwards tried to enrich themselves by driving a deep wedge between the old and new settlers there. The Edwards Brothers sought to bring others into the conflict including the Cherokees who lived nearby, the Americans, and the British. Ward personally supported plans for English colonization including one that would place 20,000 native Americans in East Texas as a barrier to American expansion. When the Fredonian escapade collapsed, Henry Ward was "abruptly" recalled to London, but Dr. James Grant remained in Mexico. By that time, he had started a Mexican family with a woman named Guadalupe Reyes. The couple had seven children together, and Grant, as did many other Texas Revolutionary adventurers, left his first family behind.

Grant, known widely by then as Diego, also set about creating his own personal empire in Northern Mexico. He swapped employers, leaving the mining company to go to work for a London-based bank named Barings as their man at the Aguayo Estates in Parras, Coahuila, extensive properties for which the bank held the mortgage. Grant entered a myriad of side businesses of his own and acquired Hacienda los Hornos for himself. In fall of 1830, he became a Mexican citizen.

Dr. Grant's politics were adamantly Federalist, and he was chosen for the state legislature of Coahuila y Texas as a deputy from Parras. Over the next four years, he advanced to legislative secretary then was elected deputy president of that body. He also became Jefe de Armas, a militia colonel. By April 1835, when Presidente Antonio Lopez de Santa Anna switched parties and political matters in Mexico had come to blows, Grant led his militia against Centralist General Martin Perfecto de Cos. Cos backed down on that occasion, but that was not the end of things. After Santa Anna brutally put down the rebellion in the State of

Zacatecas, he ordered the arrest of Federalist leaders in the north. Cos scooped up Agustin Viesca and James Grant, the top two men in the state legislature, as they were attempting to flee to the north.

The Federalist uprising across Northern Mexico was in full swing with some planning for a breakaway regional republic. Most Texas leaders, both Tejano and Anglo, still preferred restoring the Constitution of 1824 and making Texas a separate Mexican state, but both of those factions agreed the Centralists must go. Local Federalists engineered the escape of Viesca and Grant, and the doctor and a Colonel Gonzalez rode into Texas to join the siege then in progress at San Antonio de Bexar. According to John Marie Durst, a legislative deputy from Nacogdoches, it was James Grant who nudged Ben Milam to lead the assault that turned disarray into victory for the Texians. Grant served as one of Milam's four deputies. Wounded in the battle, he still helped foment the defection of a large share of Cos' troops garrisoned inside the Alamo. He was fighting for his life most likely, so why hold back?

At the same time, Mexican General Jose Antonio Mexia was landing at Tampico with 150 American mercenaries. It was all part of the grand Federalist plan in which Diego Grant was so invested. Mexia was to gather more support in southern Tamaulipas and head north toward Matamoros and Texas rallying the northern reaches of the country to overthrow the traitorous Santa Anna. Instead, bad weather and less-than-expected support brought what former Alamo curator Bruce Winders called a 19th century Bay of Pigs. The general and some men escaped, but 31 unfortunates were lined up in front of a firing squad.

More immediate trouble for Texas started after Perfecto de Cos surrendered and marched back across the Rio Grande. James Grant and Colonel Frank Johnson, an American who had been promoting a fight for the last four years, went among the Texians remaining at the

Alamo asking them to join an expedition against the city of Matamoros. That place was the northernmost large port in Mexico and a major point for tax collection. It proved to be an undertaking that destroyed the interim Texas government. That general council, unrecognized by Mexico, gave its support to Grant, but the military commander-in-chief Sam Houston and governor of the non-existent Mexican State of Texas, Henry Smith, adamantly opposed the operation as a generally terrible idea. Six companies were formed in spite of jockeying over who would lead them. Ultimately, Grant asserted that as former deputy president of the legislature in Coahuila and a jefe de armas, he was in charge of this "Federal Volunteer Army," and he was headed south to join up with his fellow Federalist rebels. He stripped the Alamo of badly needed men, arms, and provisions and marched out of the old mission compound on New Years Day 1836.

Sam Houston caught up with Grant's force on January 21st and persuaded four of the companies to stop at Refugio, leaving Grant and Johnson to continue south. Stuart Reid points out that the group was "accompanied by a senior East India Company officer, Colonel Edwards, revealing the British government's continued clandestine involvement."

The Matamoros Expeditions, since the groups were by then split, did not accomplish any of their stated goals. General Mexia's force, with whom they were to meet up, no longer existed. The few dozen men of the "Federal Volunteer Army" fought skirmishes with Centralists and Comanches, but one company lost at Mier, and the British officer Edwards was killed on February 20th. A week later, Frank Johnson made a narrow personal escape from San Patricio, but his men were surprised and killed by General Jose Urrea.

Dr. James Grant met his fate on March 2, 1836, the same day that a declaration of independence was signed at the Texas town of

Washington. Headed north from Camargo with 26 men, they were also ambushed by Urrea. Six men escaped. Placido Benavides survived and headed for his hometown of Victoria, but the other five survivors joined James Fannin at Goliad only to be massacred before month's end. Six others were taken to Matamoros as prisoners, finally reaching their destination in chains. The others were killed at the site of the engagement along Agua Dulce Creek in today's Nueces County. The general understanding is that Grant, dismounted or knocked from his horse, was stabbed in the back by a Mexican lancer.

Dr. James Grant's reputation in early Texas history is still open to debate. In his day, Sam Houston and his camp believed Grant to be an unscrupulous land speculator while his fellow revolutionary Frank Johnson called him a "gentleman, scholar, patriot and gallant soldier." Nothing prevents him from being both.

Chapter Twenty-Eight

Fort Clark

The Las Moras Springs, named for surrounding mulberry trees there, has been drawing travelers for centuries. Indigenous Indians and early Europeans were regulars. The Comanche Trail that those bands followed to trade or raid into Mexico passed through, but it was different pressures that brought the United States Army to the springs.

The Army had begun solidifying a presence almost as soon as Texas became a state. That included Fort Brown on the Rio Grande in 1846, the installation that saw the start of the Mexican War. The Texas frontier forts protected settlers from Indian tribes who were none too pleased to see hundreds of White families moving into their lands, but the settlement line did not extend into what today qualifies as West Texas. That changed with the Treaty of Guadalupe Hidalgo ending the Mexican War and even more so with the discovery of gold in California. Suddenly thousands of Americans were traveling "the government road," a southern transcontinental route from San Antonio to El Paso and beyond. Army posts needed to be close to the Rio Grande to protect those mail and stage routes from the Apache, Comanche, and Kiowa.

Where the government road crossed the Comanche raiding trail, the Army established Fort Clark in the summer of 1852. The name honored Major John B. Clark an officer who died during the recent Mexican War, and it was two companies of his old unit, the First Infantry, who came to occupy the new post. The Army did not own the land. They leased it for "not more than 20 years" from Samuel Maverick, a politician and land baron of great note.

Part of the treaty with Mexico included a promise by the United States to stop Indian raids from the U.S. side of the newly agreed upon border, but Fort Clark also allowed the Americans to keep an eye out should Mexico ever second guess its peaceful intentions.

It was not the first time people had tried to permanently inhabit the area near the springs. At the start of the 1830s, an English doctor named John Charles Beales got empresario contracts from Mexico City to bring as many as 1,450 colonists north of the Rio Grande. They were a motley mix of Americans, Mexicans, Germans, and Englishmen. Beales called his new settlement Dolores meaning the sorrows, and it was apt. The soil and climate were certainly not conducive to agriculture, and the Indians frequently killed off the intrepid colonists. The approach of Santa Anna's army of retribution in 1836 scattered those who remained. The village of Dolores was never reoccupied.

It did not take long for the Army to realize that the area was much better suited to full blown cavalry than infantry, and in 1853 began the love affair between Fort Clark and horses. Needless to say, they were a necessity for travel in the isolated spot. Mail came weekly from San Antonio, but supplies were from the depot at Corpus Christi, a 30 day round trip by wagon if conditions were good.

At first the soldiers lived in tents thrown up near the banks of Las Moras Creek, but they started constructing a fort on the limestone ridge just above. The first were log huts and jacals, but a few limestone buildings quickly followed. That included the old post headquarters that has a date of 1857 over the doorway to what is now ruins. Like most army posts dating back to Europe and including the Spanish presidios in Texas, a civilian town soon rose nearby so merchants could make money off the needs of soldiers. Oscar Brackett was the supply man at Fort Clark, and the town still bears his name.

In the 1850s, the "Indian menace" was at a peak on the Texas frontier. The western tribes were fighting for their very existence, but the more Whites they killed in asserting their power, the more armed men poured in to extinguish them. Governor Elisha Pease sent two companies of Rangers to join the regular soldiers - two companies of Mounted Rifles and one artillery company - to patrol Southwest Texas. The commander of the mounted U.S. troopers was John Bankhead Magruder, and he was the first of many Americans stationed at Fort Clark who would make their mark on subsequent history.

When Texas seceded from the Union in early 1861, Fort Clark, like all of the military facilities in the state, surrendered without a fight. Three companies of U.S. infantry handed the post over to one under-sized company of the Provisional Army of Texas. The Confederates manned the fort for just over a year before they decided that their interests lay to the east and that they were desperate for manpower. They abandoned the base in August 1862, and it sat officially empty until December 1866 when Troop C of the Fourth U.S. Cavalry resumed the job of protecting the road to El Paso. By that time the United States had another worry. The French had taken over Mexico with a large, unfriendly army.

The post was rundown. A great number of the buildings were still made of wood, and there had been zero maintenance done since the rebels bugged out. Yet no investment in the place was undertaken for a very solid reason. The Army was still renting the joint. Slowly, even a decade before the deed was finally secured, stone buildings started to replace the wooden ones. The central part of the post gained a sturdy and trim hospital, bakery, stables, guardhouse, and stone quarters for more than 200 men plus a commanding officer's house and eight officers' row duplexes to hold sixteen families. It was not until 1884 that Mary Maverick received $80,000 for the almost 4,000 acres that held Fort Clark.

By that time, the threat of Indian attacks on the audacious Texans who pushed settlement into the westernmost part of the state had passed, but getting to that point was rough and bloody. Not until 1873 and the arrival of Colonel Ranald Mackenzie to lead the cavalry did the Whites start to gain the upper hand. Since no troops were in the area during the Civil War, the tribes who had been using Northern Mexico as a sanctuary raided into Texas at will with devastating results for the Whites. Mackenzie decided to combat the trouble by ignoring the border. In May 1873, he led six cavalry companies across the river to punish the Kickapoo and Lipan Apache. The Army destroyed three villages and killed or captured 60 people including an aged Lipan chief. Many of the prisoners were Kickapoo women and children.

The Mexicans protested vigorously, but from a U.S. point of view, it was the Mexican government that had abetted the Kickapoo in the first place. As long as the tribe served as a buffer to the Comanche raids, what did Mexico City care about Kickapoos stealing horses in South Texas and murdering a few dozen Texans? Mackenzie's raids into Coahuila continued. The troublemaking Kickapoo, in exchange for their wives and children, agreed to return to the United States. Within a year, over half the tribe was confined to a reservation near Fort Sill, Oklahoma.

A major reason that the raids from Fort Clark were successful were the Black Seminole scouts. They were a people with a mix of native Seminole Indian and African heritage. Although smart and fierce fighters in Florida during the Seminole War, many relocated to Northern Mexico to escape American slave hunters. There they worked to protect the northern frontier. The U.S. Army recruited many of these men to serve as scouts, giving them full military status and the pay of privates. Their knowledge and courage proved decisive. They first served at Fort Duncan in Eagle Pass, but some of the Black Seminoles and their families were moved to Fort Clark. Lieutenant John Bullis was their commander, and he earned their respect by accepting the same privations that they did.

Black Seminole scout Ben July and family at their jacal. Fort Clark Museum

The experience of the Black Seminoles in the terrain of Coahuila was the key. They also proved themselves adept at tracking. At a fight at Eagle's Nest on the Pecos River, three of the Fort Clark scouts earned the Congressional Medal of Honor. Despite their stellar record and efforts by some champions within the Army, the scouting group was ultimately discarded, and their families, who never got title to the land where they lived in jacales southwest of the post, were left destitute.

When Ranald Mackenzie was sent north to subdue other Native Indians, command of Fort Clark's cavalry was given to Lt. Colonel William Shafter. The troops under his command were Buffalo Soldiers, direct military descendants of the U.S. Colored Troops who emerged from slavery and fought for the Union during the Civil War. After a lull in the cross-border attacks, things began to flare up again in Southwest Texas. Like Mackenzie before him, Shafter led his men across the river and even deeper into the mountains of northern Coahuila. His aggressive missions were wide-ranging and the Buffalo Soldiers under his command scoured not only around Fort Clark but west into Big Bend and up to the Llano Estacado. The entire campaign enraged the Mexican government, but, one year into the 1880s, the notion of murderous Indian raids in Texas was a thing of the past.

With that threat eliminated and a new railroad being constructed just nine miles to the south, some in the army, including General William Tecumseh Sherman, thought what he termed the "largest and most costly military post in Texas if not in the United States" should be closed. Instead, the Army doubled down on expansion and new construction. More stone quarters were built for officers along with larger storehouses and a granary that could hold 3,000 bushels. As calls for shuttering Fort Clark ebbed and flowed with American military needs, virtually every cavalry unit in the Army called it home at one time or another. By 1920, it was the Fifth Cavalry, an organization that could trace its lineage to Albert Sidney Johnston and Robert E. Lee.

In that year of 1920, the Army was adjusting to life after the First World War. It would take more than a decade, but eventually cavalry units became mechanized. Still the dusty Southwest Texas soil on the Fort Clark parade ground was kicked up daily under the wheeling drills of Army horses. Col. George S. Patton, Jr., himself a bit of an anachronism, served for a time as a cavalry officer at the fort. His superior was General Jonathan Wainwright, another famous Army leader-to-be.

With the outbreak of WWII, cavalry troopers passed through Fort Clark by the thousands, training before combat deployment. One unit was the segregated Ninth Cavalry, a Black outfit with elements that had fought on the Southwest Texas frontier in 1875. The last to leave was the Second Cavalry, the final horse-mounted unit in the United States Army. They left Fort Clark to head to Europe in February 1944. The decision to shutter the post came three months later, and it was officially inactivated in 1946.

Later that year, the old fort, with that largest collection of stone military buildings in the United States, was sold to a subsidiary of Brown & Root, and that company operated it as a guest ranch and executive retreat. It came with one of the largest spring fed swimming pools in Texas. That had been built in 1939 when Jonathan Wainwright commanded the post.

Without the thousands of soldiers, the little post town of Brackettville was dying. But in the 1950s, it became known for another reason. The town's mayor, a local rancher named James "Happy" Shahan, hit on the idea of turning the place into a location for Hollywood Westerns. He managed to get a foot in the door with a connection to Walt Disney's personal secretary, and had some success with a movie called *Arrowhead* starring Charlton Heston and Jack Palance in 1953. His jackpot, though, came when John Wayne sent his production manager, Nate Edwards, to scout Brackettville as a potential location for *The Alamo*.

Shahan drove Edwards all over Kinney County. Fort Clark would be perfect for housing and staging, but they struggled to find the exact terrain to recreate 1830s San Antonio until they swung by Shahan's own ranch to check on some cattle. Wayne and art director Alfred Ybarra came to Brackettville a week later and leased 400 of Shahan's 22,000 acres. They even hired Happy as the general contractor for the set.

Some 600,000 adobe bricks were made to create the mission and town. There were set backs due to a torrential rainstorm and even bigger ones thanks to John Wayne's funding trouble for the eight million dollar plus project. Somewhere along the way, Happy Shahan realized that if he built four sided buildings instead of the planned false fronts, he could turn his Alamo Village into both an attractive set for future movies and a tourist attraction.

When filming began in 1959, John Wayne and family settled into the Wainwright House, the old commanding officer's quarters. Top cast and crew lived in the former post barracks or other officer housing, and the old post HQ served as the base for Wayne's Batjac Production Company. Planes flew in and out of both the fort and the ranch so Wayne, taking his first crack at directing, could have the latest printed rushes. When the recreated buildings proved unsuitable for some interiors, Batjac turned a Fort Clark airplane hanger into a sound stage. Cast and crew swam at the Fort Clark pool and John Wayne hosted several barbeques under the shade trees there.

The extras and lesser lights stayed several miles south in the hamlet of Spofford, but hundreds of locals got jobs as drivers, set builders, caterers, and extras.

In the early morning of November 15, 1959, several of the Duke's closest buddies on the project were burning the midnight oil. That meant they were drinking heavily and swapping stories when one of the men quite literally stumbled into an oil-burning heater and set one of the oldest and most important stone buildings on the entire post ablaze. It was serving as the Batjac administrative headquarters, but around 20 people were also staying on the second floor. Before the local fire department, assisted by various inebriated actors and crew, could put out the fire, all but the stone walls were gone.

The Alamo Village held out through an entire generation of Shahans, finally closing for good in 2009. Fort Clark, with the word Springs added to the name, is now a gated community with a golf course, peaceful trails, and a small museum in the old guardhouse. Most of the 43 historic buildings identified in the National Register application are privately owned and occupied. The Black Seminole Cemetery established in 1872 still sits, parched and dusty most of the time but carefully maintained, off to the southwest of the post, and the charred ruins of the 1857 post headquarters building burned by John Wayne's drinking buddies still stands.

Chapter Twenty-Nine

Pauline Wells

In the current political climate, there are often fingers pointed at people who vote against their own self-interests, but most would agree that those people do so unwittingly. There are cases in history, however, of people who actively campaign to deny themselves a basic right. In Texas, one of them, who did so with a relentless fervor, is Pauline Wells.

She was born Pauline Kleiber in Brownsville during the Civil War. Her parents were Alsatian immigrants who gained a significant amount of local power. Before the war, Joseph Kleiber owned a drugstore, but once the battles commenced, he saw the opportunity to move his family across to Matamoros and make significant money selling supplies to Confederate soldiers and contraband cotton to anyone who paid.

When she was 17, Pauline married Jim Wells, the law partner of her uncle, Stephen Powers. Theirs was one of several marriages that connected the Anglo power brokers of Brownsville. The couple had four children in the decade of the 1880s, but more important to history, they also created a political power base of their own. Jim Wells relied heavily on his wife's input and advice, and he expanded their control over the Cameron County Democratic Party, something largely inherited from his partner Powers, into an ironclad handle on party politics in Hidalgo, Starr, and Duval Counties. Each locale had a hand-picked boss.

The Wells style was akin to the Mexican patron. Certainly, there was graft and arm twisting, but he also kept his constituents happy. Taxes stayed low, sketchy land claims for the right people were defended, government men protected the ranches against rustling, the railroad was promoted, and payments found their way to the poor. In return, the ranchers made sure that their Mexican and Tejano hands dutifully voted as Judge Wells asked.

Jim Wells circa 1875

In short, Pauline Wells and her husband had a good thing going, and an enemy of that was change. After 30 years of being the top political

boss in the Valley, one of Jim Wells' own pet projects was beginning
to bite him. Along with the coming of the railroad, Wells was one of
the biggest promoters of irrigation and the wide expansion of fruit and
vegetable farming. It brought a heavy influx of northern immigrants
to the borderlands, every one looking for their own piece of paradise.
The problem was that these Yankee newcomers failed to understand
two things: the importance of a good old fashioned political boss and
the easy cross-border relationship with Mexicans and Tejanos, however
paternalistic it might be. When revolution erupted south of the river in
1910, it pushed violence into South Texas. Using the murderous Texas
Ranger companies as a guide, the incoming northerners grew to distrust
and even hate Latinos. These outsiders began to erode the reliable voting
base of Jim Wells.

Add to the mix the concept of women getting the vote, and Jim and
Pauline Wells and their cabal feared that the end might truly be at hand.
As Wells put it, "No one on Earth can tell how they are going to vote, or
can control them."

There had been previous agitation in Texas for women's suffrage and
women's rights in general, but when the loudest voice for that change,
Annette Finnigan of Houston, moved to New York in 1905, things
died down. That changed in 1912. Women in San Antonio founded the
Equal Franchise Society. A year later, Finnigan was back in Texas full
time, and she joined with San Antonio's Eleanor Brackenridge to start a
statewide organization – the Texas Women's Suffrage Association.

The movement for American women to have the vote had ebbed
and flowed since the 1870s, but around 1913, it began to gain some
real traction. The Catch-22, of course, was that women required the

votes of male politicians and the male public at large in order to get
the vote for themselves. Lucky for them, there was an issue that might
do the trick. Movements to prohibit the sale and use of alcohol, ideas
rooted in American Protestantism, were almost as old as the nation, and
frequently the unsuccessful campaigns were led by women. In Texas,
after a statewide vote for Prohibition failed for the third time in 1911,
the Drys, men who favored the end of alcohol, had an epiphany: most
women wanted prohibition. The prohibitionist men began to support
giving women the vote.

Though the new president, Woodrow Wilson, opposed the notion,
suffragists saw another way forward. They mounted campaigns on a
state-by-state basis. By 1915, eleven states - Wyoming, Utah, Colorado,
Idaho, Washington, California, Oregon, Montana, Kansas, Arizona, and
Nevada -- had all given women the vote. Progressive women in Texas
mounted a major publicity campaign and lobbying effort. With the
legislature opening a session in Austin, they succeeded in getting a House
committee to back the adoption of a Texas constitutional amendment
giving women the right to vote. The issue might well be put in front of
the voters.

Then, seemingly out of nowhere, came Pauline Wells. In February
of that year, the bill came before the House. It was the third time up,
and support had grown from 10 votes to 55 to 90, just four shy of
the two-thirds needed to place the question on the statewide ballot. As
members debated, flinging various charges with both sides quoting the
Bible, the State Senate unanimously asked that "Mrs. James Wells" be
allowed to address the body. She had requested the opportunity in order
to "save the citadel of the home." Her oratory was stirring. She told the
legislators that "most women" did not want the vote in the first place,

and that giving them the power would bring "feminism, sex antagonism, socialism, anarchy and Mormonism."

Several of those words were not-at-all veiled code to play on the emotions and flat out hatred inherent in conservative Texans. Feminism and sex antagonism meant lesbianism. Opponents spoke often of the leaders of the suffrage movement being "unnatural man-haters" who would sap the "pep," meaning manhood, of American males. They spoke of innate "female tendencies" such as lack of logic, being ruled by emotions, shallowness, and irresponsibility, and how those traits would "hen peck" the U.S. government and military. These opponents, including Wells, opined that marriages and families would be torn apart if husband and wife disagreed over politics, and they added that suffragettes did not truly realize all of the joys of housekeeping they would surrender by gaining the vote.

Some of the opposition rhetoric was blatantly racist. Representative Stanley Beard of Houston warned that if women could vote, Texas will become just like California where "negroes and whites intermarry, and the children of all colors sit together in the school room."

It is virtually impossible to fully understand motivations from over a century ago. Whether those emotional arguments carried the day, or whether those Texas politicians were merely listening to their financial backers in the brewing, liquor, manufacturing, railroad, and ranching industries, we cannot know. We do know that all of those special interests and the political machine bosses very much wanted to preserve the status quo under which they were making satchels full of money. After Pauline Wells spoke, the movement for suffrage in the 34th Legislature stopped dead in its tracks.

Emboldened by success, and with the backing of the national anti-suffrage movement, Pauline Wells founded the Texas Association

Opposed to Woman Suffrage. Their aim was to publish information that would appeal to the "large majority of thinking women" opposed to female voting rights in Texas. The organization also doubled down on the notion that votes for women would increase Black voters and lead to "Negro domination" in the South. It was an argument even most Texas women in favor of suffrage agreed was a risky by-product of their movement.

The Association Opposed lost their next round when the suffragists and progressive Governor William P. Hobby managed to get a 1918 law passed that allowed women to vote in primary elections. The following year brought another chance. The pro-suffrage amendment to the state constitution finally made it to a general election ballot and came up for a vote in 1919. Wells and her anti-suffrage association distributed over 100,000 pieces of literature restating their arguments. In the post-WWI climate of 1919, the socialist bogeyman was especially effective. At the same time Texans were being asked to give the vote to women, they were also voting to take it away from Texans who were foreign born. In May, the state's voters rejected the suffrage amendment by a 25,000 vote margin.

Pauline Wells did not get to savor her victory long. Just over one month later, in a special session called by Governor Hobby, Texas became the ninth U.S. state to ratify the 19th Amendment to the Unites States Constitution. It marked the end of Pauline Wells' campaign to deny votes to her fellow women. The following year, many of her husband's investments turned sour, and the new coalition of voters in the Rio Grande Valley did indeed end his four decade reign as the region's top political dog.

Chapter Thirty

Sutton-Taylor Feud

As several modern historians have become to view it, the Sutton-Taylor Feud was not a feud in the sense of the famous Hatfields and McCoys. Many tales of post-Civil War violence have been classified as feuds when in fact they are better described as serial murders carried out by sociopathic thugs unwilling to accept that their traitorous rebellion against the United States had come up short. While the vast majority of the defeated Confederates grudgingly settled back into life, a few hundred continued killing for a decade and more after the official fighting was declared to be done. By then, however, it was not couched in war. It was cold-blooded murder, and the categorizing of these acts as feuds is as much a part of mythologizing the South as the Lost Cause.

A "persistent" rumor that the two families had known one another before coming to Texas is untrue. Some western dime novels put the dispute down to disagreements over unbranded cattle on unfenced range land. Other lazy accounts state "how it started, nobody knows."

Though the killings became very personal, what has been described as "the longest and bloodiest feud in Texas history" began quite simply as race-motivated murder on the part of the Taylors. As for the few Suttons, they entered this long-running melee on the side of law enforcement and were backed by the Unionists in Texas. As with much of the historical record that existed for a century and a half, a fair telling regarding Union factions in the South never stood a chance.

The many Taylors involved in this story were all descended from Josiah Taylor, a Virginia planter who made a stop in Alabama before settling in DeWitt County. Josiah had made an earlier foray into Texas as an officer with the Gutierrez-Magee Expedition, but he returned to the United States after the green flag army took San Antonio. Josiah came back to Texas in 1824 and the downline of his sons Pitkin and Creed became the aggressors on the Taylor side.

Creed Taylor could put his early Texas resume up against most anyone's. As a 15-year old, he was among the cannon defenders at the Battle of Gonzales, and he went with that group to the Siege of Bexar, being discharged before the surrender of General Cos' force. Taylor is said to have ridden with a group in the Matamoros Expedition then acted as a courier for the Texian revolutionaries before leading his family east in the Runaway Scrape. He also seemed eager to gild the lily of his exploits. Creed claimed that he rejoined the army the day before the Battle at San Jacinto, but he is not listed on the official roll. He is known to have fought Comanches at Plum Creek, joined a Ranger company, and battled the invading Mexican Army at Salado Creek in 1842. During the Mexican War, Creed Taylor was part of Samuel Walker's mounted Rangers and fought at four of the biggest battles in that conflict. Creed's sons and nephews, on the other hand, turned out to be anything but Texas heroes, and Creed himself ended his life as the patriarch of what neighboring ranchers called a cattle and horse stealing ring.

Creed and his sons, Hays and Phillip "Doughboy" Taylor, ran herds over five South Texas counties, and to counteract the claims that they often appropriated livestock from neighbors, the Taylors hired a force of about 80 gunmen to bring things to a stalemate until after the Civil War.

The first of the Taylor clan to run afoul of the law was Pitkin's son, Buck. He assembled a small band who attacked the Freedmen's Bureau School in Victoria in the fall of 1865, brutally beating the teacher and several students. The group then did the same in the DeWitt County seat of Clinton. They next turned to robbing travelers, committing murders near Yorktown, and finally ambushing and killing two Union soldiers. Buck then ran to Panola County in Deep East Texas to hide out.

The murders of freedmen and their White allies were rampant across Texas and the South, and the Taylors made sure they did their share. Martin Taylor, another nephew of Creed, killed a Union supporter in Victoria County, and Creed's son Hays shot down two Black troopers at a bar in Indianola then killed a Black sergeant who pursued him. For good measure, he rifled the dead man's pockets and stole his mule. Buck and Martin enlisted more like-minded criminals, and more murders and robberies were committed. On the Colorado River near La Grange, the Taylor Gang ambushed five recently discharged U.S. soldiers, killing three then tying up the other two before beating them to death and dumping their bodies into the river. They cruelly murdered freed Blacks, Tejanos, and poor Whites by the dozens across 45 Texas counties over the next several years. Usually killing when their prey was unarmed and outnumbered.

Lawmen were not wholly oblivious to the carnage. Lavaca County deputy sheriff Jack Helm was one who enumerated the many Klan units and raiding gangs to the occupying military authorities. Helm specified that despite any political pronouncements, most of these men were no more than criminal rabble, but their sympathizers continued to help the marauders. When lawmen and military wanted to act, they found themselves woefully undermanned. Many Federal troops were unmounted.

Even when the former Confederate politicians were not involved directly, they knew that the gangs were doing their bidding to destabilize Texas under Republican rule.

When Hays and Doughboy Taylor, along with fellow thug Ran Spencer, murdered the Fort Mason post commander, Major John A. Thompson, on a Mason sidewalk in November 1867, their father, Creed Taylor, hid them out, but the killing turned up the heat on the Taylor gang. The Army sent a detachment of about 50 men to scour multiple South Texas counties for the murderers, but their hired local scout was a Taylor man who ensured that the mission ended in failure. Adding insult, a Taylor relative bragged that the marauders intended to kill the Yankee major leading the pursuit.

The Taylor's reign of terror stretched across dozens of counties, and their numerous abettors continually helped them escape, but in the spring of 1868, things began to shift. After the Taylors stole a large number of horses and robbed a local widow, DeWitt County deputy sheriff William Sutton led a posse of 15 in pursuit. They found two of their quarry on the street in Bastrop. Instead of surrendering, the criminals opened fire, and the lawmen did the same. One Charley Taylor was killed and his cohort was shot down "trying to escape" on the way back to Clinton. A bystanding boy in Bastrop was also killed.

By that summer, reward money had reached $1,500 for Hays and Doughboy Taylor, and the entire gang was being sought. Former Union soldier and spy Charles Bell was one of the special detectives being paid by the Army. Jack Helm, declaring himself a thorough Unionist was back on the scene, and Bill Sutton, who had fought for the Confederacy but now swore loyalty to the United States, was dogged, as well.

It was Sutton and his friend Doc White who Buck Taylor and Dick Chisholm taunted at a Clinton saloon on Christmas Eve 1868. They erred. White and Sutton shot the two dead, though Sutton took a serious wound in his shoulder.

Jack Helm, Bill Sutton, and rancher/lawmen Jim Cox and Joe Tumlinson kept up the search for the rest of the Taylors. Many local lawmen, including in places like Lavaca and Goliad Counties, sympathized with the anti-Union and racist raiders and refused to join any pursuits. Evidence shows that the Taylor element founded Klan groups, and their political allies were happy to tolerate the gang's non-stop thieving, rustling, and murder. Citizens meanwhile clamored louder for help. A Goliad County judge said he could not even convene his court without federal troops to protect him.

While the Taylor gang laughed at how easy it was to elude capture, Helm and Bell began to adopt some tougher tactics. In the summer of 1869, their group surrounded the house of Taylor gang members in San Patricio County. Though one of the desperados used his own wife as a shield, the lot of the criminals were killed in a storm of gunfire. Not long after, the lawmen went to Creed Taylor's ranch in Karnes County. Most of the gang escaped in the ensuing shootout, but Hays Taylor took shotgun and pistol fire before a round to the skull dropped him for good. Creed Taylor, described by Detective Bell as "a very bad man," was arrested and taken to the Army post at Helena where he remained for a month before being bonded out.

The numbers of the lawlessness in Texas were staggering. Not all the state's counties filed reports, but among those that did, more than 1,000 murders were reported between 1865 and 1868. Close to 500 were Whites against Whites, and some 400 were Whites murdering Blacks. Only 10 showed as freedmen killing Whites. With the ex-Confederate Governor Throckmorton replaced by Union man Edmund J. Davis, the cries of a terrorized populace were finally answered. In 1870, Davis formed a State Police force to go after outlaws like the Taylor gang. In the first month, there were 978 arrests including 109 for murder. The force was multi-ethnic – White, Black, and Mexican American. There were veterans of the Union and Confederate armies. There were also loud and unceasing cries of overreach and much outrage against the officers of color despite the policemen's success. Charles Bell was not part of the force. Complaints and whining from the former rebels had disgusted him enough that he moved from the state.

The biggest accusations were leveled against Jack Helm who was accused of killing several men after he had taken them prisoner. Helm was dismissed from the police, and though he kept his sheriff's job in DeWitt County for a bit longer, Bill Sutton filled the leadership void in the chase for the Taylors.

In 1871, a teenager named John Wesley Hardin joined the Taylor gang as a prime enforcer. He filled the murderous role vacated by those who were killed earlier.

The local lawmen under Sutton and the State Police used whatever methods they could to bring the serial murdering members of the Taylor gang to justice. It was an unknown party who lured Pitkin Taylor from his home by ringing a cow bell in his corn field one night. Pitkin was shot but lived another six months. At the funeral, his son Jim Taylor and other relatives swore revenge with Sutton, Cox, Helm, and Tumlinson as primary targets.

Three Taylor men fired a shotgun at Sutton through an open window at the Banks Saloon and Billiard Hall in Cuero in April 1873, wounding the lawman badly. That same month, the ex-Confederates who were back in charge at Austin repealed all authorization for the State Police. The famed Leander McNelly and more than three dozen other out of work officers joined the Texas Rangers. Though many Confederate apologists subsequently wrote of political bias and murderous overreach by Edmund Davis' police force, the evidence does not support those charges.

The Taylors failed with another ambush of William Sutton that June. Some 40 of them later attacked a sheriff's posse. When Jim Cox was shot from his horse, Taylor men slit his throat. Shortly afterward, Jim Taylor and Wes Hardin shot down an unarmed Jack Helm in a blacksmith shop. They laid siege to Joe Tumlinson's ranch near Yorktown, but were talked down by the new sheriff. That brief peace ended within months, and more killings and sieges followed.

William Sutton, with growing concern about his own family, moved to Victoria, but that did not bring him safety. On March 11, 1874, Jim and Bill Taylor rode up to the Indianola steamship dock where Sutton, his wife, and their employee Gabriel Slaughter were buying tickets for themselves and passage for a herd of cattle. The Taylors shot the two men down in cold blood.

Laura Sutton was pregnant when her husband was killed. Later she gave birth to daughter Willie, their only child.

Bill & Laura Sutton. University of
Houston Victoria

Leander McNelly, by then tubercular, led Company A of the Texas
Rangers and Washington County militia. In 1874, with the violence in
DeWitt and nearby counties well out of hand, Governor Richard Coke
sent Adjutant General Steele to investigate. Just four days after Steele
got back to Austin, Coke ordered McNelly and his volunteers south to
restore order amidst what McNelly called "a perfect reign of terror."
The lawmen arrived on August 1, just two days before the district court
was set to hand down a slew of murder indictments against men on
both sides. The Rangers patrolled the area for some months, eyeballing
the "grog shops," and some order was restored, but always with the
knowledge that murder would erupt again the moment they left. That

happened in March after a large gang of bandits from Mexico looted, burned, and killed their way through the outskirts of Corpus Christi. Before he left, McNelly reported his thoughts on peace in DeWitt County: "With the present incumbents, there is no hope." The district attorney "is drunk most of the time & when sober is of no earthly account."

The Taylors continued their vow to kill all of the lawmen who had come after them. Rube Brown, the marshal of Cuero was assassinated, but just after Christmas in 1875, Jim Taylor and two of his friends were killed in Clinton. As one of McNelly's Rangers put it, "The men of both factions are men accustomed to righting their own wrongs, and they object decidedly to any interference, even should that interference be lawful."

By that fall, McNelly was abed with the consumption, Richard Coke was off to the U.S. Senate, the 400-pound Jumbo Hubbard had taken over the governor's office, and Lieutenant Leigh "Red" Hall was in command of McNelly's company of Rangers. Though they were chasing trouble elsewhere in Texas, they had not forgotten the last of the Taylors.

In the dark of night on September 19, 1876, a masked group of men burst into the home of the respected Doctor Philip Brassell, took him and his son, George, down the road a piece, and executed them. With indignation at a peak, Hall and his Rangers arrived in the DeWitt County seat of Clinton to face a hostile sheriff and few willing witnesses. Two of the killers were deputy sheriffs. In spite of the obstacles, warrants were secured and served in the midst of a wedding party when most of the murderers would be in one place. The armed Rangers also lined the courtroom walls when Judge Henry Clay Pleasants denied bail and ordered the eight defendants to out of town jails.

None of the men Hall rounded up saw justice, though. Some were acquitted. Others had convictions overturned on appeal. Charges were dismissed on technicalities, but the biggest blow came when court records mysteriously went missing. The lone conviction that stuck was pardoned by the governor without ever serving a day. As historian Robert M. Utley put it, the gov "could not bear to see an old Confederate veteran committed to Huntsville." Thus ended the "feud" in 1899.

But that ignores a major player in the long and bloody saga – John Wesley Hardin. He was such an important gunman for the side of the unrepentant Confederates that many contemporary write-ups called them the "Taylor-Hardin faction." Scads of Hardin relatives lived in DeWitt and Gonzales Counties.

Hardin is celebrated as the most legendary of Texas gunslingers with good reason. The tales are tough to sort, but he shot down between 20 and 50 men. Hardin was a slightly built control freak with "an unlimited capacity for self-justification," and in his mind, all of his victims had it fairly coming. He started killing United States soldiers while still a teen, was particularly fond of killing sheriffs and state policemen, especially those of color, and he murdered bar patrons for having the temerity to offend him when he was drunk. In one such shooting, with Jim Taylor by his side, a liquored up Wes Hardin killed Brown County Deputy Charles Webb in the town of Comanche.

Forced to flee Texas, Hardin adopted the alias of John Swain and fled first to Alabama and then to Pensacola. A Dallas policeman named Jack Duncan and Ranger Lieutenant John Armstrong tracked him there. With the help of the local sheriff and eight hastily deputized men, John Wesley Hardin was overcome and arrested in a train car. He was delivered back to Travis County, Texas before a murder trial in Comanche for killing Deputy Webb. The sociopathic gunfighter received 25 years at Huntsville, eventually becoming a "model prisoner" and studying law and theology before Governor Jim Hogg pardoned him some 16 years into his sentence.

Hardin's life out of prison did not last long. He moved to El Paso where he started a law practice and continued to frequent the other kind of bars. In August 1895, just a year removed from incarceration, Constable John Selman entered the Acme Saloon and put three .45 slugs into Hardin. The motives are still debated.

Gulf Coast

Padre Island National Seashore. NPS

Chapter Thirty-One

The Brothers Laffite and Their Loot

The list of people who have active organizations named in their honor two centuries after their deaths is not a long one. The Laffite Society of Galveston, a group that describes its members as "history buffs and serious scholars," has been around for thirty years. That's almost ten times as long as the Brothers Laffite stayed on the island. On the other hand, the rollicking history and legend of Texas' most famous pirates does seem to be a bottomless well for study.

In many ways, the Laffites, Jean and Pierre, are a complete unknown. Historians cannot determine their birthplace or ages. There are even arguments over how to spell the last name. The spelling of Laffite is used by the society based on how the brothers signed their names. As to their origins, the most likely possibility is that Pierre and his younger brother Jean were born near Bordeaux, France, with Jean coming into the world around 1780. There may or may not have been a third brother named Alexandre who was involved in the family business. To add to the confusion, before they showed up in New Orleans, there was another Jean Laffite who had a son named Jean.

The golden age of piracy with the Jolly Roger, Blackbeard, and Captain Kidd was over a century past by the time the Laffites made a name for themselves in New Orleans. A more apt description of Jean Laffite, generally accepted as the leader of the outfit, was more of a mafia kingpin. Like other organized crime families, the Laffite operation was diversified into piracy, smuggling, slave-trading, and fencing illegal goods. Much of the open seas raiding of ships was done under a letter of marque from the short-lived revolutionary government of Cartegena, Colombia, which technically, in the eyes of some, made the Laffites privateers rather than outright pirates. Though his Louisiana headquarters were at Barataria, south of the city, the Laffite Brothers conducted regular business in town and were occasionally accepted in New Orleans society.

When the British Army and Navy came calling in the fall of 1814, they approached Jean Laffite about helping them fight the Americans. Since the U.S. government was looking to crack down on the brothers' far flung criminal enterprise, the British offered amnesty for previous crimes. They sweetened the pot with 30,000 pounds and the offer of a captaincy in the British Navy. Jean Laffite said he would get back to them. In spite of declining the British offer, the United States Navy raided and sacked Barataria.

Laffite wrote Louisiana Governor William Claiborne offering to instead assist in the defense of Southeast Louisiana in return for an American pardon. Though the governor was inclined to accept, the state legislature voted no. Once the British arrived on land, General Andrew Jackson accepted Lafitte's offer and placed the pirate gunners, considered among the best in the Gulf of Mexico, aboard navy ships and on land.

Whatever contribution the pirate crews made, Jackson earned a victory in battle and Lafitte a presidential pardon from James Madison. The good feelings did not last. The United States, particularly the Navy, wanted rid of pirates and slave smugglers.

The Laffite operation moved to Galveston Island, a spot undeveloped by nations, and a place with which the brothers were already familiar. Entering the harbor with seven ships, the Laffites co-opted an existing operation run by Michel Aury. Much like in Barataria, Laffite established a permanent settlement near where the present Port of Galveston lies. There were huts for his hundreds of sailors along with warehouses for stolen goods and saloons, gambling houses, a slave market, and places to house visiting shoppers. Jean Laffite also continued his political fluidity, siding variously with Mexican revolutionary filibusters while sometimes spying for Spain. There was even a letter penned by Jean to American Secretary of State James Monroe announcing that he was the governor of Galveston appointed by "the Supreme Congress" of the Republic of Texas, though nothing of the sort existed.

Along present day Harborside Drive, Jean Laffite built himself a home to oversee the criminal empire. Today there is a state historical marker, but the ruin at the location is from a later, unrelated building.

In 1818, a brutal hurricane, that great peril of the Gulf, wiped out Jean Laffite's town, which he called Campeche after a Spanish port in the Yucatan. Some accounts claim that half the population was wiped out and all of the wooden structures swept into kindling or out to sea on the tidal surge. The Laffites built a lesser community in its place, but they did not get to enjoy it long. In May 1820, the U.S. Navy showed up in Laffite's Spanish harbor. They were tired of the pirates attacking American shipping, and they persuaded the brothers to vacate the northern Gulf. After a final celebration, Laffite's crews did exactly that, but not before burning the town of Campeche to the ground.

The end of the Brothers Laffite is as murky as their beginnings. While Jean headed south toward a new potential base in Colombia, Venezuela, or Argentina, Pierre went to Charleston, South Carolina to acquire a new ship and crew. He established a lair on Isla Mujeres by the Yucatan Coast, but Spanish authorities, in their death throes in Mexico, did not want him either. Pierre was severely wounded in battle and died as a result.

No definitive evidence is known to establish the death of Jean Laffite. He shows up in several records in 1822, fighting an English brig, daringly escaping confinement, capturing an American ship, and gaining a commission in the Colombian Navy of Simon Bolivar. Over the next few years, various tales of his demise appear. Take your pick.

The Laffites' primary impact on history came after their death in the form of myth and legend. In 1826, two different books about *the Buccaneer* Jean Laffite appeared. Others followed. A 1930s movie cast Frederic March as the swashbuckling pirate, and the film was remade 20 years later starring Yul Brynner. The most exciting tales, however, passed mostly through word of mouth.

The notion that criminals who rob and pillage for a living would carefully bury their haul for a rainy day is rather far-fetched to begin with. The idea that those treasure boxes would remain unfound for 200 years in a metropolitan area of eight million people is downright ludicrous. In spite of the gossamer-thin logic, stories of buried pirate treasure around the edges of Galveston Bay have abounded over the years.

After the Laffite Brothers left Galveston, some of his men probably stayed behind to pursue a calmer life or returned in the 1820s before real settlement of the island began. It is likely that a handful of those Texans of the 1830s and 40s claiming to have sailed with the pirate band may even have been telling the truth, but separating undocumented fact from whiskey-infused fiction is impossible. Galvestonians of the time claim the number was six, and local historians of the pre-Civil War era offered some details, though what portion was exaggeration is unknown. They wrote of Captain Jim Campbell, who lived at Virginia Point, local butcher John Lambert, Charles Cronea, and Steve Churchill, who ran the ferry at the west end of the island, as former sailors for Laffite. Tales of treasure ran rampant, and over the years, maps on both sides of Galveston and Trinity Bays have changed hands, and nefarious midnight digs have taken place. There is as much mystery as with the Laffites themselves.

One of the more interesting enduring tales is that of Crazy Ben Dolliver. A New Orleans newsman described him thusly in 1847: "Dollivar's face looked like a piece of mahogany carved into human semblance. His nose is sharp and crooked enough to have served as a boat hook in an emergency, and his mouth, cheeks, and face are covered with a thick, dark beard. His little grey eyes twinkled in their sockets with a semi-piratical ferocity. His forehead is scarred and full of wrinkles, and a seer might discover in them lines written by vice on the tablet of crime. The police know him to be one of the crew once under the command of the celebrated Lafitte."

Dolliver lived in a sailcloth lean-to on the bay side of the island, or according to another account, at a shack near Seabrook. Whether caused by a saber cut or something else, one author wrote that Crazy Ben was intellectually impaired. The story went that young Dolliver had already chased a band of Seminoles through the Everglades before he met up with Jean Laffite's band around 1810 in service of the abortive Republic of Cartegena. He served on a gun crew, fought at New Orleans, and, in the Galveston saloons, Dolliver mumbled those stories in his whiskey fug along with snippets of boarding spikes and cutlasses and sacks of gold dust secreted in the Hotspur's bilge.

As far as stories go, they were easily dismissible, except for the part where Crazy Ben routinely paid for his drinks with Spanish doubloons. Sometimes the barmen carefully counted out his change, and other times, when Ben was especially in his cups, they were less precise. Many a Galvestonian followed Ben Dolliver on his wanders or dug holes in the sand near his hovel in hopes of finding his cache. Depending on the type of ending desired, Crazy Ben and his golden sea chest were lured away by some ruffians, including a man claiming to be Laffite's nephew, in July 1858. Others prefer the other tale in which Crazy Ben took the location of his buried treasure to his grave.

Chapter Thirty-Two

Hector P. Garcia

An overlooked fact of United States history is how much change has been effected by military veterans following major wars. Some of that societal flux was ugly, and even bloody, especially after the First World War, but much of it brought needed progress. Once WWII concluded, the largest number of soldiers, sailors, and Marines in American history came back home, and they shaped the nation for the next sixty years. One of those positive influencers was Hector P. Garcia.

He was born in Tamaulipas, Mexico, and like many other leaders, he was the child of teachers who grew up knowing the never ending value of education. The family crossed the border when Hector was three, fleeing the violence of the Mexican Revolution. He grew up in the Valley town of Mercedes and graduated from the local high school as valedictorian. Garcia later said a primary impetus for his studious school work came when one of his teachers said, "No Mexican will ever make an "A" in my class."

After time at Edinburg Junior College, Garcia went on to the University of Texas where he got a bachelor's degree in zoology and then moved to UT Medical School at Galveston. Because of a racial quota system, he was the lone Hispanic medical student in his class. Upon graduation, no Texas hospital would accept the "Mexican" doctor for residency, so he served that part of his training at Creighton University's St. Joseph Hospital in Omaha.

Captain Hector P. Garcia

Garcia had been involved in the Citizens Military Training Corps since age 15, and he stayed with it. Reaching the rank of lieutenant in the organization. After the U.S. entered WWII, Dr. Garcia enlisted in the regular Army and served as a captain in the Medical Corps in North Africa and then Europe. It was in Italy that he met his wife. His service earned him a Bronze Star. He also noticed that a lack of education and proper training might be putting many of his fellow Mexican American soldiers at risk on the battlefield. They did not always understand the instructions. Garcia felt that was a wrong that might be righted.

In 1946, back in the States with his new wife, Garcia opened a medical practice in Corpus Christi. Garcia, who finally received his U.S. citizenship that same year, became known to some as the "doctor to the barrios," sometimes foregoing payment from his most impoverished patients. He also joined LULAC to get involved in the fight against injustices being foisted on the Mexican American community in South Texas, but Garcia noticed areas that particularly added to the struggles of veterans.

Latino vets were rarely able to access or navigate the benefits of the GI Bill. They were often turned away from getting needed medical care at VA hospitals. When the Hispanic men did get admitted, it was to a segregated ward. The ex-soldiers were being denied burial benefits and schooling. They were turned down for home loans being readily handed out to their Anglo counterparts. The doctor decided to do something about it. In March 1948, a year after serving a term as local LULAC chapter president, García founded the American GI Forum. By year's end, there were Forum chapters in 40 Texas communities. Dues were 25 cents a year.

One typical incident that happened in the South Texas town of Three Rivers in 1949 proved pivotal. In spite of the fact that Mexican-Texans were a majority there, the small burg's lone funeral home and cemetery operator refused to hold a wake or allow interment for Felix Longoria, Jr., a 25-year old decorated war veteran who had been killed by a Japanese sniper in the Philippines. The only explanation given the family was that "The Whites wouldn't like it." Not only did Garcia step in, but the

matter quickly came to the attention of newly-elected Senator Lyndon
Johnson. Though each man applied stubborn opposition to the funeral
home's decision, they got their satisfaction elsewhere. Senator Johnson
pulled the necessary strings, in spite of a flurry of criticism, to have
Longoria's remains buried at Arlington National Cemetery.

Bitter feelings over the Longoria Affair continued in Three Rivers
for decades, and many among the local Anglos denied that racism ever
existed in their community. It is a story that continues to play out in
Texas.

The Longoria incident brought national press to the American GI
Forum and the plight of Mexican Americans in the Southwest. He
was suddenly attracting real attention to his causes. One profile article
described Hector P. Garcia as "a man who in the space of one week
delivers twenty babies, twenty speeches, and twenty thousand votes."

The higher profile also brought an expansion of the Forum's mission.
The group began to focus on the problems facing all Latinos, not
just war veterans. They worked against poll taxes and other forms of
segregation. In 1954, the Forum was a supporter of the Hernandez
v. Texas case that fought systematic exclusion of Latinos from juries.
Following the Brown v. Board Supreme Court case, came a cascade of
follow up cases in Texas when citizens had to return to the federal courts
in order to make local school districts apply the new laws of the land.
Cisneros v. Corpus Christi Independent School District came up in
1966. The American GI Forum and the Corpus chapter of the United
Steel Workers were the primary backers in that effort. It took four years
before the plaintiffs were able to make the case that the lion's share of the
city's Tejano children were being forced into substandard schools.

After fighting what seemed like the same battles repeatedly for years,
Garcia had hope that new elected leaders might change things. He

was one of the coordinators for the "Viva Kennedy" clubs during the presidential campaign of 1960. He was disappointed that JFK did not push for Latino issues, but in 1964, he was back working for "Viva Johnson" efforts. This time he was rewarded with the Civil Rights Act and Voting Rights Act, both of which impacted Mexican Americans just as it did the country's Black citizens.

President Johnson appointed Dr. Garcia as an alternate delegate to the United Nations, and in 1967, when he spoke to the General Assembly in Spanish, he became the first U.S. delegate to ever address that body in a language other than English. He also served on LBJ's Civil Rights Commission. President Carter named Garcia to a federal judgeship nominating committee.

Doctor Garcia's work did not go unrecognized. He was the first Mexican American to receive the Presidential Medal of Freedom when Ronald Reagan awarded it to him in 1984. Pope John Paul II named him to the Order of St. Gregory the Great. After his death a dozen years later, there were more celebrations of his life. Schools bear his name. South Texas PBS produced a documentary about his work called *Justice for My People*. It follows the struggle for Mexican rights in Texas through his eyes. The Dr. Hector P. Garcia Memorial Foundation carries on his work through scholarships, educational grants, and other community-building efforts.

Of all of the ways in which Dr. Garcia has been honored for his efforts, the statue on the Texas A&M Corpus Christi campus, in his home town, is especially fitting. It includes the motto that he crafted for the American GI Forum: "Education is our Freedom, and Freedom Should be Everybody's Business."

Chapter Thirty-Three

Shanghai Pierce

The glib might say that Shanghai Pierce was the greatest Texas cattleman ever born in Rhode Island, but he was much more than that. He became a ranching legend thanks to bold chances and an outsized personality. What would a Texas legend be without those?

His family were New England Puritans, and perhaps not overly sentimental. Or possibly with nine children, his parents simply needed to thin the household. Around the time Abel Head Pierce was 14, with no more than a few winters spent in a one-room school at Little Compton, RI, he was shipped to Petersburg, Virginia to work in the store of his namesake uncle. He likely brought the nickname of Shanghai with him. Pierce was tall and lanky, and the joke was that he looked like a Shanghai Rooster. One thing for certain, he grew bored of the mercantile life and having swallowed "too many doses of sanctimony," took off for New York City. There he stowed away on a Texas-bound schooner. Lucky for Shanghai, he was not discovered until the vessel was at sea, and the captain put him to work handling cargo.

He was 20 years old when he landed at Indianola, and he soon made his way to Port Lavaca. Pierce later wrote that he was "poorer than skimmed milk." It was 1854, and contrary to visions of vast western Texas, the lion's share of ranching in the state was still being done on the coastal prairie. Large cattle operations covered much of Harris County and places both east and southwest of there. At roundup time, the herds were either loaded on ships at Galveston or driven across the many rivers and marshes of Louisiana to be disposed of in New Orleans.

At Port Lavaca, young Pierce met Richard Grimes and went to work at that man's ranch splitting rails. Grimes was one of the largest cattlemen on the Gulf Coast, and his headquarters were not far from the mouth of the Colorado River. Shanghai did not know a thing about the ranching business, but at 6'5", he was bigger and stronger than most everyone else. Soon he graduated from hauling and tool work to breaking horses. He proved to be a fast learner, and Pierce was soon buying a few head of cattle for himself and branding them AP. Some of the cattle, and even small parcels of land, Shanghai acquired from Grimes in lieu of pay.

Pierce chose cows with young calves, thinking it would increase his holdings faster. J. Marvin Hunter wrote an article about Pierce for *Frontier Times* in 1951 and described the first ventures: "These cows were poor culls which the budding cattle baron bought for $14 a head when the pick of the range was worth $7. A severe winter followed and spring found Pierce relieved of all responsibilities as a cattle owner. This is what Grimes called 'teaching a Yankee the cow business.' But Pierce proved to be one of those rare pupils who profit by their lessons."

Around 1860, Shanghai invited his brother Jonathan to join in his Texas adventure, but the Civil War intervened. Both of the New Englander Pierce brothers spent some time in a Confederate cavalry company under command of a recently arrived German. When they returned, they found that their cattle holdings had evaporated like a July puddle. The range cattle had been left to their own devices, and those that survived were said to be as wild as the jack rabbits who shared the coastal prairies and just as skinny, but the Pierces stubbornly started again from scratch.

They also got married at war's end to two sisters - Fanny and Nanny Lacey. The girls' father, a signer of the Texas Declaration of Independence, had established his own operation in Matagorda County, but died about the time a teenaged Shanghai Pierce was being apprenticed in Virginia. The Lacey girls' mother took the family back to Kentucky, but they returned to Texas just in time to catch the eye of the Pierce brothers.

Just a few years later, Shanghai and Jonathan established their first real ranching operation. Called Rancho Grande, it was near Deming's Bridge across Tres Palacios Creek near today's town of Blessing. Cattle operations were still open range, and the brothers were branding cattle across 50 square miles. That brand changed over time. Originally it was a B, then BB, UU, and finally a simple D.

The Pierces realized that the markets for beef were in the Northeast. Instead of the pre-war trailing and shipping of herds to the east, they were among the early ranchers to head their cattle north to the new transcontinental railroad. There the story might have stagnated, if not for the death of Shanghai's wife and infant son in 1871. He converted his cattle into hard currency and moved to Kansas for a year and half, but by then Texas was in his blood. Shanghai Pierce returned to the Gulf Coast with a new resolve.

The business was changing. Open ranges in South Texas were no more, and Shanghai Pierce began buying up land under the name of the Pierce-Sullivan Pasture Company, an outfit he headed. That included snatching up spreads that had been owned by men who had doubted that a Rhode Island Yankee could succeed in the Texas cattle business. In the days of Reconstruction and tough times, the hard currency he handed over was heavenly manna for many of the poor Texans, and they often jumped at Pierce's offers.

The story was that he traveled with an African American man leading a mule weighted down with bags of silver and gold coins. Those would be poured onto a blanket and counted out to meet the agreed upon price for acreage or stock. While he waited, sometimes as long as a week, for the newly acquired cows to be rounded up, Shanghai sat around the chuck wagons and campfires and loudly told stories that no doubt stretched the blanket of truth.

He was a natural giant of a man, but he made his height even greater by wearing broad-brimmed, high-peaked hats. Unlike the normal Texan on the range, he often opted for monogrammed shirts and brocade vests. Combined with his booming voice that was rumored to be "so loud he could be heard a ½ mile away," and his penchant for self-promotion, it earned him more than a few detractors in South Texas and beyond.

He was prone to brag about his accomplishments, claiming that he controlled "nearly all the cattle in Christendom once." His skin was thick, though, and the bad mouthing did not seem to bother him. He was said to have remarked more than once: "By God! If I was to stop to fight with everybody who cussed me, I would be fighting all the time, but while they are busy cussing me, I am busy getting their money."

Still, he had a touch for associating with his ranch hands. Writer Hunter described his vocabulary as "picturesque, rather than elegant." Numerous raconteurs of the West wrote that Pierce frequented gambling halls and barrooms not only in Texas but at the end of drives to Abilene and Wichita. "The whiskey barrel at his home was never empty," and he was comfortable raising a glass with pistol-toting Texans anywhere. Still, he was said not to imbibe to excess. It was a good policy as he remarried in 1875, and he and his new wife, Hattie, soon had a daughter whom they named Mary Frances.

Shanghai's cattle company sent thousands of Texas cattle north on the trail and, once the New York, Texas & Mexican Railway built 90 miles of track from Richmond to Victoria, the Pierce-Sullivan outfit shipped out thousands more by rail. That track ran right across the northern part of his empire, and Pierce granted right of way on the condition that he was allowed to hand pick the loading points. Shanghai then ponied up his own cash to build more rail on his property at his own expense.

He also started his own town, originally called Pierce's Station, in 1881. Eventually the name was changed to just Pierce. He had grand plans for the hamlet. He tried and failed to get the Wharton County seat moved there, and he also struck out with his bid to have a railroad from Eagle Lake to Bay City make Pierce a crossroads. He financed a church, several houses, and a three-story hotel, and by 1892, the town of Pierce had 50 residents. The hotel never became much of a going concern, but it did stand there until 1980. By then most of the homes were gone, too.

There was another town called Shanghai that sat down a railroad spur on the west side of the Colorado River not far from Wharton. Pierce decided to farm that area of his holdings, and in 1897, he contracted with the State of Texas for convicts to cut timber and burn the canebrakes. The spur was built for that purpose and later served the cotton gin that he constructed. That spur was retired by the Southern Pacific in 1940, and the old convict quarters, with bars still on the windows, was turned into a barn for the Pierce Ranch.

Shanghai Pierce tried to expand his holdings into banking and railroads, but that, along with damage from the Great 1900 Storm cost him more than one and a quarter million dollars. A sizable chunk of change at the turn of the century.

For all of the colorful legends about Shanghai Pierce and the Texas coastal prairies, there is one change he promoted that can still be readily seen on Texas ranches.

In 1868, just as the famous cattle trails from Texas north to the middle-American railheads were heating up, northern animals began dying of a mysterious malady. It was soon determined that the disease was being transmitted by herds driven to northern climes from the south. The English *Veterinarian* magazine pronounced it "fatal in every instance," and they were almost right. Though the infected animals were found across the entire Southeastern quarter of the United States, as far away as Virginia, it was dubbed Texas Fever. Quickly, states began quarantining Texas herds, railroads segregated cattle cars, and in 1885, Kansas placed a flat prohibition on any Texas cow crossing its border.

Louis Pasteur and Robert Koch did yeoman's work on bacteriology, but not until the 1880s, and it was a decade after that before the pathogen that caused Texas fever was isolated. Somehow the Texas Longhorns were developing an immunity, but when these apparently healthy animals arrived on the plains of Kansas and Illinois, they turned out to be carriers of the fever. Ranchers needed answers right away. If they could not cure the disease, perhaps they could find cows that would not catch it in the first place.

Shanghai Pierce suspected that the cause might be ticks. He performed rudimentary experiments by removing ticks from certain animals. It did not render definitive answers, but it was enough to send him to Europe in search of a breed that was "immune to ticks." His ultimate conclusion was that Brahman cattle from India were the answer. One tale which is almost certainly not true was that Pierce bought two old Brahman bulls from a circus, and saw that, in the words of Marvin Hunter, "there was a line beyond which even a Texas tick refused to go."

Pierce was not the first Texas cattleman to import Brahmans. Crossbreeds were in Hays County as early as 1860, and there was a Brahman bull included in a bankruptcy settlement just down the road in Comal County two years later. The King Ranch brought in some Brahmans and mixed breeds in the early 1870s. The first record of Shanghai Pierce's Brahman purchases were five animals brought into Indianola in 1875. Still the numbers brought in during the end of the 19th century were small.

Shanghai Pierce, the towering cattle baron, died of a cerebral hemorrhage in December 1900 without ever knowing if he was 100% correct about the Brahman cattle, but his nephew, A.P. Borden, headed to India not long after Pierce's death and bought 51 of the big animals. After a quarantine period in New York Harbor, during which 18 of them died, they became the first large scale importation to Texas. Because of the deaths in New York, future Brahmans came through Brazil or Canada, not directly from India. But the Pierce Ranch was eventually breeding them with Herefords and shorthorns and finding animals that were indeed more resistant to ticks and disease. The heat-loving Brahmans, generally drawled as Bray-mas in Texas, also put on weight because they kept grazing when other breeds were lounging in the shade.

The Texas Brahman Breeders Association is over a century old, and the state has more of the animals than any other. Most are cross breeds such as the Santa Gertrudis or Beefmaster, and there are also Brafords, Simbrah, and Charbray. They make for big animals who are easily recognizable with their prominent dewlaps and humps.

That aspect of Shanghai Pierce is likely known only to a few thousand cattle raisers, but no one can say that the man did not try to ensure a bit of immortality. In the early 1890s, he hired sculptor Frank Teich to create a 6'5" marble likeness and mount it on a ten-foot-tall piece of granite. He told all who would listen, "If I don't do it myself, they'll forget Old Shang."

The marble Shang stands on the bank of Tres Palacios Creek and today marks his grave and those of his first wife and infant son. At one time there was an old weatherboard church, but there is still a grove of live oaks with Spanish moss swaying "gently to the caress of a Texas breeze." Most of the visitors today are Braford cattle since the Pierce Ranch still operates, if only on what Shanghai may have considered a modest 32,000 acres.

Brahmas at Pierce Ranch 1906. Pierce Ranch House

Chapter Thirty-Four

William Wharton

Stephen F. Austin quite deservedly is looked upon as the leader of Americans in Mexican Texas. For his first decade in his new nation, Austin repeatedly stressed his loyalty to the Mexican Republic, wrote his documents in Spanish, and urged his colonists to do the same. In private, though, Austin often suggested that loyalty cut both ways. The government in Mexico City must continue to do right by Texas. Still, Austin knew that his fledgling colony in Texas was not remotely strong enough to stand alone as "an independent speck in the galaxy of nations."

Another of the early newcomers from the United States arrived with a more combative attitude. He was a newly minted lawyer from Tennessee, and if he did not arrive in Texas with enough privileges, he soon acquired them. William Harris Wharton and his little brother, John Austin Wharton, were orphaned as children and raised by a generous uncle, Jesse Wharton, in Nashville. They were provided with a top-notch education. Almost as soon as the older boy, William, passed the Tennessee Bar, he lit out for Mexican Texas. In December 1827, at only 25 years old, William married Sarah Ann Groce, the daughter of the richest man in

Austin's Colony. When Wharton took his new bride back to Tennessee, the father-in-law offered a sprawling plantation in Brazoria County as an inducement to return. It was 16,000 acres of rich alluvial soil on Oyster Creek just a dozen miles from the Gulf of Mexico.

William and Sarah Ann dubbed it Eagle Island. The couple replaced the log house with an elaborate building made of imported lumber. They landscaped the grounds. The layout was patterned after a home in Mobile. For functionality, a sugar house with two cook kettles and redundant machinery was constructed. That entire operation was eventually run by more than 130 slaves.

The splash William Wharton made in Austin's Colony was not due to his wealth. It was because of his mouth and his pen. He was intelligent, eloquent, and often short-tempered. It was a combination that gained him a small but loyal following among the colonists.

On April 6, 1830 a law went into effect that sent the new American settlers in Texas into a tizzy. It came about because the government in Mexico City was concerned by the overwhelming response to the empresarios' offers to land-hungry Americans, a system the government had put in place. They wanted colonists to populate the country's frontier border with the United States, but when they saw that those newcomers were simply bringing American customs and politics with them, the Mexican leaders realized they had let the proverbial snake into the henhouse. Manuel Mier y Teran, the general who had been sent on a northern inspection tour, made several suggestions on how to regain a balance in Texas. That included paying all expenses to get people from the interior of Mexico to move to the northern reaches of Coahuila y Texas.

The outrage was not so much over the ideas of Mier y Teran but over the provisions that foreign minister Lucas Alaman y Escalada added to

the law. Article 11 looked to shut down further immigration from the
U.S. Mexico's president, Anastasio Bustamante, was no friend to the
Texans, but Stephen F. Austin attempted to work around the law by
gaining exemptions for himself and fellow empresario Green DeWitt. As
a member of the state legislature at Saltillo, Austin walked a tightrope
between the competing Mexican political factions of Centralists and
Federalists. He and virtually all American Texans sided with the latter,
but it was the Centralists who held power.

William Harris Wharton

Though Austin believed that restraint was needed, those who thought
like Wharton disagreed. In addition to the stoppage of immigration,
Mexico had ended the years-long customs exemption that had existed in
Texas. The man in charge of collecting those taxes at the small port of
Anahuac was Juan Davis Bradburn, a Kentuckian who had been in the
Mexican military for a decade. His ham-fisted tactics brought sentiments

there to a boil, and him granting asylum to runaway Louisiana slaves
made things worse. Led by lawyers Patrick Jack and William B. Travis,
the Texians resorted to armed skirmishes, and when settlers on the lower
Brazos tried to ship a cannon to Anahuac, men died on both sides.
Though it is not definitive, many historians believe William Wharton
was among the combatants at Velasco.

That agitating faction pushed for a political consultation at San Felipe
in October 1832, and adopted a list of reforms they wanted. The asks
included separate statehood for Texas without being a part of Coahuila
along with the lifting of all immigration restrictions and the ability to
organize a militia. A provisional constitution for state government was
drafted and William Wharton wrote the official request to be forwarded
to authorities. Though the Mexican government deemed the entire
meeting to have been illegal, the same figures met again the following
year, and this time they doubled down by choosing Wharton to preside
over the convention. It is easy to lose sight of how small the population
of the American colonies in Texas was, and how outsized the voices
of a handful of accomplished men could become. By 1833, William
Wharton was decidedly one of those men. Despite the clear shift toward
Wharton's radicalism, the consultation elected Stephen Austin to carry
its requests to Mexico City.

By that time, the younger Wharton brother, John, had settled in
Texas. He jumped right into the political maelstrom by starting up a
newspaper at Brazoria called *The Advocate of The People's Rights* to give
William a platform for presenting his radical views. Mainly, the paper
railed against Stephen Austin as being too cautious and conservative.

Austin had bigger troubles because he had been arrested for treason
on his way home from delivering the consultation's petition. After some
kindnesses extended at Monterrey by General Pedro Lemus, Austin was

sent back south to Mexico City under an armed guard of seven soldiers. There some months of solitary confinement awaited, but he managed to send a spate of letters before he left Monterrey. His calls for prudence and quiet instead of revolutionary actions were heard in Texas.

John Wharton's paper started an editorial by pledging a sentence worth's of support "so long as he continues to be a true friend to Texas." Wharton, who may have arrived only a matter of months prior, then quickly changed his tone. "...but should he be actuated by an inordinate ambition for wealth and power, should he be disposed to sacrifice the interests of thousands to promote his own private views, he will find in me... a Brutus with an arm uplifted against him." Such belligerent words did not bring the desired groundswell, and the *Advocate of the People's Rights* ceased publication by the end of March. The more lasting result was that the Wharton's anti-Austin rumblings prompted Gail Borden, Jr. to establish the *Telegraph & Texas Register* at San Felipe as a moderating counterpoint.

Austin's imprisonment in Mexico continued, but he managed to gain transfer from the Inquisition Prison to a more favorable spot with a window. Allowed to write letters home, Austin told his brother-in-law, James Perry, that he would have been released except for allegations put forth by his personal enemies, Anglos back in Texas. Though he had no proof, he suspected Thomas Chambers and William H. Wharton. Austin called men such as those "political fanatics... vain talkers, and visionary fools."

When those allegations found their way to print, Wharton vehemently denied the charge then lashed out with an articulate tantrum against the jailed empresario's "disgusting self conceit" and "inconsistent stupidity." As Gregg Cantrell put it in his definitive Austin biography, "the quick-tempered Wharton vowed that 'when this obeyer of instructions[,] this man of so many personal friends, this disinterested benefactor of Texas, this oracular weathercock,'" ..."this maker of mottos... this presumptuous dictator" comes back from confinement, Wharton would "brand him on the forehead with a mark that shall outlast his epitaph."

The younger Wharton brother went beyond threats in the newspaper. Later reminiscences from Brazoria County mention various potential catalysts, but suffice to say the Whartons had a serious chip on their shoulders when it came to people with the surname Austin. Not long after a distant Austin cousin and most all his family died in a cholera epidemic, John Wharton allegedly raised a glass at a dinner party and offered the drunken toast, "The Austins, may their bones burn in hell." Present at the dinner was William T. Austin, the brother of the departed man. A duel of pistols at 10 paces was soon arranged.

The consensus was that John Wharton was an excellent shot, but William Austin could not shoot worth a damn. His second, Warren Hall, relentlessly trained his friend and stressed that Austin must fire first or die. William Austin heeded the warning, fired as soon as his pistol was level, and hit John Wharton in his right wrist. The bone was shattered almost to the elbow, and Wharton's pistol dropped to the ground. He was treated by close friend Dr. Branch Archer, but ever after, John Wharton was obliged to write left-handed.

Stephen F. Austin's entreaties for the Texans to remain "quiet" may well have extended to them not pressing overly hard for his release according to biographer Cantrell. By the summer of 1834, though, the ayuntamientos, the councils of the Texas population centers, had gathered petitions and selected two Anglo lawyers, Peter Grayson and Spencer Jack, to deliver them to Mexico City and lobby for Stephen Austin's release. They also brought along a letter from Juan Jose Elguezabal, the new governor of Coahuila y Texas. Among the signatures on one petition was that of William Wharton. Stephen F. Austin sent him a note of thanks.

On Christmas Day 1834, Stephen F. Austin was given his freedom...of sorts. He was required to stay in Mexico City until the Mexican Congress and then the courts granted a final amnesty. He returned to Texas in September 1835 with a different attitude, convinced that his Anglo Texans could not trust the government of Mexico to do right by them. He now understood that Texas would eventually have to fight, but he still believed that it should wait until the "violent political convulsions of Mexico" would shake Texas loose "like a ripe peach." When word came that General Martin Perfecto de Cos was coming to Texas with troops and an enemies list marked for arrest, Austin grew serious. He wrote to a committee at Columbia that "war is our only resource."

By that time, the Wharton Brothers and several others were loudly calling for complete independence. They gained the name of the War Party, and they sought out the dissatisfied and new arrivals. The majority of Texas leaders still favored a more moderate approach. They wanted the republican constitution of 1824 restored, and they still wanted separate statehood for Texas within Mexico. Those men believed they had strong Federalist allies across Northern Mexico. Another consultation was called at San Felipe de Austin, but the unexpected battle at Gonzales at the start of October 1835 intervened. Stephen F. Austin was elected to command the "Army of the People," and William Wharton was picked as judge advocate. Both men headed west to besiege the Mexican troops at San Antonio de Bexar.

Wharton did not stay long. He resigned his commission with the army still trying to take San Antonio, and soon after, Stephen Austin was called back, as well. Those two men, along with Branch Archer, had been named by the Consultation as commissioners to the United States. They were to rally the cause of Texas, and above all raise money for a fight. Wharton and Austin were far from friends, but they agreed on one point - the declaration of causes that the Consultation had ratified was weak. Wharton declined his appointment outright, and Austin was on the verge of doing the same. Only an agreement to hold a convention on the matter of independence convinced the men to change their minds. They left for the United States the day after Christmas.

By and large the grand trip up the East Coast of the U.S. was a failure. The big bankers of New York, Philadelphia, and Nashville along with the politicians at Washington, would not commit major funds to back Texas with things in such flux. The already established connections at New Orleans brought the only cheer. Austin was reduced to paying hotel bills for himself and Wharton out of his own pocket, much of which was spent on liquor and cigars. The biggest positive to come out of the trip was that by its end in June, both Branch Archer and William Wharton were devoted friends of Stephen F. Austin. When the election for first President of the Republic of Texas was held in the early fall, Wharton wholeheartedly backed his old enemy. It mattered not. Austin finished a distant third to the hero of San Jacinto, Sam Houston.

Houston, though, was smart enough to utilize the talents of the best men in Texas. He appointed Austin Secretary of State and selected

William Wharton to be the first minister to the United States. The goal was to secure recognition for the new nation of Texas with the ultimate prize being annexation to the U.S.. Wharton resigned from his seat in the first Senate of the Republic to take the post.

William Wharton lobbied earnestly for the good of Texas and wrote a lengthy report home in January 1837. He assured his government that both Britain and France would remain neutral in the beef between Mexico and Texas, and that he expected annexation to the United States was but two years away. He felt that incoming president Martin Van Buren would push it through. Wharton also wrote of a somewhat fraught meeting with sitting President Andrew Jackson whose decision to delay recognition of Texas was costing the new country dearly in terms of financial credit. Jackson took the words to heart, and recognition was won on March 3, 1837, Jackson's final day in office. On the topic of annexation, Wharton was incorrect in his optimism. Texas would go it alone for another eight years.

William Wharton resigned as minister and headed for home. After a month long journey from Washington to New Orleans, he was able to hitch a ride on the Texas Navy ship *Independence*. Following a week at sea, the little schooner was abreast of the mouth of the Brazos, only four miles up the coast, and in sight of its destination of Velasco, when two Mexican navy ships appeared and boxed it in. The Texas ship, its sailors, and its important passenger were taken prisoner and sailed to Matamoros.

John Wharton immediately demanded that President Houston secure his brother's release, but Houston pointed out that since Texas and Mexico were still technically at war, there was not much to be done. Sarah Ann Wharton tried to ride to Mexico herself, but broke her leg in a fall from her horse before she could make it. It was a letter from William

Wharton himself that first suggested that the Mexicans might be open to a prisoner swap, and Sam Houston agreed to finance a boat and send 30 of the soldados still held from San Jacinto as the price of exchange.

Leading the mission was John Austin Wharton, but before they could get permission to land in Mexico, a storm ran their schooner aground. They were hidden and fed by Father Michael Muldoon, an Irish priest who had lived in Northern Mexico for decades and was a great friend to many of the Anglo Texans. The good father also provided news – William Wharton had already escaped. That was thanks to Muldoon smuggling him clerical robes that allowed him to walk out of confinement dressed as a priest. A few days later, Muldoon managed to sneak John Wharton and his party of Texans back across the Rio Grande.

Back home in Brazoria County, William Wharton was again elected to the Republic's Senate. True to his pattern, he resigned from that office in May 1838 but was reelected later in the year. Tragedy struck that December when his brother John died of a fever. William, though, did not have long to mourn the loss. Just three months later, he was dismounting from his horse at the home of his brother-in-law, Leonard Groce, when the pistol he was wearing accidentally discharged. The wound proved fatal. William Wharton was 36 years old.

He left behind one child, a boy who he and Sarah had named John Austin Wharton after his brother. Left with perhaps the most valuable estate in Texas, the gallant and rich young Wharton rose to the rank of major general during the Civil War. Like his father, he married very well. He had a bright political future ahead of him when he was gunned down by a fellow officer whom he had angered.

Chapter Thirty-Five

Seito Saibara

This is a tale of technology, whales, steamships, and samurai warriors. It was the intersection of that unlikely grouping that set the stage for the Texas rice industry, and it begins in Japan.

The samurai were initially a disciplined warrior class, but they transitioned from the battlefields to administrative and bureaucratic roles during a centuries-long peace presided over by a military dictatorship. The samurai were only one level of a rigid caste system, but they gained a great deal of power. Under their protectionism and their code of stoicism and ritual, a robust merchant class emerged in Japan, and urban centers grew with wonderful roadways between them. Edo, later renamed Tokyo, had a population of one million people. The thing was that virtually no one outside of Japan was allowed to see it. Feudal lords, fearing both the growing influence of Christianity and a possible loss of military power, sealed off the country from Westerners in 1639. For over 200 years, those foreigners, or barbarians as the Japanese viewed them, were turned away with force.

With the advent of the Industrial Revolution, though, the United States needed oil to lubricate machinery, everything from pocket watches to locomotives, and that oil came from whales. Hundreds of whaling ships left New England ports and sailed around the Horn of South America to the Pacific on years-long journeys. They brought back a product that filled American lamps but also provided a non-corrosive oil that operated in a wide temperature range to keep factory gears and pistons running smoothly. Many of the sought after sperm whales lived in waters just north of Japan, and the sailors needed provisioning stations and an occasional safe harbor. The closest, most logical place for that refused to let them in. Even Herman Melville wrote in *Moby Dick* of "that double-bolted land, Japan."

The American answer to the problem was gunboat diplomacy. Using an approach that has never gone out of style among global powers, the plan was to utilize a show of force to achieve a desired goal. Other American ships had tried and failed to "open" Japan, but in 1853, President Millard Fillmore sent Commodore Mathew Perry. He was a younger brother of a War of 1812 hero who had himself fought in the recent Mexican War. Most importantly, he was stubborn, determined, and in command of four warships, two of which belched thick black smoke from their steam boilers. The Japanese were astonished by the new machines, and since they had not fought a war in 250 years, they were wholly unprepared to resist them. Perry and 300 officers, Marines, and musicians went ashore and presented U.S. demands to the shoguns with a promise to return soon for a response. When Perry came back in March 1854, he brought nine American ships bristling with guns. Gifts were exchanged, banquets enjoyed, and a treaty signed. America got its two ports of call, and Japan was opened to the West. It was the death knell for the samurai and brought about a political revolution.

That new Japan was where Seito Saibara was raised. As a youngster, he developed an interest in the Western world, and he entered an English school, something that did not exist a mere five years before his birth. Emerging from education as a lawyer, Saibara became a judge and a member of the Japanese parliament in 1898. While living in Kobe, he converted to Christianity, and, within a year, was heading a Congregationalist university. It made him the only Christian member of the Japanese government.

The Christian leadership in the country asked Saibara to give up his seat in the Diet and go to the United States to study theology. He agreed. In 1901, Seito entered a seminary in Hartford. It did not take long before he decided that he wanted to remain in the United States. The opportunity for that was presented to him by the Japanese consul general at the request of the Houston Chamber of Commerce and Southern Pacific Railroad. Those entities wanted to increase rice production in Texas. They were looking at examples set by the Carolinas and Honduras, places where rice fields were producing 18 to 20 barrels an acre. If Southeast Texas could manage the same output, there was money to be made from both the growing and the shipping. The consul, Sadatsuchi Uchida, suggested the distinguished Seito Saibara as the man to teach rice production to local farmers. He arrived in August 1903.

Rice farming was not entirely new to the Gulf Coast. Though the Carolinas and Georgia were the primary places in the U.S. that farmed rice from a Madagascar variety brought over in the late 1600s, Louisiana and then southeast Texas prairies saw some rice fields around the time of the Civil War. David French of Beaumont was the first major Texas rice farmer. New railroads to move agricultural products, the introduction of widespread irrigation, modern combines to harvest, and updated mills to process the grain all moved things along nicely. By 1900, Louisiana and Texas produced 99% of American rice. Land on the Gulf prairies was cheap, and the East Coast rice operations shut down. Still, yield per acre was mediocre, and business leaders in Houston felt things could be even more profitable. They banked on the Japanese effort to up their game.

Seito Saibara leased 1,000 acres of land at Webster on the southern edge of Harris County and founded a colony to run it. His wife, Taiko, and son, Kiyoaki, came to Texas and brought a few hundred pounds of shinriki rice seed. It was a superior variety gifted by the emperor himself. Thirty colonists from Japan also arrived in Webster. Their first harvest, in 1904, yielded 34 barrels an acre, almost doubling the previous output. The majority of that rice was sold to farmers in Texas and Louisiana for seed.

Seito Saibara's (in hat) well and irrigation 1904. UTSA Special Collections

The quick success allowed the Saibara farming operation to expand, and they soon purchased the leased land. More Japanese families emigrated to the Texas coastal counties, but not all stayed. The culture shock was overwhelming to some. There had been only 13 Japanese people in Texas in 1900, but the census a decade later showed 340.

The Saibara family was relatively well accepted in the tiny community of Webster. They joined the Presbyterian church. Their children and those of the other Japanese families went to the local school, and the Galveston School Board granted permission for Kiyoaki to attend Ball High. By 1909, that young man was ready to marry. It was arranged that he meet the daughter of a family friend from Japan, a samurai who arranged for the girl to be trained in English and Christianity. Kiyoaki Saibara traveled to San Francisco to meet Shimoyo Iwasaki, and the two agreed to marry. The ceremony was held in Webster.

The family rice business continued to grow. Kiyoaki and his young family moved to New Mexico for a time to start an operation there, and Seito opened a nursery in Mobile, Alabama. With Seito Saibara as the recognized leader of the effort, Japanese immigrants were growing rice all along the upper Gulf Coast.

All of the personal success could not overcome U.S. immigration policy, however. No matter what Seito, Taiko, and Kiyoaki achieved in building for themselves, no matter how many other Japanese farmers they brought in, or even how much money they made for American businesses, they remained aliens under American law. The Naturalization Act of 1790 was meant to codify citizenship requirements and make the United States a friendly new home for would-be merchants and idealists, but it also limited the chance at citizenship to White males. The Chinese Exclusion Act had set the premise that unlike Hispanics, the Chinese were not considered White under the law. That thought was extended to all Asians. The Saibara men might do whatever they wanted short of voting and the like.

In 1917, another act was passed that stopped all immigration from an "Asiatic Barred Zone," but that did not include Japan. The family could still bring immigrants to Texas to join in their agricultural operations, but that reprieve was short lived. The Johnson-Reed Act in 1924 fully embraced growing American xenophobia. Japanese immigrants were prohibited. Seito Saibara's vision of a faith-based Japanese agricultural colony was on hold indefinitely. As frustrated as the immediate family was, Seito declined an invitation to return to Japan and serve as minister of education.

Instead, he chose another option to cultivate - Brazil. There had been a trend of Japanese immigration to that country, and Seito and Taiko ultimately spent eight years establishing agricultural settlements in the Amazon. As most countries were tightening immigration policies, Brazil loosened theirs, and it worked for many nationalities to move to South America. At the same time, Seito corresponded with his son who was still operating the family business in Webster.

In 1932, Taiko Saibara returned to the family's home on the Texas Coast, and Seito moved to Taiwan, then known as Formosa. After just a brief stay, he returned to live in Tokyo. That did not last long either. Seito, then in his middle 70s, grew seriously ill. He sailed from Kobe to Los Angeles in the early fall of 1937, and came home to Webster. His final year and a half was spent near his family. Seito died in April 1939 and was buried at League City in Galveston County. He was eulogized not only by the Texas locals; his obituary ran in newspapers from Florida

to Hawaii. In those increasingly tense days just before WWII, several
headlines identified him as a "Japanese liberal."

Kiyoaki Saibara still remained at Webster, and he proved himself a
worthy successor to Seito. Like his father and mother, who died in
1942, Kiyoaki was still a Japanese citizen, and under Franklin Roosevelt's
order, that made him an enemy alien. When thousands of other Japanese
in that situation were being herded into internment camps, Kiyoaki
Saibara was in Webster, Texas broadcasting to Japan on shortwave radio.
He told his own story of a Japanese family that had prospered in
the United States and was an indelible part of their local community.
He urged the Japanese government to give its own "enemy aliens and
prisoners of war the same kind of treatment as is accorded to us." His
messages were an influential factor in Japanese Americans enlisting into
the U.S. military.

Kiyoaki's two oldest sons, Robert and Warren, joined the Army, and
Robert rose to Lieutenant Colonel, the highest rank ever attained at
the time by a person of Japanese ancestry. The youngest of Kiyoaki
and Shimoyo's sons was Harvey. He was killed during Army Air Force
training.

Saibara's work to help Japanese-American relations did not go
completely unappreciated in Washington. It did not hurt that diplomats
from Tokyo had routinely visited both he and his father on the Gulf
prairies. Though it took quite a while, in 1952, several lawmakers
pointed to him when they finally allowed Japanese to become American
citizens. The following year, just shy of 50 years after his arrival in
America, Kiyoaki Saibara was sworn in as a U.S. citizen at a ceremony
in Houston.

One the family's favorite stories involves John Glenn, a Mercury and Gemini astronaut who trained and lived at nearby NASA. After Glenn's first orbit of the Earth, he went on an international goodwill tour that included a stop in Japan. In preparation, he met Kiyoaki Saibara who said, "Colonel Glenn, when you get to Japan, if you should meet the Emperor, would you give him my regards?"

Glenn could not fathom that the Emperor of Japan would have the slightest clue about some old man raising rice in Webster. As the memoirs of his granddaughter put it, "But when Mr. Glenn did meet the Emperor, he thought there was no harm in trying it, and said, 'Your Majesty, do you know a Mr. K. Saibara in Webster, Texas?' The Emperor immediately flashed a big smile and said, 'How is my dear friend, Mr. Saibara?'"

Kiyoaki retired from actively farming rice and raising cattle at age 79. He died in 1972. That year Texas rice production totaled two billion pounds. Though Texas now ranks sixth among rice producing states with Arkansas far out in front of the pack, it is still a major crop in the state and elsewhere along the Gulf Coast, and much of the credit for establishing that enterprise lies with the Saibara family who brought superior seed and technique to the flat prairies near Webster.

Chapter Thirty-Six

The Coming of the Telegraph

For many centuries, long distance communication was a hurdle for mankind. People walked then managed to tame animals to carry them and their information. Indigenous people in the Americas, Asia, and Australia sent signals with smoke. As early as 2400 BCE, Egyptian pharaohs began using couriers to deliver their messages. The Persians and presumably other dynasties in the region followed suit, and the Romans stole the idea to bring it to Europe. The couriers were still not widely available to the public. Mothers hoping to write their sons who had left home to be a gladiator or galley slave were generally out of luck.

In 1520, Manuel I of Portugal, the king who sent Vasco de Gama to India and started a Portuguese Empire, ordered the creation of a public mail service. The Polish got on board with the idea a few decades later. Though Henry VIII had appointed a Master of the Posts, the English public did not get access to mail until the 1660s and the first two Kings Charles.

Still, there existed a need for something faster than what postal workers could provide. By the late 1600s, multiple locales had developed a system of towers and semaphore flags or fires that relayed messages across the horizon. It was the French who applied the word telegraph, and some called it an optical telegraph. The United States Congress even considered funding such a system between New York and New Orleans in 1837 but decided against it. By then a couple of intrepid but less than dedicated American inventors, building on recent electromagnetic inventions of Englishman Michael Faraday, had dabbled with an electric telegraph before giving up on the idea.

In that same year, painter and inventor Samuel F.B. Morse and two colleagues, Leonard Gale and Alfred Vail, came up with a better system. Also in 1837, a British team had independently developed their own electric telegraph. Theirs used five magnetic needles to point at letters on a fixed panel. Morse's was much better. He came up with a code of dots and dashes, and an operator who learned that alphabet of impulses could send, receive, and transcribe the messages. Morse got his patent and sought financial support for a long-distance public demonstration.

Timing is everything, and two events in 1837 greatly impacted the new telegraph. The first was a severe financial panic. It was brought on by rampant market speculation, tightening of British credit, the bursting of a real estate bubble, and a giant drop in cotton prices. The downturn was hugely exacerbated by the fact that Andrew Jackson had successfully waged political war against a central bank, leaving the government with no independent entity to stop the freefall. Forty percent of the nation's banks soon shuttered, and any chance at capital to implement his new invention slipped through Samuel Morse's fingers like smoke.

Another of the biggest news items in North America in 1837 was the beginning of a new Republic in Texas. About the time that the U.S.

Congress declined to underwrite Morse's demonstration, the inventor sent a proposal in writing to Memucan Hunt, the new Republic's blue-eyed, thin-lipped Minister and Envoy Extraordinaire to the United States. In the letter, Morse offered to give "the perpetual use of my new Electro-Magnetic Telegraph" to Texas "as evidence of my interest in the rising character of the new and independent state." Morse wanted to see his invention in use and was willing to give it away if Texas was willing to be his showcase. For good measure, Morse closed his letter by saying that he hoped "your fine country may be as distinguished for your religious, moral, and intellectual character as it is for that of courage and energy." Morse might be forgiven his optimism about Texas morality. He was from New England.

The Republic of Texas, just beginning its journey to bankruptcy thanks to the aforementioned Panic, never responded to Morse. In 1860, the inventor wrote then Governor Sam Houston to rescind his kind offer. By then, the telegraph was in use across much of America and was already gaining a foothold in Texas although via private enterprise.

The first electro-magnetic telegraph connection to Texas came to Marshall in January 1854, ten years after Morse established the nation's first intercity connection between Washington and Baltimore. Morse initially tried to bury the telegraph lines, but they broke, so he followed the British example and used poles. Telegraph lines in the East had been on poles for a decade, but they were slow coming to the West. The lines running to the original telegraph office in Marshall did not wait for the time and expense of poles. Wires were strung between tree tops. Texas telegraph operators were often required to close their offices and personally make repairs when wind blew the branches and caused breaks in the wires.

The company providing the service was the Texas and Red River Telegraph Company. If potential customers in Marshall wished to send a wire to a fellow Texan, they were initially S.O.L. The line only ran to the company's facility in Shreveport, and from there on to Alexandria, Natchez, and New Orleans, but progress was coming. In a matter of just a few months, wire was run south to Henderson, Rusk, Crockett, Montgomery, Houston, and Galveston.

The newspaper in Houston was coincidentally named the *Telegraph & Texas Register* since 1835, two years before Morse's experiments, and the editor there was positively gleeful. That writer used the arrival of the new technology for an "in your face" attack against Antonio Lopez de Santa Anna. He reminded readers that the Mexican President and General had burned the town of Harrisburg, but that the area "rose like another Phoenix." Furthermore, the *Telegraph* opined, the new "lightning messenger" joined with "the shrill whistle of the steamboat and locomotive" as "the embryo city" of Houston moved forward.

Like the rest of the nation, Texas soon saw companies racing to build telegraph lines. In 1856, the Texas and New Orleans Telegraph Company began construction of lines from Galveston to San Antonio and Austin, but it took years before Austin had any direct connection to New Orleans. The piecemeal approach and questionable corporate structure were both impediments.

Another issue was as old as time – greed. The money for the Texas and Louisiana enterprise had largely come from Houston and Galveston, and it was not long before visions of fatter wallets pitted backers against one another. Charles C. Clute went to Louisiana announcing himself the owner of the line between Alexandria and Natchez, and he presented a bill of $300 for carrying messages over his part of the telegraph route. Before long, his crew showed up in Alexandria and began planting poles in the middle of sidewalks and cutting down venerable shade trees without permission.

Meanwhile, another Houston investor, T.C.H. Smith, claimed ownership of the same line, and he was the man who had collected $4,000 of a pledged $5,000 from the citizens of Alexandria. Clute tried to talk the city fathers out of another $1,300, this time paid to him. Alexandrians stopped just short of running Clute out of town in a tar and feather jacket and riding on a rail. As one local paper put it in September of 1854: "Since the day that the line was completed to the present time, it has not been in working order three weeks at any one time. For all the benefit that our citizens or the traveling public have derived from this line, it could easily be dispensed with, for as uncertain and irregular as the mails are, they afford a more certain and expeditious medium of communication." The editorial ended by saying that the Alexandria stockholders "were unanimously of the opinion that they had been basely swindled."

It was indeed T.C.H. Smith who had completed the line in the first place, but the company's operators and contractors were obliged to ride through desolate and empty country almost every day to repair breaks in the wire. Soon the Texas and Red River company was deemed a financial failure, and the tangible assets were sold for debt. Aside from the portion between Houston and Galveston, the wires were ordered to be taken down. The final indignity was that there was little wire to be found. Enterprising farmers had carted it off to use for mending fences and bailing hay.

C.C. Clute remained involved as superintendent of the portion between Galveston and Houston, but it was another telegraph line, opened in 1860, that can be called the first permanent one in Texas. That was also the first in the state to run along a railroad right of way as most successful lines back east had done. In this case it was the tracks of the Galveston, Harrisburg & Houston Railway. The earlier attempt paralleled stage coach routes, but railroad trackage was much better suited to maintenance efforts.

The telegraph line in Houston about 1860. University of Houston Special Collections

There is a very interesting sidebar to Charlie Clute and the first permanent telegraph line in Texas. Clute was from Ontario, Canada, and he came to Texas, along with his brother, John, expressly for work in the new technology sector of telegraphy. He also hired a Canadian friend named George Ellsworth who had learned telegraph operation as a teenager and was said to have been exceptionally good at it. In April of

1861, all three of those men were listed as directors and players for the first ever baseball club publicly announced in Houston. They had been meeting at least three days a week at 5:00 AM for ball practice before work.

When the Civil War broke out, Northerners and Canadians like the Clutes and Ellsworth were faced with a choice. Often that came down to weighing moral convictions against monetary and personal investment. John Clute opted to leave the Confederacy, but his brother Charlie joined the rebels as a "telegraphic superintendent," reaching the rank of captain. Captain Clute oversaw building of a second telegraph line along the Texas & New Orleans Railroad between Houston and Beaumont. That and the line between Houston and Galveston were the only ones operating in Texas for the first part of the war.

George Ellsworth turned out to be the most famous of the bunch. He joined the Bayou City Guards at the outbreak of the war, but Ellsworth soon chafed at the idea of serving as a mere infantry private. He resolved to put his telegraphic skills to work, and deserted his unit. Fleeing Houston on a hand car under the pretext of "going out to repair the telegraph line in the direction of Sabine Pass," he ran all the way to Mobile with the plan to offer his services to the famously daring Confederate raider John Hunt Morgan.

Re-enlisted, this time in the 2nd Kentucky (Confederate) Cavalry, Ellsworth soon became indispensable to his new commanding officer. He proved particularly adept at cutting into telegraph lines, imitating other operators, and sending reports that placed Morgan's raiders dozens of miles from their actual location. Ellsworth's great speed at the telegraph key earned him the nickname "Lightning."

Once the fighting was well underway, the Confederate troops in Texas saw the pure necessity of the electromagnetic telegraph. The

United States troops were well connected by lines, and those Union forces were trying to get into Texas. The South needed to counter that advantage. Rebel Colonel L.C. Baker oversaw building a line from Shreveport to Crockett, and Colonel D. P. Shepherd, who later became a telegrapher in Houston, tore down an old line "he had built, from nowhere to nowhere, in Louisiana and Arkansas" and rebuilt it to connect Crockett and Houston. That allowed the major players in the Confederate Trans-Mississippi Department to rapidly communicate.

When the Civil War ended, Texas and the South was occupied not only by the Union Army. They welcomed a rash of telegraph companies, as well. The South-Western Telegraph Company bought the line from Galveston to Houston and extended it to New Orleans. That company later consolidated with the American Telegraph Company. The biggest new player to come to Texas was the Western Union Company. That firm was started in Rochester, New York under a different name, but they soon began buying up and uniting small regional competitors. In 1861, Western Union completed a telegraph line across the entire nation with President Abraham Lincoln sending the first coast to coast message.

With the war over, Western Union quickly moved into the South. Within less than a decade, they owned eighty-nine of the state's 105 telegraph offices, and ran some 1,500 miles of wire. Telegrams cost a quarter if the distance was under 25 miles, and Western Union soon added the ability to wire money from one place to another. It made telegraph offices, along with banks and Wells Fargo Express boxes, tempting targets for hold-ups.

Newspapers also thrived on the telegraph. Prior to the invention, newspapers sent copies of their editions to other cities by mail, and stories were often weeks old by the time they got widespread coverage. Once the wires came to town, newspaper offices could dispatch items in hours. States east of the Mississippi used the tool as early as the Mexican War, and the practice kept growing with every new connection. The *Galveston Daily News* and the *Dallas Morning News*, owned by the same man by 1885, even went so far as to lease its own wire between the two cities to transfer items back and forth.

By the end of the 19th century, old telegraphers, on the verge of being made redundant by the telephone, would sit and swap stories. They recalled the earliest days when an operator might tap out only half a dozen messages a day and spend the rest of his time whittling. They recollected the trouble caused by wagoneers hauling down a pole to pry a stuck wheel out of the mud or no-good youngsters shooting out the glass insulators atop the poles.

The most famous among them did not wholly disappear from the news. "Lightning" Ellsworth became a wanted man for drunkenly murdering a barkeeper in Kentucky. He then dropped from public view only to possibly reemerge as a train robber and desperado in Montgomery County, Texas. Later speculative reports had Ellsworth working as a telegraph operator back in Houston. He was reported to be one of the men captured for robbing the Texas Express office in Willis. Eventually, he surfaced for certain at New Orleans where the *Times-Democrat* published his memoirs in their pages. Eventually, George Ellsworth died at the telegraph key in Antonia, Louisiana.

Houston

*Buffalo Bayou and Downtown. Bry0909 via
Wikimedia Commons*

Chapter Thirty-Seven

Mamie Ewing

It should be well known that women did not get a universal right to vote in the United States until 1920, but there was a patchwork of women's suffrage well before that date. Wyoming Territory gave women equal voting rights in 1869, and a handful of other states followed, all of them in the far West. Texas did not get on the bandwagon until 1918 when Governor William Hobby pushed through the right for women to vote in primary elections only. Of course, in a state that famously swore a yellow dog could get elected if he ran as a Democrat, the primary was all that mattered.

Women had to assert themselves outside of the home in other ways, and to say customs and popular thought were stacked against them would be an understatement. One notable exception was in the realm of schools. Women had been getting teaching jobs since the end of the Civil War, and in 1900, for the first time, female teachers in Texas outnumbered men. Still, they were expected to do as they were told by male supervisors. For women who preferred more power, they started private schools albeit limiting enrollment to girls and young boys.

Texas cities were growing fast, and none of them saw greater leaps in school overcrowding than Houston. Public schools at the dawn of the 20th century were run by the city itself, and those outside the limits were divvied up into thirty something rural county districts. In the fast-expanding city, buildings were erected on often dismal, treeless, and muddy lots.

The answer was Mothers' Clubs. They formed to provide things that the public coffers were slow to cover, but their birth in Houston was tied to one specific event in 1904 at the upscale Fannin Elementary in the city's South End.

School lunches were a have and have not situation at the start of the century. When male workers and their school-aged children left home for the day, most of them packed a lunch. Though some of the more well-to-do grownups had fancy baskets or multi-piece metal pails, for schoolchildren, a lunchbox was often a used tobacco or coffee tin with a handle bolted onto it, and milk was brought in all sorts of rinsed-out bottles. Usual fare was a piece of bread, a hunk of cheese, and a few strawberries or pecans. The poorest students generally went hungry.

Hot lunches were rare. Four Houston city schools allowed third party vendors on campus to sell meals. Longfellow Elementary, on the east edge of downtown, let youngsters go unattended to the restaurant next door. At Fannin, street cart vendors pulled up at the gate of a noontime and sold candy, pickles, "pink ice cream, impossible 'hamburgers,' sausages of questionable origin and other alleged eatables." The bacteria came home to roost in the form of chili con carne that sickened a number of the "silk stocking" kiddoes.

The words "sanitary" and "hygienic" lunches became a rallying cry. The suddenly unified mothers set themselves up at the school and began providing "wholesome nourishment" to the children at cost. They served more than 300 grade schoolers hot soups, roast beef and bread, hot chocolate, tea, and coffee. The Fannin mothers were still running the lunchroom a decade later when the school district finally began to get involved. By then the Mothers' Club movement, under the leadership of Mamie Ewing, was one of the strongest forces in Houston. They flourished at both city and county schools, and active groups had started at eight of the city's segregated Black schools, as well.

Once empowered in the Magnolia City, the mothers expanded the scope of their efforts.

Beautification of the school yard was one early task. Mothers' money and work turned many a patch of dirt or spotty grass into "pretty and inviting flower gardens." They took up collections for shade trees and sidewalks that the school board had failed to provide.

Mothers' clubs bought the latest technological advancements for their children's schools. They furnished stereopticons to fire the imagination visually and "graphophones with records of music of a high classic order" to "enable children to get in touch with the best music." They gave books, globes, maps, sewing machines, and even an occasional piano.

The clubs also became enamored with monstrous contraptions called outdoor gymnasiums. For a cost of $225, elementary schoolyards gained "two swinging trapezes, two pair of acting rings, two rows of swinging rings, four climbing poles, two hand-over-hand ladders, and two parallel bars." And those were the small ones. Larger ones contained uppermost perches as much as 15 feet in the air. Despite the fact that the behemoths would be a modern insurance company's nightmare, school officials called them "a constant source of profit and pleasure to the pupils."

Principal Helena Holley at Houston's Reagan Elementary found other benefits: "They have proven of inestimable value. The pugnacious propensity of the boy has been expended on trapeze and climbing pole instead of on his fellow student. As a consequence, fights have been few and far between, while the boy in the school room has been quieter and more attentive to his books."

By the end of the decade, there was a collective organization of Mothers' Clubs under the leadership of Mamie Ellen Ewing, the wife of prominent Judge Presley Kittredge Ewing. She was born Mary Ellen Williams but began going by Mamie early in life. Both Ewings were raised in South Louisiana's Lafourche Parish. Presley rose to be Chief Justice of the Texas Supreme Court and was backed by some state boosters for a national judgeship. Presley and Mamie had two daughters – Vesta and Gladys – and they lived in a fashionable home at Clay and Fannin south of downtown. In the 1910 census, Maggie Hooks, an African American girl the same age as 17-year old Gladys, was a live-in servant. The Ewing home was such an important household that they hosted the famous William Jennings Bryan when he passed through town in 1897.

In a Southern city in the first decade of the 20th century, Mamie might be expected to confine herself to Houston's social whirl. The Ewings were at the head of the city's Z.Z. Club and oversaw many annual debutante affairs, but her broader accomplishments took no back seat to the judge's. Mamie was active in the Child Welfare League, the Texas Humane Society, Christ Church Parish, and the Ladies Reading Club through which she established a system of circulating books into rural areas. She took part in medical conferences aimed at ending tuberculosis. Though not as well-known today as Texas leaders such as Minnie Fisher Cunningham, Annette Finnegan, and Hortense Ward, Mamie was an equally high-profile backer of women's suffrage throughout the state.

Her work did not end with club work and causes, though, nor did they begin with the Mothers' Clubs. In October 1901, when Mamie was in her late 30s, the *Galveston Journal*, the official publication of Galveston labor organizations, ran an item that was steeped in friendly familiarity. "We are pleased to note the return of Mrs. Presley K. Ewing and family from an extended trip through California. Mrs. Ewing is an honorary member of Local 165, and is one of the most earnest workers for the cause of justice and right in grand old Texas." That local represented retail clerks, and Mamie had been working on their behalf to secure shorter work hours.

She also received three patents for devices to improve street sanitation. It was a contraption that improved the suction of street sweepings and immediately ignited and disposed of them in a contained vehicle.

By 1912, the associated Mothers' Clubs had joined the Texas Congress of Mothers, and Mamie Ewing oversaw their statewide convention in Houston that year. Shortly afterward, the local group became part of the national Parent-Teachers Association. That school mothers group started in the Northeast in 1897, so Houston's all-in attitude just seven years later made it an early adopter. Harmony was not to last, though.

Houston's PTA experienced a major rift in 1913, and the catalyst was Mamie Ewing's progressive ideas. At the top of her list was the radical notion of allowing women, who couldn't yet vote, to serve on the school board. Ultimately, Mamie led the walkout of 25 like-minded women after a "spirited discussion" at a meeting held at First Presbyterian Church. The more "standpat" members led by Mrs. George Heyer remained behind.

Not only did Ewing and her crew quickly establish the United Mothers Council, they demanded their names be removed from all PTA rolls and their dues be refunded. The new council promised that every school in Houston would be represented in their membership, but they did not want teachers among them. Mrs. Ewing believed "in the freedom of persons to vote their honest convictions," and she told newspapers the city's teachers were "dominated by powers higher up." In other words, they could not speak out because they were under the thumb of the man.

MRS. MARY ELINOR EWING.

Mamie Ewing

The first attempt at putting women on the school board in Houston came in 1904, at the same time that the Fannin Elementary mothers were cooking up their first school lunches. Mamie and others in local women's clubs managed to get the ear of a majority of city council members, and they voted down two appointments that Mayor Andrew Jackson expected would be routine. It was a fine bit of lobbying for people unable to vote in elections, but just a week later, the two men were approved.

Dallas and San Antonio were the first large Texas municipalities to add women to their school boards. Adella Kelsey Turner and Ella Isabelle Tucker in Dallas and Anna Hertzberg and Jeanette Noyes-Evans in San Antonio each entered office in 1908. Houston, however, stood at an impasse. As the ladies groups continued to press their claims, Mayor Jackson told city council that women were not even legally eligible to act as school trustees. In opposition, Judge Noah Allen offered a lengthy citation of why it would be perfectly legal for women to serve. Two mayors down the road, the situation remained unchanged.

Perhaps emboldened by the split from the staid PTA, Mamie Ewing went on the offensive. She flatly accused the all-male Houston school board of being derelict in its duties. Her mothers organization submitted a lengthy list of problems and neglect at the city's schools. Detail-oriented and concerned women would bring better results.

Though their reasons were no burning desire for gender equality, many Houston men agreed. One editorial submitter wrote "no matter how unruly a child may be, the soft tender appeal to the child from a woman's voice has ninety-nine times out of a hundred a better effect than the harsh, abrupt, stern command of a man... Every child looks to the gentler sex, the women to guide it to its destiny."

On the side of unwaveringly against was Dr. S.C. Red, one of the two men who was briefly denied his school board post by city council back in 1904. He was a medical doctor with impeccable credentials, and he summoned the press to denounce Mrs. Ewing's rabble rousing, calling her claims of negligence "grossly exaggerated." The salivating Houston newspapers ran the feud verbatim. No wonder given Mamie Ewing's gift for words.

"Dr. S. C. Red has had a disturbing nightmare," she said. "He evidently sees in the vision of women on the school board a disappearance of himself and similar ornaments. Dr. Red treats it as a fundamental that women should simply rely on men like babies on their mothers. A man who is inspired that way in this progressive day, face to face with the great independent work being done by women in the world, writes himself down as so antiquated that he ought in justice to the spirit of the age retire from public service. Dr. Red says, in his opinion, that 'the sanitary condition of the Houston Public Schools are as good as they are in any public school buildings in cities of equal size.' ... It means if you have a vile smelling, unforgivable stench in your own home, be comfortable and don't bother if your neighbor has one equally bad. Ye gods, what a philosopher!"

It had no effect. Mayor Ben Campbell offered no more than a metaphorical pat on the head and reminded citizens that "The school system is the most important branch of the city government. It has the disbursement of funds aggregating from $350,000 to $375,000 a year. The present board is made up of good business men."

The women definitely knew the law. They had a petition drafted to put the matter before Houston voters under a new home rule act to amend the city charter via referendum. It required signatures from 10% of registered voters – a number just over 1,000. When Mrs. Ewing next came before council, she said she was "back like a bad penny," and she handed in a petition with almost twice the number of signatures needed.

The fight to the polls was a rough one. The Labor Council, a powerful force in Progressive Era Houston, backed the measure, but most of the powerful politicians did not. Neighborhood rallies were held, and the two largest Houston newspapers supported the women. The sitting board president, Rufus Cage, threw gasoline on the fire by saying, "We now have 283 women and 60 men teachers in the schools,... it would seem that the female influence is already fully represented."

Mamie was blunt in her response: "It would be amusing, if the life and health of little children were not involved... The school board for twenty years and more have had their man's ideas and ambitions turned to their own personal affairs, giving only one night a month for school affairs, and I am convinced from my personal experience with them, forgetting the needs of the schools as soon as the night's session closed."

Just days before the vote, Mayor Campbell stepped it up. He cut deals with other interests to drop his opposition to several other measures if those interests would oppose the Mothers' Council. One day out, the *Houston Chronicle* rescinded their endorsement and came out against the ordinance. Mamie Ewing was left with no time to reply.

On election night, Houston voters decided on 29 amendments to the city charter. Only three of them failed, and one of those was the chance to put women on the school board. The 441 vote margin was the biggest loss of the day, even worse than the amendment to raise the salaries of city commissioners. Among the things passing that day were free textbooks for city schools, an eight hour work day, and city ownership of public utilities.

Politics is fluid, however. By the time the more progressive J.J. Pastoriza took office in 1917, an elected school board had once again become the law in Houston. Mamie Ewing declined to put her name forward, but Blanche Scholibo and Emilie Dwyer, each past P.T.A. presidents at South End Junior High and Dow Elementary respectively, took office at the end of May. One barrier had tumbled, but it was another 50 years before a woman was elected to a position other than school board trustee in Houston.

Mamie Ewing continued to be involved in her community beyond the revolving circuit of social teas. If there were any hard feelings over the school board fight, they did not show publicly. Mrs. Presley K. Ewing was one of only two women who joined Houston's top bankers, industrialists, and newspaper publishers to raise funds for a large Sam Houston statue, the fruits of which now stands as a gateway to Hermann Park.

She died on April 1, 1919 after a brief illness that kept her "semi-conscious" at home. It was one year before American women won the universal right to vote. A brief Associated Press wire story ran in most Texas newspapers saying that "Mrs. Ewing is known throughout the South as one of the leaders in the development of women's influence." The hometown *Post* was more loquacious. "She was a woman of engaging personality," the paper wrote. "Optimistic, public-spirited, and fond of society."

Chapter Thirty-Eight

Gold Star Records

In spite of Austin's claims, the musical history of Houston is much richer and broader, and an objective observer might say the race is not even close. Houston gave birth to some of the greatest early horn players in jazz, pioneers of hip-hop and rap, iconic blues players, and stars of Tejano music. For all its Louisiana roots, the first zydeco record was made in Houston. Beyonce. Kenny Rogers. ZZ Top. Clint Black. The Geto Boys. Even Willie Nelson recorded his first two hits when he lived in Houston.

A great many of those artists, plus hundreds of others, passed through a recording studio on Brock Street in Southeast Houston not far from MacGregor Park. It was never much to look at from the outside, but it is the longest running music studio in the United States. For over 80 years, the studios, boasting both state-of-the-art and vintage equipment, have turned out hit records in a dizzying number of genres.

Bill Quinn started the business under his own name in October 1941, and took on the Gold Star moniker nine years later. His introduction to sound equipment came with a touring carnival. After car trouble stranded him in Houston, he started a radio repair shop, but he was fascinated by the recording process, and he taught himself on outdated or improvised equipment through trial and error. When he first began charging people for his services, the clients were radio advertisers or the random sailor looking to record a special message for his girl, but in 1944, Quinn created the Gulf Records music label. When the Gulf label failed to take off, he changed the name to Gold Star Records.

His one-man operation in an old gas station/grocery took on White musicians in hillbilly and Black musicians in blues. Both were styles flourishing in Houston. Gold Star became the most successful independent label in the South and the first in Texas to produce a national hit.

That song was the Cajun waltz standard "Jolie Blonde," but Bill Quinn misspelled it on the record label as "Jole Blon," and so it became famous. For good measure, Quinn misspelled the artist Harry Choates' name as Shoates. That recording was the only Cajun song to ever crack the *Billboard* Top 5 in any category, and there was such demand for the vinyl around Southeast Texas that Quinn was forced to set up a license deal for the pressings.

Though Quinn tried, there was no second big hit for Harry Choates, but a more reliably hit-producing star was in the wings. Centerville-born Sam Hopkins, who was known to everyone as Lightnin', lived not far away in Houston's Third Ward. He had first recorded for Aladdin Records based out of Los Angeles, but Lightnin' did not like to travel, so the actual recording sessions took place at Gold Star. After about 40 records, Hopkins started working directly with Quinn. He cut more than 100 songs at the Telephone Road studio with the "booth" set up in the far right hand corner. "Short Haired Woman" was his first, then "T Model Blues," and "Tim Moore's Farm" both made the *Billboard* R&B Top 15. Lightnin' was prolific, and whenever he needed money, "he would go over to Gold Star to 'make some numbers,'" many of them were songs now considered essential for the blues fan.

It was a Hopkins B-side that marked the first recording of zydeco music. Once again, Bill Quinn's Massachusetts ear proved incompatible with Gulf Coast accents, but "Zolo Go" was Lightnin' singing about a zydeco dance. Not long after that, the "King of Zydeco," Clifton Chenier, recorded at Gold Star. Other Texas blues artists flocked to Quinn's studio. Lil' Son Jackson had the biggest hit with "Freedom Train Blues" in 1948, and L.C. Williams had success, but many of them failed to produce a profit for Bill Quinn.

Lightnin' Hopkins. Wikimedia Commons

The same need for fast cash that drew Lightnin' Hopkins to Gold Star also lured him to other labels. He and Quinn split. That was followed by a disagreement with Lil' Son Jackson, then a resulting hiccup with the Internal Revenue Service. Bill Quinn gave up his storefront on Telephone Road and moved around the corner to his family house. He set up a studio downstairs, and he, his wife, and boy lived above it. Quinn was done with running a record label and decided to concentrate solely on getting paid for recording. He also dropped all vestiges of his own name from the business and named the new studio to match his former record label.

Though country music was Bill Quinn's first targeted genre, his early hits were in Cajun and blues, but when another Southeast Texas artist, Port Arthur's George Jones, recorded "Why Baby Why" in 1955, that changed dramatically. The song featured Tony Sepolio on fiddle and Herb Remington on steel guitar, both now in the Texas Western Swing Hall of Fame. Regular Gold Star session guitarist Glenn Barber went on to a solo career, but the other singer, Sonny Burns, was a drunken no show, a trick also already perfected by Jones. Bill Quinn doubled the tracks to get George to sing his own backup vocals. The song became Jones' first hit single, and was followed by six more: "What Am I Worth", "You Gotta Be My Baby", "Just One More", "Yearning", "Too Much Water" and "Don't Stop the Music", all within the next two years.

Another Golden Triangle kid, J.P. Richardson known as the Big Bopper, recorded "Chantilly Lace" in 1958. It was intended to be the B-side, but disc jockeys preferred it to the novelty number on the flip. The song spent 22 weeks in *Billboard*'s Top 40.

With the money that he was bringing in, Bill Quinn built a huge metal addition to the house at the end of the 1950s. It was 22 feet high and had 48 by 53 feet of parquet floor. There were acoustic tiles and heavy drapes

that had been sewn by Quinn's wife. The control room was elevated for
a view of the entire studio.

Not long after the "Big Room" was complete, another young man
came in to record. At the time he was not long out of the Air Force,
living in Pasadena, and driving across town most nights to play gigs at
the Esquire Ballroom on the old Austin Highway. His name was Willie
Nelson, and he had given up work as a DJ to try to further his recording
career. His first two official hits were cut at Gold Star in 1960: "Family
Bible" and "Night Life." It was the latter that proved to be his musical
epiphany. Others had often been unsure of Willie's guitar phrasing and
style, but as they readied for "Rainy Day Blues" and "Night Life,"
Quinn held three good musicians over from the previous session. They
understood the piece musically, and Nelson, feeling a new confidence,
said, "It was a cut above what I'd been doing." Producer Pappy Daily
thought it was not country enough, and refused to release it. Willie and
Paul Buskirk managed to steal the masters.

Bill Quinn recorded several early Texas Rock songs, and none were
bigger than "Treat Her Right" by Houstonian Roy Head. It hit #2 on
the *Billboard* Hot 100. The Sir Douglas Quintet followed with "She's
About a Mover" which made it to #13. The producer on those songs
was Huey P. Meaux, and International Artists soon worked a deal with
Quinn that led to more psychedelic rock bands such as the 13th Floor
Elevators, Red Krayola, The Bubble Puppy, and The Moving Sidewalks
which was the first big band for Billy Gibbons.

In the early 1970s, after the two-year ownership by International
Artists ended with stock fraud and jail time, Huey Meaux, fresh out
of jail himself, bought the place. Meaux launched several major music
careers from what he renamed Sugar Hill Studios. One of the biggest was
Freddy Fender, a Mexican American from San Benito. Fender recorded

21 hit songs at Sugar Hill including his two biggest hits "Wasted Days and Wasted Nights" and "Before the Next Teardrop Falls." That last song was single of the year at the 1975 Country Music Association Awards, was the top track on the first ever platinum country album, was the first ever bilingual country single to chart, and the first to appear simultaneously in *Billboard*'s country and Top 40. The legend is that it happened by accident when Fender dropped his English lyrics, notes he wrote on a yellow legal pad, as the music tracks went into the second verse. Fender improvised in Spanish. He picked the paper up at the next break and finished the song in English.

Huey Meaux was very publicly arrested in a police raid in January 1996. Ultimately he pled guilty to various counts of child pornography, sex with a child, and drug possession. The offenses were all on Meaux's part and unbeknownst to the engineers and staff at Sugar Hill, but it tainted the reputation of the place for a time. Things came back to normal as the situation was understood, and quality righted the ship.

The list of stars who recorded at Gold Star/Sugar Hill seems mind boggling when a person considers the non-descript studio on a dead end street in a completely forgotten part of Houston. Early R&B stars O.V. Wright, Joe Hinton, and Junior Parker, who had recorded at Don Robey's famous Duke-Peacock studio across town, were there as were blues greats like Albert Collins and Bobby "Blue" Bland, after Robey began to lease the Gold Star space around 1959.

Asleep at the Wheel did "Miles and Miles of Texas" at Sugar Hill and Kinky Friedman and his Texas Jewboys cut an album there. Such modern day mega-stars as Little Wayne, Paul Wall, and Megan Thee Stallion graced the microphones at Sugar Hill, as did Texas singer songwriters including the likes of Guy Clark, Doug Sahm, and Lucinda Williams. Tejano stars have always been a staple at the studio including big names like Little Joe y La Familia, and it was the home base for Emilio Navaira and country singer Johnny Rodriguez.

After the raid in 1996, there was another ownership change. Studio engineers Rodney Meyers, Andy Bradley, and Dan Workman bought the place. Hard core music and tech afficionados, they made certain that the hodgepodge of buildings, including the remnants of Bill Quinn's old house, were lovingly preserved even as they remained busy with clients. Not long after that, the author of this book went in with his two bandmates in the PC Cowboys to master the group's second album with Meyers. During a break in the all-day session, one of the other partners told the boys about a group of young girls who had come in to record a few weeks earlier. As they warmed up, one in particular was obsessive about finding her exact best location to maximize the sound of the vocal mic and the resonance of the room. The engineer's silent head shakes turned to admiration and awe when Beyonce, Solange, and Kelly, the group Destiny's Child, started to sing.

Chapter Thirty-Nine

Joseph Finger

Houston business leaders in the 1920s and 30s wanted to project the image of a modern city on the rise, and a prime way to accomplish that was through the architecture of their many new buildings. It was a boom time for the Bayou City, and their two busiest commercial architects were Alfred Finn and Joseph Finger. Finn was the favorite of the powerful Jesse Jones, but that did not prevent Finger from getting the biggest municipal commissions of the era. Both men were masters of the most modern genre – the form later dubbed Art Deco.

The style was sleek, geometric, and often utilized rich palettes of material to gain color. It used accents of chrome, stucco, aluminum, terra cotta, art glass, and steel. There were stylized figures or flowers and bold zigzags or waves, lightning bolts and sunbursts. There were curves and chamfers and setbacks. Before there was even a name for it, some architects were calling it the vertical style in reference to the windows. Art Deco or Art Moderne was not some revivalist rehash of the ancients. It was new. It was its own thing, and that was a perfect metaphor for Houston.

Joseph Finger was born in a part of Austria-Hungary that is now Poland. His father was hoping that Joseph would take over the family dry goods business, but the son had other ideas. He emigrated from Vienna, where he studied at the Royal School of Art, to New Orleans as a wannabe architect still in his teens. Finding lots of closed doors, he wound up in Houston in 1908 at the age of 21. It appeared to be a land of opportunity.

At first, Finger partnered with other architects including Dallas-based C.D. Hill and local men Lewis Sterling Green and Lamar Q. Cato. By the early 1920s, Finger was a hot architectural name on his own. His 1929 Houston Turnverein clubhouse and bowling lanes on Almeda Road was a true head-turner for Houston. There were definite early elements of Deco, though the architect called it a combination of German Secession and Art Nouveau. The Turnverein's National Register status could not save it from demolition in 1993. A remaining example of Finger's early work is the Lawndale Art Center that was originally a commission for Barker Brothers Studio. He designed Byrd's Department Store in 1934 and a new building for the Parker Brothers Company.

His best known works are his Art Deco and Modernist designs from the 1930s and 40s. Some of those structures were for the Weingarten's grocery chain that became his greatest cash cow. He designed over 30 buildings for Abe Weingarten, a man with whom he went to temple. Weingarten's mansion on South MacGregor Boulevard was one of Finger's few residential designs during the peak of his career. The grocery stores themselves sometimes anchored what could be described as some of Houston's first strip centers. Modern residents should not hold that against him as these neighborhood groceries, retail stores, and car dealerships included graceful curved lines and smooth stucco and metal.

Many of them still stand but with such alterations and cladding that they are no longer recognizable.

Though Finger was all about commercial jobs, there were a handful of Finger designs for rich friends in River Oaks, the city's most lofty neighborhood. Many more of them were in Riverside Terrace, the neighborhood for wealthy Jewish Houstonians who were restricted from owning in River Oaks. The most famous home he built was for oil, lumber, and cattle baron Jim West. It was done in the 1920s in an Italian Renaissance style. It overlooked Clear Lake and cost a rumored $750,000.

Finger was responsible for a succession of Houston hotels. The De George on Preston Avenue was one of his earliest major commissions. It was followed by the Ben Milam, Plaza, Auditorium, and Texas State. All except the Ben Milam still stand. The Auditorium was so named because it sat across Texas Avenue from City Auditorium, a structure that was replaced in 1966 by the modernist Jones Hall. Finger's hotel creation is now the Lancaster, a remodeled, upscale landmark of the Theatre District.

The Works Progress Administration placed $11 billion in spending around the United States to give steady employment and help the nation's recovery from the Great Depression. Over its eight year lifespan starting in 1935, the WPA built a myriad of public buildings, bridges, dams, airports, roads, and parks. Joseph Finger and Alfred Finn, the city's other top architect, combined on the Jeff Davis Hospital complex that graced Allen Parkway for decades. It was one of the largest federal public works projects built in Houston as part of the New Deal. Harry Hopkins, an ex-social worker who was a long time crony of Franklin

Roosevelt, was in charge of the WPA, but Houstonian Jesse Jones, another administration official, perhaps exerted some influence.

Where Finn was conservative and restrained in his Deco and Moderne tendencies, Finger was often "exuberant." He more visibly embraced the aspects of modernism. One of Finger's first WPA jobs was the Montgomery County Courthouse in Conroe. It replaced an 1891 building done by Eugene Heiner, a Houston architect of an earlier day. In that courthouse, Finger embraced the emerging WPA modern style of public buildings with vertical window lines and horizontal setbacks. That Conroe courthouse began to be obscured by modern additions in the 1960s.

One of Finger's great improvements for his hometown was the 1940 terminal and hangar at Municipal Airport which today is an aviation museum. Finger used graceful curves and added reliefs that depict the evolution of air travel over its first four decades. Above the main door is a colossal, globe-spanning winged Mercury with a strategically placed airplane. Houston's air travel needs outgrew Finger's sleek stucco and steel terminal in just 14 years, but at the museum, it is easy to imagine locals decked out in their finest to catch a roaring Constellation or DC-3.

The crowning achievement of Joseph Finger's career was another WPA federally funded project that pitted Finger and Finn against one another.

Historically, Houston City Hall was combined with a food market on downtown's Market Square, but as Houston grew, they needed more space for city government. In the late 1920s, plans for a Civic Center on Bagby Street were floated. Renderings show several Italian Renaissance style buildings encircling a reflecting pool. The Julia Ideson Library building was the first and only one actually constructed. Plans were sidelined by both the Depression and Houston voters. Finally, in August of 1937, WPA money was awarded for the project.

The location at the west side of Martha Hermann Square was chosen by Mayor Richard Fonville, but hizzoner lost out on the architect. Fonville wanted Finn and objected to Finger's "ultra-modern" design. The architect's answer was that Americans build "for the masses, not the classes." The City Commissioners gave him the job.

Houston City Hall in 2018. Michael Barera

The beautiful Houston City Hall which opened in 1939 still shows off the classic vertical windows and light sconces of Art Deco and Moderne, but the real glitz of City Hall lies in the details. Marble elevator lobbies gleam with hidden lighting. Texas gum tree wood is utilized for some interior doors and trim while polished walnut appears in panels and inside the elevators. Nickel, silver, and bronze highlight various areas, and interior signage is done in curving chrome and glass. The central lobby boasts a mural on the ceiling highlighting Houston's culture, law, and industry. It was done by Daniel MacMorris of Kansas City with assistance from local artists Grace Spaulding John and Ruth Uhler.

Outside, Finger placed 27 friezes and reserved the prime spot facing the reflecting pool installed in Hermann Square for two cowboys taming a wild mustang. Texas bobcats adorn the top. Specially made aluminum finishes cover the doors, and they are crowned with grillwork that depict history's great givers of law: Hammurabi, Julius Caesar, Moses, England's King John, and America's Thomas Jefferson.

The whole thing set the taxpayers back about $1.7 million and all labor was union. The mayor got a private elevator, and the city commissioners got private showers.

Later in his career, Joseph Finger sometimes partnered with George Rustay but maintained an ever more modern sensibility. The pair did an industrial job on the west side of downtown, away from Houston's normal factory sector. It was a remodel and expansion of the Carnation Dairy on Waugh Drive. That one was just around the corner from Finger's earlier Clark & Courts Printing Plant that featured a grand center tower and some of the finest 1930s signage in Texas. The Carnation Milk plant was demolished in the 1980s, but Clarke & Courts lives on as trendy office lofts.

Joseph Finger was very active in the local Jewish Community, designing buildings for Congregation Beth Yeshurun, specifically an education center with Rustay that later became HISD's Lockhart Elementary School. His most important faith-related work was for his own Congregation Beth Israel, the oldest Jewish congregation in Texas. In 1924, he designed a new Egyptian-inspired synagogue, a sturdy, columned structure at Austin and Holman Streets. Eleven years later, he created the mausoleum in their cemetery. It was where Finger was interred upon his death in 1953.

Chapter Forty

Ashbel Smith

The Republic of Texas attracted much more than rough-hewn frontiersmen. Contrary to portrayals in popular culture, some highly educated men found their way to Texas, and one of those was undoubtedly Ashbel Smith. Yet for all his polish, Smith was also a bundle of contradictions. Texas historian Harry Hewitt called him "the Yankee rebel, the hot-tempered diplomat, the gregarious loner, the idealistic politician, the home loving rover, the bachelor father, the slave-owning humanitarian, and the peace-loving soldier."

Ashbel Smith was a Connecticut native who graduated Yale at age 19 as a Phi Beta Kappa Society member and with the accolade from the college president that he was the best Greek and Latin scholar ever to study there. His first job was teaching in Salisbury, North Carolina, and indications are that Smith did not enjoy the place. After a year and a half and a foray into the study of law, he returned to Yale to get a degree in medicine. With that qualification in hand at age 23, he came back to Salisbury to begin a practice, but again wanderlust took over. Smith went to Europe in 1830 and stayed for three years studying at the top hospital in Paris. He recorded detailed observations during a cholera epidemic, joined the Societe de Geographie, and started to amass a personal library. Once again he returned to Salisbury.

Along the way, Smith made the acquaintance of J. Pinckney Henderson, a North Carolinian who had moved to Texas, and Mary Louise Phifer, a woman who rebuffed his marriage proposal. Both played a role in the fact that when the job of head surgeon of the Texas Army opened up and Henderson offered it to Smith, the young doctor jumped at the chance to relocate for good. He found himself in the brand new town of Houston, the nation's capital, just in time to join the fraternity of ambitious men looking to make a mark on the world.

The Town of Houston was being built from scratch, and the tiny population was disproportionately made up of government officials and those who wanted to be. Among the many people Ashbel Smith met was President Sam Houston, and the two soon became fast friends. It did not hurt that Smith arrived in Texas with the recommendation of Houston's mentor Andrew Jackson who called Smith "a Gentleman of useful, varied and eloquent intelligence." Houston and Smith shared a house together while Sam was a bachelor. Though they drank together, Smith was no match for the president at a bar, but Ashbel possessed a "redoubtable talent for mixing classical quotations with frontier profanity." The two grew to be best pals, and it was Smith who loaned the ex-president $250 for him to make the journey to Marion, Alabama to marry Margaret Lea.

Within three years of his arrival in Houston city, it seemed that Smith had his hand in almost every institution of potential uplift. He was a founding officer of the Philosophical Society of Texas. He bought a one-acre property that held the town's hospital. When a devastating epidemic of yellow fever hit, Smith observed the effects and oversaw autopsies of the dead so he could write a book on the subject. In 1840, he encouraged a cousin named Henry Gillette to start one of the first schools in Houston. Family was important to Smith, and his brothers George and Henry joined him in the new country. After becoming acquainted with the surroundings, Ashbel bought property and made his home near the wide waters of Goose Creek in what is today downtown Baytown. When the chance to make a peace treaty with the Comanche arose, President Houston selected Ashbel Smith to get it done. The agreement, which would have established the Comancheria as a recognized sovereign territory, was not ratified by the Texas Senate.

Smith's diplomatic career was just getting started despite some decidedly undiplomatic behavior. At one point he beat the president pro tem of the Senate with a horsewhip on the floor of Congress. It did not stop Sam Houston, returned for a second term as the Republic's president after having been displaced by Mirabeau Lamar, from appointing Smith minister plenipotentiary to Britain and France. He managed to smooth things with the French and met with Pope Gregory XVI in Rome, but the English proved more of a challenge.

The Republic of Texas rented digs above Berry Bros. & Rudd, London's oldest merchant of wines and spirits. Various parts of the building had served as a brothel, a gambling hall, and the courtyard out back once held cock fights and bear baiting. It was an appropriate venue for a rough-edged upstart of a country.

Lord Aberdeen, the Foreign Secretary and future Prime Minister, left Smith hanging for some weeks on important questions before finally getting back to the new diplomat. The British were polite, but eventually admitted that the Texas Navy blockade of Mexican ports when Britain was Mexico's largest trading partner was not viewed all too favorably. Smith retorted that Texas did not appreciate the fact that two warships were being built for Mexico in British ports, and accused abolitionists of being behind the construction. Aberdeen did not admit the truth of that, but replied that Texas was free to pay the Brits to build warships for her, too, or buy anything in his majesty's government stores, for that matter. The two imposing ships were not only completed, but sent to Mexico with British captains and partial British crews.

Great Britain was wholly committed to eliminating slavery, and Ashbel Smith was adamant in telling Lord Aberdeen and others that Texas would not negotiate to end the institution, and he "expressed (his) utter dissent from and opposition to all operations then carrying on in London, having for their object the abolition of in Texas." Sam Houston admonished Smith not to overdo his protests. The president wrote his friend that "when your hand is in the lion's mouth it is safest to withdraw it quietly without slapping the lion on his nose."

Ashbel Smith in the 1840s

The short of it was that in the summer of 1842 Britain was not yet ready to sign on to full diplomatic relations. Their dealings with the United States might still turn hostile, and if so, the Brits needed Mexico, and Mexico wanted Texas back. On the other hand, Mexico wanted Texas as both a buffer and a cotton-producing competitor of the U.S. In the end, Smith wrote his superior, Texas Secretary of State Anson Jones, "The cause of Texas is not regarded with favor at this time in England. I have been several times assured that the public sympathy is with Mexico."

Before his time in London was up in 1844, the British had signed a treaty of commerce and amity with the Republic. It earned Smith a promotion. He came home and became Secretary of State to Anson Jones who, thanks to term limits, had become President of Texas.

When it came to the vital topic of annexation to the United States, Ashbel Smith started out in the Lamar camp – he believed Texas should remain an independent republic. It was overwhelmingly the minority opinion among the populace, but by the time 1845 dawned, both Smith and Jones could best be classified as ambivalent on the matter. Smith was sent to Mexico to negotiate yet another deal, and he came back in May with the Cuevas-Smith Treaty in hand. In it, Mexico recognized Texan independence in return for Texas forgoing annexation to the United States. In June, the Texas Congress considered both options and forcefully chose the Americans. Ashbel Smith was burned in effigy in Galveston and San Felipe.

With annexation complete, war between the United States and Mexico was inevitable. When it came, Ashbel Smith volunteered as an

Army surgeon in the forces of General Zachary Taylor, a connection he later put to use. At war's end, he served a term as president of the board of visitors at the U.S. Military Academy.

Smith did not spend all of the war with the Army in Mexico. In 1847, he was receiving letters from Margaret Houston. Sam was away at Washington, D.C. serving in the United States Senate, and Margaret was managing the raising of a toddler and a baby at Raven Hill, a plantation in the woods 14 miles east of Huntsville. Several times she experienced horrible pain and swelling in her right breast. One account even states that the tumor burst. Though he was hesitant to operate with Sam far away, Dr. Smith knew surgery could not wait. Margaret, an inveterate Baptist, refused whiskey and endured a partial mastectomy while biting down on a silver coin. Medical writings of the day indicate that survival rate without recurrence was much less than 10%, but she lived another 20 years without the cancer resurfacing.

Elsewhere, Smith was his usual energetic self. At the start of the 1850s, he worked with Gail Borden to develop a dried beef biscuit. He was a founder of the Texas Medical Association and chaired the committee to draft its bylaws. Though that group experienced a hiatus of more than a decade, Smith was involved when it returned, as well. He went to London representing Texas at an international fair, chaired a fair in Corpus Christi, and was the first president of the Texas State Agricultural Society. Smith got himself elected as Harris County's representative in the state legislature, the first of three terms, each about a dozen years apart. As a member in the 1850s, he championed railroad construction and improvement of common schools. By decade's end, he was also superintendent of the private Houston Academy and served on school boards around his home by Goose Creek. He even headed Harris County schools for a time.

Ashbel Smith was all in on his neighborhood at the top of the bay. He acquired Mosely Baker's plantation called Evergreen in 1848, and kept adding more land in several counties until he owned well over 100 square miles of Texas. Smith also held as many as 40 slaves at a time, and he remained a vocal proponent of the institution. He tried to temper his denial of human freedom by giving extra hours off, some transitory privileges, and one acre garden plots, but otherwise, Ashbel Smith was unapologetic for owning others.

He embraced his agricultural operations just like everything else. Tiring of cotton farming, he opted for livestock and owned cattle and hundreds of hogs. Smith was one of the first landowners to raise sheep in Texas. He was so enamored with those wooly creatures that he wrote a scientific paper about it as well as others about growing peaches in South Texas and the virtues of oxen over horses.

When most Texans began clamoring for secession, Ashbel Smith, the Connecticut Yankee, was right there with them. By that time, his brothers, George and Henry were long since living in Memphis, Tennessee where they faced danger for loudly espousing support of the Union. Ashbel did not hesitate in going against the United States. Though 56-years old, he organized his own company of troops, the Bayland Guards. He oversaw their drill himself at Evergreen, and outfitted them in especially spiffy uniforms. Smith, still with his hair temper, sometimes "danced, swore, jingled his sword and denounced the object of his wrath in words that burned holes in the surrounding atmosphere." But he prepared his young men as best he could.

Disobeying his father's wishes, Sam Houston, Jr. joined the unit to fight under their family friend, Smith. The Guards were soon rolled into the Second Texas Volunteers, and Sam Houston, Sr., deposed from the Governor's Mansion because he would not swear allegiance to the Confederacy, often sat forlornly at Galveston and watched the unit of both his son and best friend march and train. As they prepared to depart for the fighting, Sam dressed in his old San Jacinto suit and gave a farewell valedictory.

The Bayland Guards found themselves in the thick of it at Shiloh in April 1862. Sam, Jr. was wounded and captured, and Captain Ashbel Smith was shot in the arm. He recuperated in Texas gathering conscripts for the unit, but when General Grant attacked Vicksburg, Smith, now promoted to colonel, was sent back to command a crescent-shaped earthwork known as the Second Texas Lunette. They withstood two direct assaults, but Vicksburg fell on the 4th of July, 1863. Smith finished the Civil War overseeing various coastal positions. At war's end, he was in charge of defenses at Galveston. Six weeks after Lee had surrendered in Virginia, with the Trans-Mississippi Department the only rebellious Americans still under arms, the governor of Texas, Pendleton Murrah, sent Smith and William Ballinger to New Orleans to negotiate peace with Union officials.

The first known image of Ashbel Smith shows him clean shaven, but later ones do not. Famous writer Marquis James wrote this about the doctor: "Smith was a wiry man of medium stature whose indifference to his wardrobe was redeemed by the care he bestowed upon a close-clipped professional-looking beard." This was Ashbel Smith, senior statesman, who jumped into the post war world with both feet.

In 1866, he helped his educator cousin, Henry Gillette, start the Bayland Orphanage to care for the children of deceased Confederate veterans. One the first charges there was a girl named Anna Allen who suffered from an eye ailment that Smith believed he could help fix. The two developed a bond that filled a void for the childless doctor. He moved her into his house at Evergreen, and when she married, Smith gifted the young couple 75 acres of his property. After the Goose Creek Oil Field was discovered at the start of the 20th century, Anna Allen Wright became one of the richest women in Harris County.

Smith had been a champion of better educational opportunities for years, but he devoted himself to the cause following the war. Texas had never had a truly universal public education system until the occupying Union forces and the Unionist governor Edmund P. Davis established one. It was the Freedmen's Bureau who first created widespread schooling for Blacks in the South. While many Texans vociferously decried it, Ashbel Smith voiced wholehearted support.

Another Texas governor, Richard Coke, appointed Smith as one of the commissioners to establish an "Agricultural and Mechanical College of Texas, for the benefit of the Colored Youths." The men chose a location east of Hempstead, and the school was begun as Prairie View A&M.

His push for educating was not confined to children. When the Southern Historical Society was organized in 1869, Smith was vice-president for Texas, and a year later, a group met in Houston to establish a Texas counterpart. Ashbel Smith was chosen as president. He also wrote a book called *Reminiscences of the Texas Republic*. At that point, Smith had outlived most of the important figures of that era and could talk about the old days without fear of contradiction. He did so every chance he got. When baseball teams from Houston and Galveston met at the battleground on San Jacinto Day in 1868, Ashbel Smith rose to commemorate the holiday before the first pitch. He spoke for well over an hour.

Recognition for the Yale-educated and accomplished Texan extended to the national stage. When the United States held a Great International Exhibition in Philadelphia to honor the nation's centennial, Ashbel Smith was chosen as a judge for the awards being handed out. Two years after that, President Rutherford Hayes named him one of two honorary commissioners to represent Texas at a similar exposition in Paris. With his fluency in French, Smith was named one of the judges of agricultural products.

Ashbel Smith was past 70 by this time, but he still had a last act left to play. A doctor friend of Smith's, George Red, started the Stuart Female Seminary at Ninth and Navasota Streets in Austin in 1876. It was first run entirely by Red and his family, but as the elder Red developed health trouble, a board was appointed, and they chose Smith to lead it.

Smith was already spending a good deal of time in Austin because he had once again successfully run for a seat in the legislature. His issue was to establish a first-class, liberal arts-focused, state university that included an equally prestigious medical branch. The seeds of the state university went all the way back to 1839, just two years after Ashbel arrived in Houston fleeing from lost love. Texas politicians found the dream of the school easy to defer over the years, and it was not until the Sixteenth Legislature that the enabling bill was finally passed.

It was 1881, and Smith was chosen as president of the first Board of Regents for the new University of Texas. He set about recruiting the best professors available. He also argued diligently to have the medical school placed in Galveston where he had already reorganized a medical college. In mid-November the physical foundation of the large gothic Main Building of the university was complete, and a ceremony was held to place a cornerstone at the West Wing. Down the hill to the south, the enormous new state capitol was also under construction, and it must have been the most grand scene to showcase Texas' ambitions.

As usual, Ashbel Smith was called upon to give the remarks. He could not have known about the Permanent University Fund that thanks to a few million acres of land, fortuitous oil strikes, and shrewd investments would by present day top $45 billion, well more than double the next closest public university endowment. Nevertheless, Smith's words about the new University of Texas can be viewed as prophetic: "Smite the rocks with the rod of knowledge, and fountains of unstinted wealth will gush forth."

Chapter Forty-One

O.P. DeWalt

To be a civil rights leader when the cauldron of Jim Crow burned its hottest must have felt like rolling out of bed each day to bang your head against the wall, but perhaps those blows, seemingly going nowhere, are what loosened the bricks for bigotry's later setbacks. Such a thought would be cheering to O.P DeWalt.

Olen Pullman DeWalt was born in the late 1880s. No one knows the date for sure. The surname was a common one in Polk County, Texas at the end of the 19th century, and evidence shows that the many Black DeWalts descended from people enslaved by Kerr Boyce DeWalt, a South Carolinian by birth who moved to Texas shortly after statehood and later became a Confederate officer in the Civil War. The DeWalt plantation was on Menard Creek east of Livingston, and that remained the seat of those freed people after Emancipation.

O.P. attended the rural school offered in the area then entered Prairie View College in 1907. He graduated three years later with high honors. He was living that year with his mother, Caroline, in the Independence Heights area north of Houston. After graduation, O.P. worked for T.M. Fairchild, a man involved in real estate and who later operated one of the top Black undertaking parlors in Third Ward. DeWalt left after a few years to become principal at Independence Heights Colored School, though whether there were any other teachers there at that time is unclear. In 1912, O.P. DeWalt did something that would change both his own life path and the city of Houston. He became a charter member of the Houston chapter of the National Association for the Advancement of Colored People. Not long after, O.P. married Maud Pernetter. His trajectory was looking up.

A few years later, a small group of Black entrepreneurs bought a former theatre downtown, and DeWalt was a part of the effort. The building at 711 Prairie Avenue had opened as the Olympia Opera House in 1903 then became the Standard before giving up on show business entirely to become a brewery warehouse. The new investors wanted to turn the place over to movies and vaudeville. They also built two floors above the auditorium to lease to Black professionals and fraternal lodges. DeWalt himself garnered one of the upstairs offices.

Not long prior to this, the movie business was itinerant, especially for African Americans. A man with a projector and a reel of film would take over an abandoned building after dark and charge people a nominal price to stand and watch the show. A year before the Lincoln venture, the New Sun Set had opened on San Felipe Road, soon to be renamed West Dallas Street. That one was in the heart of Freedmen's Town, the epicenter of African American life in Houston, but the Lincoln's ownership knew that the city had a large enough Black population to support more.

Even though the plan was to show "all colored" silent films, the ownership group wanted a White manager for their new theatre. DeWalt persisted that he should run the operation, and he eventually won out. The films were mostly from Lincoln Motion Pictures and the Foster Photoplay Company, pioneers of Black cinema. The auditorium and its balcony were upgraded, and a bas relief of Abraham Lincoln was added. Maud sold the tickets, and O.P. tore them at the door. Soon there was a Lincoln Barber Shop and a Lincoln Café next door. The venture was decidedly good for the Black Houston economy.

The theatre business and some continuing real estate forays led DeWalt firmly into Houston's thriving Black middle class, but it was his work with the NAACP that gave him notoriety.

WWI saw 370,000 African Americans enter the military, and, at the conflict's end, many of those soldiers believed they had earned consideration on civil rights. The backlash from Whites was fierce. The Ku Klux Klan saw a nationwide resurgence. It was especially strong in states like Indiana and Oregon, but no place took a backseat to the South. KKK marches and rallies were held openly in every city and town in Texas. In Harris County, a deputy sheriff led a mob that castrated an outspoken Black dentist, and for good measure, they beat up his White lawyer.

In 1921, the Democratic party voted to deny Black voters the opportunity to participate in the primary elections, and two years later the state legislature backed them up. Two lawsuits were filed, one in El Paso and one in Houston, against the blatant disregard of the 15th Amendment that gave freedmen the right to vote. O.P. was one of dozens of successful businessmen and NAACP members who resolved to fight back as the cases worked their way through various appeals.

DeWalt also had to speak out in defense of his business practices. In 1922, DeWalt wrote an editorial for the *Houston Informer,* the city's predominant Black newspaper, speaking to "the brethren," as he called members of his race. The issue was complaints about the prices he was charging at the Lincoln theatre, a place he boasted was "the finest strictly colored theatre in the country." The entire piece showed that O.P.

DeWalt had a way with words: "Yet these self-same hyphenates talk more race pride in a minute than they'll practice in a lifetime. Listen, brethren, once and for all; unclog that old rusty think tank of yours and let her hit on all four cylinders. It is necessary for us to charge more because it takes more to run a first class house."

Olen P. DeWalt was elected president of the local NAACP in 1924 amidst a difficult time. On top of the Klan threats and popularity, there was trouble within the Black community itself. Membership was not even close to what chapter officers wanted. The wealthiest African Americans in town barely contributed any money to the cause, and Black preachers were mostly hesitant to rock the boat by supporting civil rights goals.

There were victories. A man named Luther Collins was accused of raping a White woman, a recipe for almost certain death in the South. It mattered not that the initial description from the woman was "a yellow Negro about five feet ten" and Collins was 6'5" tall. The Houston chapter under DeWalt raised over $2,000 without help from the national office. They hired attorneys to appeal the inevitable conviction in Harris County. There were two new channels of approach presented – arguing the evidence and presenting affidavits that the White accuser was of poor character. It took several years, but Luther Collins was eventually set free, a staggering result.

As the White primary cases unspooled, DeWalt and J.B. Grigsby, owner of both an insurance company and the Black Buffs baseball team, filed an injunction against the Harris County Democratic Party. The national NAACP persuaded the pair to drop the suit because they believed it conflicted with another effort. It was a losing fight as the legislature was allowed to simply pass a modified version of their law which stated that a "private" political party had total power to decide who took part in its primaries. Blacks in Texas would stay shut out until 1944.

In June of 1928, the Democratic National Convention came to Houston. It was the first national political confab to come to Texas and the first anywhere in the South since half of the nation's Democrats met in Charleston on the eve of the Civil War. Jesse Jones, the city's richest man and biggest booster spread a liberal amount of cash to secure the meeting for his home town.

On the veritable eve of the event that was to bring true national attention to the bayou for the first time in history, there was the exact sort of racial incident that business leaders were desperate to expunge from the state's permanent record. Lynchings had been endemic to the South since Emancipation, and Texas had its hotspots. Harris County was not among them. Nor was it completely blameless and immune.

The law enforcement community in Houston and Harris County was notoriously racist, and those behaviors threatened to upend the positive convention spin. A street conflict between Houston police and a small group of Black men turned violent, something to which many in the city's African American community were all too accustomed. This time, detective A.W. Davis was shot and killed. On the night of June 20th, one of the suspects, Robert Powell, was dragged from his bed at Jeff Davis hospital by a large group of White men and hanged from a bridge some six miles away, where Post Oak Road crossed Buffalo Bayou.

Anti-lynching reaction was swift with much criticism falling on HPD. City Council appropriated $10,000 to investigate the crime, and the

NAACP chapter under DeWalt offered a thousand dollar reward. Seven murder charges quickly followed, and Houston returned to putting on its best face for the arriving delegates.

The city pulled out all the stops to welcome their guests. Red, white and blue bunting almost suffocated downtown, and organizers hired real cowboys to roam the streets, riding horses and showing off rope tricks. The city was bustling with activity, and smiles and hospitality were everywhere. But a few months later, when those murder charges came to trial, it proved to be the same old Houston. The defendants offered the excuse that they were close friends of the slain detective. None of them were convicted.

O.P. DeWalt was a talented communicator, maybe the best ever to come out of Jim Crow Houston, but his editorial for the *Informer* on October 13, 1928 following the first two acquittals of Powell's murderers was perhaps the height of his eloquence.

"Some of us were just as sure of the course those lynching cases would take as we were that the sun is going to shine on a cloudless morning in May – in spite of the deafening noise of law and order advocates to the contrary," he began. "We were aware at the time that the big fuss was intended for visitors and the outside world."

DeWalt, though, was just getting warmed up. He went on to define two "classes of lynchings." Legal and illegal he wrote. The illegal ones were self-evident, and created a self-perpetuating mob tendency even in unborn babies brought to the spectacles, the "free-for-all celebrations" by their parents making all pre-destined as "born lynchers." "The victims of illegal lynchings are numerous," he continued. "But they dwindle away to insignificance when compared to the number of legal lynchings. If all lynchings were put in the column where they belong, the total number of Negroes that are lynched in the South annually would startle Americans."

The legal ones were more insidious according to DeWalt. They took place inside courtrooms. "It is commonplace to read about negroes who are accused of crimes against white folks being captured, indicted, tried, and sentenced to the electric chair in the span of a few hours." Those sham trials were held in a stately building on the town square "surrounded by a howling mob, threatening to take charge at any time if the results do not meet the fancy of their strained imaginations." "A Negro's life and liberty are about the cheapest thing on the criminal market."

DeWalt was speaking for the NAACP branch which he helmed, but it is impossible to miss his own personal anger, frustration, and hurt contained in his poetic words. He began the penultimate paragraph of the two-column piece with this: "The most dangerous lynchers are not always members of the bloodthirsty mob. They belong to the class which makes our complexion the sole excuse for withholding the rights that we are entitled to as tax-paying, law-abiding American citizens. These people lynch our manhood, our self-respect, our spirit, soul, and everything within us that is worthwhile."

DeWalt was a regular speaker before bodies like the Houston Business Association and the Negro Chamber of Commerce, important groups of the city's top Black leaders, and he did not hold back his thoughts on much of anything. He chastised Black business owners for looking at their peers as competition when the White business were ready to "step in and grab most of the bones of contention." He spoke against chain theatres and stores as places that "undermine the principles upon which this government was founded. The resultant centralization of power is gradually but surely destroying the independence and ideals of the American people... There are three things from which to choose: Break the chain; Establish a cooperation method of competition; or, become members of the chain gang in the form of hirelings and menials." They were timeless words that were aimed at all races in 1930. He often spoke of "better interracial understanding," and he served with several top White leaders on an interracial commission of businessmen.

Part of DeWalt's job as head of the NAACP was the ongoing struggle of fundraising, and the group held annual drives. He wrote editorials asking that "Houston's large colored population...not wait to be solicited." They could bring their contributions to the NAACP headquarters which was located on the second floor of the Lincoln Theatre Building, or, if they were pressed for time, hand them in at the theatre's cigar stand in the lobby.

Lincoln Theatre. Story Sloane Collection

He minced no words about the organization's work to "extend and perpetuate the vital principles of citizenship to every Negro in America" and the duty people had to financially support that work. "Negroes who have this information and don't subscribe liberally," DeWalt wrote in November 1929, "are racial parasites and should be weeded out and labelled as such." People must "make an investment in the manhood and womanhood of your race."

The feature picture on Thursday, April 24, 1931 was *Hell Harbor* starring the steamy Lupe Velez, and it ended about 11 PM. As the patrons departed and the theatre was darkened, the live-in janitoress, Evelina Simms, stood on the sidewalk with Harold Payton, the porter from the Barber Shop. They were listening to band music pouring through the open doors and windows of the nightclub across the street. Allen Orange was running the coffee shop across an alley, and Parris Sinkler was closing up the cigar and candy stand for the night. Some heard two gun shots, but all heard screaming which they soon realized was coming from upstairs near the projection room. Simms and Payton saw Julius Frazier and another boy, Alan Turner, rush down the fire escape and race off in opposite directions on Prairie. There was confusion over whether Frazier was still holding a gun.

Sinkler was the first to find O.P. DeWalt slumped against the wall at the top stair. A blood trail showed where he had dragged himself from the operating booth. He told all who crowded around him that Julius had "fooled" him up to the booth by saying there was a mechanical problem with the film. The other boy had a hammer, but it was Frazier who shot him twice. Police later said the .45 was wrapped in cotton to deaden the sound. The shutters from the booth to the theatre, always open, had been closed in advance. Both shots hit DeWalt below the waist, suggesting he had been knocked to the ground first. The bullet through his thigh likely cut his femoral artery. As the ambulance men carried him down the stairs and out through the lobby, by-standers could see that O.P. DeWalt was covered in blood.

He was taken to Houston Negro Hospital, the segregated facility on Elgin in Third Ward. DeWalt, still president of the NAACP chapter and described by White newspapers as the "wealthiest Negro in South Texas," died the next morning. The *Houston Informer* ran a huge headline that screamed "Thousands Throng DeWalt Funeral." People spilled across the streets outside Trinity AME Church by the hundreds to solemnly watch the procession, adorned by an estimated $1,500 worth of flowers. After the services were held in Houston, there were more in Livingston, where DeWalt was buried.

Almost immediately, the word assassination began to circulate surrounding the shooting of DeWalt. He was no doubt a vocal civil rights leader, and surely many among the White elite would like to have him silenced. DeWalt spoke to police and family before he died and never suggested a possible motive. No evidence to support the conspiracy surfaced, but the theory remains in circulation to this day.

Julius Frazier was working as a projection operator as early as 1920 when he was just 19, and had been "taken care of by DeWalt" for 14 years. He lived with his divorced mother near Dallas and Sampson Streets in Second Ward, walking distance to the theatre at Prairie and Milam. When prosecutors got him on the witness stand, he claimed self-defense.

Frazier said DeWalt had hit him in anger over a lens or perhaps a letter, and that he grabbed a pistol that was kept in a drawer, shot twice then fled. Alan Turner did not back Frazier's story.

Frazier was sentenced to just two years for the murder of DeWalt and was out in barely one. The state had asked for the death penalty, and Frazier's attorney for a suspended sentence. The jury deliberated about three and a half hours. Black citizens were outraged. *Informer* editor C.F. Richardson wrote on the top of the front page that "Human life gets cheaper and cheaper in these United States. Cheaper still if the life involved is housed under a black skin."

Frazier did not stay away from prison very long. Two years after his release, he killed Emma Casey, a "crippled" 56-year old woman, by beating her with a pipe and robbing her of just over $100. This time Frazier got 99 years.

Julius Frazier died at Halloween in 1970. Through the last of the 1930s and most of the 1940s, he had bounced between Huntsville and prison farm units such as Ramsey and Darrington, but he was transferred back to Harris County, and appears to have gained his parole in 1947. He found work as a TV repairman, married, and was living in a small house in Third Ward when he passed.

A year and a half after the shooting, Maud DeWalt's photo was splashed large across a page of the *Informer* with a story about her efforts "despite depression." She was said to be "carrying on to successful fruition her original plan to see to it that Negroes of Houston were not deprived by a cruel fate of their only modern, up-to-date playhouse of their own. She is giving employment to Negro boys and girls, she advertises in Negro newspapers, and she is contributing her all to the uplift of Negro Houston."

The DeWalt family commitment to the place did not last forever, though. The Lincoln Theatre eventually became the Texan and then it went quiet at the end of the 1960s. Aside from one stubborn dentist, the office space upstairs had not been leased in over three decades. In 1972, the *Chronicle* ran a story about the reopening of the movie house. Alvin Guggenheim, a longtime movie promoter, and an investor announced they would pump as much as $100,000 to "recapture some of the 1916 flavor." They spent $12,000. Guggenheim christened it the Majestic in honor of the recently closed downtown movie palace, and the 600-seat house reopened later that summer with "first run movies at popular prices." In this case, they rode the Blaxploitation trend. One of O.P. DeWalt's nephews was interviewed for the short reopening article, and told the writer that Stepin' Fetchit had played on the Lincoln's vaudeville stage. Hardly the role model for civil rights.

The last showing at O.P. DeWalt's theatre came on September 11, 1977 – a quadruple feature of *Cornbread, Earl and Me, Cooley High*, and *Sheba Baby* for a dollar. A few weeks later, the venerable old building that had once been so vital to Houston's Black community met the wrecking ball.

Chapter Forty-Two

Fairgrounds Park

It is nigh on impossible to believe that the Texas Longhorns and Oklahoma Sooners would meet at a neutral state fair site in Houston, but perhaps credulity could be stretched far enough for Big Tex to straddle Buffalo Bayou slathered down with mosquito repellant. For that is precisely where the First Annual State Fair of Texas took place. It was mid-May of 1870 under the auspices of the Agricultural, Mechanical, and Blood Stock Association of Texas. It went so well that they determined to upgrade after only one year. Leaders decided that "larger grounds must be purchased, suitable buildings and sheds erected, the grounds beautified", and with a can-do approach, they made it so.

By the following year organizers had laid out the groundwork for new fairgrounds located near where Main Street petered out onto the bald prairie south of town. It was called the head of Main. The foot was at the north, where the street intersected Buffalo Bayou, the location of the bustling city docks. On a modern street grid, the gates to the new grounds were just past Hadley, at the southern edge of town, and the fair spilled away from that intersection to the southwest.

Eager crowds toured the 80-acre grounds in anticipation of the
upcoming festivities, and city leaders promised a "State Fair such as Texas
has never experienced before." The fairgrounds had a one-mile racetrack
with a grandstand. There were permanent exhibition halls. Newspapers
trumpeted "beautiful fountains, grassy knolls, clumps of shrubbery and
beds of flowers, along which the hard rolled gravel walks and carriage
ways wind in graceful curves, while floral hall, pagodas and booths are so
tastefully arranged as to present to the eye of the gazer a most picturesque
appearance."

Unlike fair season today, the annual event was held in May, but the
event boasted exhibitions of the newest machinery and competitions
were held for items that included canned meats, quilting, crochet work,
stoves, cakes, jewelry, dentistry, beer, fruit, and flowers. There was a
livestock show for horses, mules, cattle, and "milch cows." Organizers
offered a music pavilion. Visitors could even see prize winning terriers
and taxidermied ducks.

For all of the goings on, one event drew the largest crowds. It was the
baseball games in which Houston's top nine defended the city's honor
against teams from other Texas towns. Specifically noteworthy was the
rivalry with Galveston. Since baseball had only settled itself in the Lone
Star State just prior to the Civil War, these competitions were the first in
Texas that could be considered statewide.

Exactly where on the grounds the ball games took place is not clear.
Observers mentioned the "luxuriantly green and thickly sewn" Bermuda
grass, so it is easy to imagine a pastoral setting. It seems likely that
the field sat near the modern intersection of Travis and McGowen.
As early as 1877, that crossroads was listed as the location of the

Houston Agricultural Grounds and Driving Park, the latter being a late nineteenth century term for a horse racing track.

Baseball, horse racing, and the other events kept the Fair Grounds lively and popular throughout the decade of the 1870s. When the Fair first moved to its new location, stable owner Michael Westheimer ran horse drawn omnibusses for the public at the fare of a quarter. The city government soon usurped the private business by adding streetcars that were drawn by mules. Riders paid a nickel for the mile and a half trip from the center of town. Cars departed every ten minutes during the run of the fair, and the trek took fifteen minutes.

The State Fair brought thousands of people to Houston each spring. It also brought the unsavory. By 1877 some attendees, many of whom were heavily engaged in betting on the races and ballgames, complained of rampant pick-pockets. The fair organizers counted on a sure-fire financial success until 1878. That year it was plagued by bad weather and a brief yellow fever scare. It was the first monetary loss on the venture, but it was sufficient for the citizens of Houston to discontinue it. The state fair concept remained dormant in Texas until the city of Dallas took it up in 1886, and it has remained there to this day.

Since the time of the Allen Brothers, Houston has been focused on development and making a buck. Even before the fair met its demise, the city's newspapers had called for the Fairgrounds to be turned into a year-round park for the people. The city did not bite the apple fully, but they did enter a five-year lease agreement in March 1876. It was the first such public parks effort in the town's history. Modern day Houstonians can probably anticipate what came next.

When the city's lease expired, visitors to the Fairgrounds could stare southward across the prairie and see new development. Suburban farms of 10 to 14 acres had totally surrounded the original fair complex. Within less than six months, most of the land where Texans enjoyed their first fair had been sold and subdivided as Fairgrounds Addition, but there was one six-block exception.

The rest of the 80-acres may have been undergoing a gradual sell off, but the small plot that streamed roughly southeast from the corner of Travis and McGowen remained vibrant with baseball competition. Newspapers in both Houston and Galveston still referred to the place as "the Fair Grounds" when those cities met. It was also the spot used for the start of the professional Texas Association of 1884, the state's first attempt at establishing an intercity sports league. Sam Hain, owner of the Houston team and one of the driving forces behind the league, paid to build out the grounds which was the site of a storied first game between Hain's Houston Nationals and the league entry from Galveston.

The development of the rest of the former Fairgrounds was not immediate. In 1885, Messrs. Raphael and Whitrock leased some of the property for an ambitious operation that promised to be going "full blast every afternoon and night" for the summer. "They propose to make the grounds a place of summer resort, and are now putting the track, pavilion, baseball and cricket fields in first class order. The place will be free to all, except on special days, the management, no doubt, expecting to get a return for their outlay in the sale of refreshments. Sunday is the day for the opening. A band will be in attendance." The following winter, another partnership rented a portion of the place for a skating rink.

Eventually, money talked. By the end of the 1880s, most of the old State Fair grounds had sprouted houses and small businesses. Only the six-block ballpark site remained. "The Fair Grounds" continued as one popular moniker for the ballpark, but in a town growing as fast as any in the region, recent history might as well be ancient to the newcomers.

Unlike today, there was not a fixed name for the ball yard. When the Cincinnati Red Stockings faced the local Houston squad in an exhibition on March 6, 1888, it was identified as the "Houston Base Ball Park." It was also regularly referenced by local sportswriters as "League Park," "Travis Street Park," and the "Base Ball Park at Travis at McGowen" just to list a few. There were, however, naming rights on the horizon. In the mid-1890s, with William H. Bailey, the editor of the short-lived newspaper *Houston Herald* as part of the ownership group, even the rival *Post* was referring to the action at "Herald Park."

The grandstand of the ball park on Travis burned in 1889, and the cause was never discovered. It certainly didn't crimp the play of the Houston baseball club. They rolled to the city's first ever league championship in any sport. Judging by the usually accurate bird's eye map of Houston, the grandstand was a straight affair that ran only along the third base line.

For some years, the land underneath the ball park shared ownership with the firm that ran the city's streetcars. Though they were essential public transportation, they were not publicly held. It was a business model that could be found across the United States in the late nineteenth century. The streetcar company upped their ridership by owning and promoting suburban attractions that made people want to pay to ride the streetcar.

That company also charged rent to the local baseball club, and in April 1892, the Houston manager announced that he was open to competitive bids for his team to play someplace else. Two bidders emerged - E. L. Coombs who owned property on the southern edge of the Heights, and Henry MacGregor, president of the street railway company which still owned the established ball park. Like Bud Adams and the Oilers a century later, the negotiating ploy resulted in the team staying put with promises that "The old park will be remodeled and new fences built." Furthermore, there were technological improvements for the fans as "Electric cars in abundance will be placed on the line running to the park, and the crowds will have no cause to complain as they did heretofore when the mules balked and kicked."

In 1895, a block away from the ball park, at the northeast corner of Main and McGowen, the city opened a large municipal auditorium with great fanfare. Houston had needed a large civic hall, but the immediate catalyst was the Confederate Veterans Convention to be held in the city. World famous John Philip Sousa and his band were brought in as the opening day entertainment, and the honored guest for the big meeting was Winnie Davis, the daughter of the late Confederate President, Jefferson Davis.

Like the Adams and Oilers saga, the team did not remain satisfied. E.L. Coombs had kept whispering in the right ears and Opening Day of 1895 found the ball club at the new Coombs Park near where Heights Boulevard crossed White Oak Bayou. The planned community of Houston Heights was less than five years old, but it was already booming with new housing, business, heavy industry, and a nearby military encampment.

There was a streetcar line that ran out Washington Avenue, but it was not enough. Houston lost to Galveston at their new home in front of "a crowd that was by no means large, considering it was the opening of the season's league contest." Less than 24 hours later, the local nay-sayers were letting their thoughts be heard. "The distance of the grounds from the city, rendering them inaccessible to the foot brigade and the fear of inadequate transportation facilities, particularly at the close of the game, undoubtedly kept many away who would have otherwise been on hand. Some of the old timers and most enthusiastic cranks were missed yesterday." Just four days later, the team's manager signed "a lease with the International and Great Northern Railroad for the old Lee grounds at the foot of Congress Street and today the lumber to fence in the park and build the grand stands will be on the grounds. ...This new park will be convenient for several reasons. it is not only accessible by streetcars, but people can walk back from the park if car service is short. Besides the trains from Galveston can unload their passengers right at the grounds."

Larger events intervened, however. By 1895, the Houston City Street Railway Company had sunk into serious financial trouble, and local lumber magnate John Henry Kirby was appointed receiver of the company. Not long after inspecting the firm's properties, Kirby also purchased part of the Houston baseball team. Unsurprisingly, the ball club, with a highly organized and capitalized ownership group, announced plans to return to the "old" ground at Travis and McGowen.

Work was underway within two days after ownership's incorporation. New fences were built along the McGowen and Milam street sides, and the old fence in other spots was being repaired. "The trees have been cut down and thus the space between them and the right field fence, which was formerly unused, will be utilized. The grounds are 403 feet long and about 310 feet wide," manager Jack Garson reported.

The new seating was spacious. "The two grand stands, one for ladies and their escorts and the other for gentlemen only, will be at the Milam

Street and McGowen Avenue corner of the park and will be entirely
of modern construction. The combined seating capacity of the two
grandstands will be about 2500. The bleachers will be erected along the
side of the right field fence and will be able to accommodate about 200
persons." Wire netting was in place to prevent fouls from hitting the
grand stand occupants, and a box for the press and scorer was placed atop
the stands. After a request from Black ball fans, a segregated section of
bleachers was installed.

With concern for propriety among the fans high, the directors agreed
that "under no circumstances will there be sale of intoxicants at the ball
park." Evidence suggests that people brought their own.

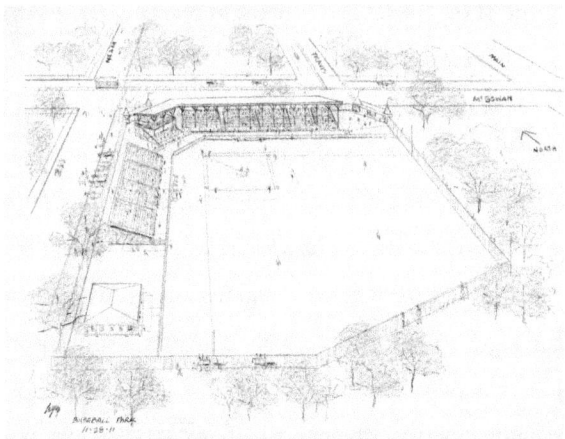

Birdseye view of the ballpark in 1896. Patrick Lopez
artwork

The old clubhouse was moved to a spot at the southwest corner of the
property, past the rightfield corner. For the first time, water connections
were run there for a nice shower bath "which will be quite a treat, indeed."
Considering players wore flannel uniforms throughout the Houston
summer, that may be an understatement. Another move toward a true

MIKE VANCE

professional venue was the removal of some trees that had stood in foul ground beyond first base so there was "no danger of getting hurt going after foul hits."

Admission was paid at the new ticket office by the Travis Street entrance, the location nearest the streetcar stop, or advance tickets could be purchased at Otto Taub's cigar stand downtown. Covered seating cost extra. True to human nature, plenty of would be patrons chose to save their money and scam the system. *Houston Post* writer James Quarles wrote an entire article on the freeloaders.

Along the Milam Street side, "There is a motley crowd. I counted no less than a dozen animals, the owners standing on the saddles and looking over the fence being given an opportunity to see what transpires within. Some of the horses had as many as two to carry. Boys ranging in age from 8 to 15 are seen all along the fence looking through convenient cracks or holes that have been whittled. They watch through these cracks for a foul ball, and when one happens of the high fence – as is often the case – there is a scramble, whites and blacks joining in the rush to recover the sphere, the possession of which gives them free entry into the park."

Along the outfield wall, where Dennis Avenue would one day cut through, was another crowd. "The first seen is a number of buggies – old ones, new ones, dilapidated ones, some with tops and some without, each having from three to a half dozen occupants who are perched about on the wheels and tops anxiously watching each successive play of the game... Next is seen a delivery wagon carrying upon the side the familiar sign of a well-known Houston business house. Upon the roof of this wagon, which should be used for the more legitimate purpose of distributing its cargo of fine silks, laces and dress goods, is roosting the driver and his friends"

Two men parked a buggy with a "portable grand stand" then sat in their homemade seats holding umbrellas to shield themselves from the sun.

"Nature has assisted others. Just behind the portable grand stand is a large tree, a gnarled oak, which has grown throughout the time of many years... Its spreading branches have a seating capacity of about twenty-five, and the limbs are crowded. Men and boys, white and black, congregate among its foliage every afternoon and watch the game."

Other fans employed a bit of daring with their mooching. "Out in McGowen avenue I saw a small boy at the point of a deserted telegraph pole. A seat had been arranged on this pole and he was comfortably ensconced upon it."

The crowds at Fair Grounds Park were too enthusiastic for some of the neighbors. One resident of a nearby house filed suit over the disturbing noise of applause. He was granted a temporary injunction to stop all ballplaying at Travis Street Park. The order was issued by a judge in far away Anderson and was soon overturned by a jurist who understood that the ballyard had been there long before the complaining neighbor bought his house.

Amateur teams frequently utilized the ball park, and football, rapidly gaining popularity across Texas, was also to be found at Fairgrounds Park when baseball season ended. There was a sprucing up of the place just two years after the new structures opened. Turnstiles were added to the gates, and a "gaudy" new paint scheme was applied with the seats of the grandstand painted orange and the inside of the grandstand painted red and orange. Signage was sold on the outfield fences, and barbed wire fencing was added 25 feet east of left field in an effort to cut down on the freeloading rabble.

All good things come to an end, however. After a team ownership change and two years that saw a split in the Texas League, the facilities at Fairgrounds Park began to deteriorate. The final straw came when Otto Witte bought the land from the Houston Electric Streetcar Company in February 1904 with the intention of developing the six blocks. He granted the ball club a stay of execution until June. Damn the fact that June was halfway through the baseball season. It resulted in the Houston club trying to play games at the horse track near Harrisburg Road and Milby Street then attempting to finish the season entirely with road games. In the end, there was barely a squeak about the demise of the city's first professional sports venue.

At least one man would miss the place. Rienzi Johnston, who had once been part owner of the ball club, ran the *Houston Post*. The byline for a farewell article was that of his 20-year old son, Harry, but the thoughts were likely those of the father:

"The old league park, after many years service to the sunkissed athletes of the National game, has faded into the dim past. The dull sombre roar of the base hit, the wild and thrilling yell of the fanatic, and the spicy field play, which have marked a period of twenty years at the famous old park will no longer be looked forward to, but, instead, will be remembered only as seen in the fast fleeting past.

"There will always be something about the old park that holds one's attention as he passes there, although handsome residences will occupy the space once used as the diamond - a diamond on which the greatest ballplayers of the country have played."

Substantial houses sprung up within a few months. Those yielded over the next decades to upscale apartments, a car dealership, and then high end Midtown restaurants. A final reminder of its first use lives on, however, in every deed record for those blocks. The tiny six-block neighborhood south of downtown was platted and developed under the name Ball Park Addition.

Deep East Texas

Big Thicket National Preserve. NPS

Chapter Forty-Three

Vernon Dalhart

Anyone searching for the answer to the riddle of where country music intersects with Thomas Edison should look no further than Vernon Dalhart. Or more accurately Marion Try Slaughter, who adopted Vernon Dalhart as his stage name when an agent suggested that his real moniker was not very catchy. Slaughter picked two West Texas towns he recalled from his youth.

Marion Slaughter was born in Jefferson in 1883 and learned about family tragedy at the age of 10 when his uncle, Bob Castleberry, murdered his father. The brief newspaper accounts that circulated through East Texas put the trouble down to "an old grudge." Two years later, the family decamped Jefferson for Dallas.

In Big D, the young man developed a love of opera. That might have been out of place on the ranges of the Panhandle where he went to earn money punching cattle. It was there he saw both Vernon and Dalhart up close. He likely did entertain the other cowboys with his harmonica and jaw harp.

Still in his teens, Slaughter returned home and studied voice at the Dallas Conservatory of Music. In 1901, at age 18, he married Sadie Lee Moore-Livingston. The couple would eventually have two children.

In 1910, Slaughter moved his young family to New York City where he soon became Vernon Dalhart. He got a job in a piano warehouse while he pursued occasional singing gigs. His goal was to put his classical training to work and become an opera singer. In 1913, he got small parts in a production of Puccini's Madame Butterfly and a Gilbert & Sullivan show.

Not long afterwards, Dalhart applied to Edison Records, answering a newspaper ad for singers. Thomas Alva Edison had very strong opinions about what constituted a good singing voice, talking a great deal about tremolo, but often applying more of an "I know it when I hear it" approach. The story is that Dalhart auditioned for the great man himself. Whoever the decision maker was, they had Vernon Dalhart sing for Edison Records.

The story of the Edison disc is an interesting one. Edison had invented the phonograph using cylinders, and the company stuck to that technology until companies like Victor and Columbia began having greater success selling discs. At his core, Edison was an inventor, of course, and his shop devised a new system that used thicker discs with more verticality in the grooves. On the plus side, they provided much better fidelity. The company held live concert hall shows in the 1910s during which the singer and their recording were both on stage. The lights were then doused, and the audience asked to determine if they were hearing a recording or a live person. Spoiler alert – it was always the recording.

There were two large negatives. The thicker Edison discs were more expensive, and they could only be played on an Edison machine. Imagine a 1910s version of the Betamax. The Edison Company held third place in the record market for a few years before fading away around WWI.

Dalhart made over 400 recordings for Edison and other labels, including Columbia, between 1916 and 1923. His primary genre was classical music and popular dance band vocals. Often he recorded under various other pseudonyms, a common practice in an industry that frequently did not even list the artist on the cylinders until about 1910. Dalhart also showed great skill singing in dialects. That included his first Edison release called "Can't You Heah Me Callin', Caroline?" He became a true journeyman on records, covering styles from Black minstrel music to Hawaiian.

In 1924, Vernon Dalhart made history. He went into the studio, such as it was, to record two sides for the Victor Talking Machine Company. Victor, which later merged with RCA, also manufactured the Victrola which was so popular that it was the eponymous record player for many years.

Vernon Dalhart's song for the "A" side was "The Wreck of the Old 97," a ballad about a Danville, Virginia train wreck. For the flip side of the disc, Dalhart chose "The Prisoner's Song." He claimed that "Prisoners" was written by his cousin Guy Massey, but as Tulane musicologist Bill Malone said, "nobody knows for sure." That is because Guy Massey claimed to have heard it from his brother Rob who had in turn probably picked it up in prison. Dalhart took 95% of the author's royalties and gave his cousin the other 5%. Victor's new executive for the nascent country music department, Nathaniel Shilkret, claimed until the 1950s that he had rewritten the unusable version supplied by Dalhart. Shilkret ultimately failed in his efforts to get a cut. "The Prisoner's Song" was later recorded by artists including Hank Snow, Brenda Lee, Bill Monroe, Johnny Cash, and Loudon Wainwright III. It lived in both the book M*A*S*H and a Buster Keaton movie.

For Victor Records in 1924, however, all that really mattered was that the song was a gigantic hit. The Dalhart recording sold seven million copies, maybe more. As a single, that puts it on par with Michael Jackson's "Billy Jean" and Queen's "Bohemian Rhapsody." It was the number one song for 12 weeks, and it is purported to be the biggest selling single in the first 70 years of the industry.

The success of the record totally changed the course of Vernon Dalhart's career. For the next nine years, he became a country artist, or more commonly known at the time as hillbilly. He recorded many songs as the Vernon Dalhart Trio, with violinist and singer Adelyne Hood and guitarist/singer/songwriter Carson Robison. On his own, he made more than 5,000 singles, often under different names on different labels. He was Al Craver at Columbia, Tobe Little at OKeh, Jeff Fuller on Vocalion, and Vernon Dale, Frank Evans, Hugh Lattimer or Bob White elsewhere. At Grey Gull Records, Dalhart used the name Vel Veteran that was also used by other singers.

The biggest and lasting impact on America was that Vernon Dalhart's success proved that people across the country liked southern hillbilly music. Northerners had long been intrigued or amused by Southern accents, and Tin Pan Alley songwriters routinely cribbed Stephen Collins Foster imagery, but country music was virtually non-existent. Texan Eck Robertson had recorded what is credited as being the first country single only in 1922. When Dalhart's songs took off, record producers were suddenly scouring the South looking for more like him. Ralph Peer held a famous recording session in Bristol, Tennessee in 1927 that included the Carter Family. Combined with Jimmie Rodgers, it changed American music forever.

"You can't overemphasize the impact that Dalhart had on American music," said that country music professor Bill Malone. "He just revealed to the entertainment trade that the music he was doing had an appeal, that people wanted to hear it."

With his new found money and success, Vernon Dalhart bought a big house in Mamaroneck, New York. He recorded some songs that he recalled from his Panhandle days and lots of songs based on current events such as the Floyd Collins cave saga and the John Scopes Trial.

Vernon Dalhart promo shot

Some Dalhart music lives on even if he is largely forgotten. His song "The Runaway Train" became a perennial favorite in the United Kingdom thanks to its use in a popular children's TV show. Dalhart also had a hit with "Big Rock Candy Mountain," but it was hardly the sanitized kid's number made famous by Burl Ives. Originally it was an unromanticized picture of a rail-riding hobo's dreamscape. Dalhart's version starts out: "One evening as the sun went down and the jungle fire was burning, down the track came a hobo a-hiking, and he said boys I'm not turning." At the big rock candy mountain of 1929, down-on-their-luck men found cigarette trees, little streams of alcohol trickling down the rocks, bulldogs with rubber teeth and railroad bulls who were are blind. Dalhart sang of a place "Where the handouts grow on bushes... where the boxcars all are empty."

He remained popular into the 1930s, but what ended his career was the perception that this native of Jefferson, Texas was somehow not an authentic Southerner. His opera training and the years of trying to lose his accent showed through, and he was widely denigrated over it. Though some of his songs were sung with conviction, country music lovers no longer found him genuine.

"It was hard for Dalhart to compete since he seemed artificial, stilted and condescending perhaps," Bill Malone said.

The irony was reflected in comments from the famous Ralph Peer who summed up what Vernon Dalhart had done for the genre in the first place: "Dalhart had the peculiar ability to adapt hillbilly music to suit the taste of the non-hillbilly population...He was a professional substitute for a real hillbilly."

After 1933, Dalhart had only one more recording session - for Bluebird in 1939. He moved to Bridgeport, Connecticut and worked as a factory watchman and a nighttime hotel clerk. During the day, he gave voice lessons to local children. He died on September 14, 1948 of a heart attack at the age of 65. He is buried next to his wife at the same burial ground that holds P.T. Barnum and Tom Thumb. His tombstone bears the name Marion T. Slaughter.

Vernon Dalhart was posthumously elected to the Nashville Songwriters Hall of Fame in 1970 and the Country Music Hall of Fame in 1981.

Chapter Forty-Four

The Caddo

Most modern Americans know about native Indian peoples in vagaries and broad strokes. By nature, it is difficult history since it was not written down, but as Texas tribes go we can be more familiar with the Caddo than others for two very simple reasons - the Caddo were here longer, and they largely stayed in one spot. The Texas portion of the Caddo confederacy also came in much more frequent contact with the newly arrived French and Spanish than did their kinsmen to the north and west. Remnants of La Salle's doomed expedition wandered through their territory at the end of the 1600s, and almost 150 years before that, diarists among the Hernando de Soto entrada wrote about the Caddo, too.

When first contacted by Europeans, the Caddo tribes of indigenous Texans were made up of at least 25 bands in three confederacies on both sides of the Red and Sabine Rivers. Specifically, the Hasanai people were those who lived in Texas. Kadohadacho groups were found to the north around the Great Bend area, and the Natchitoches groups were on the Red River near the town in Louisiana that bears their name. It was the way many tribes lived, separate bands of people related along maternal lines, though marriages were between different clans.

The Hasanai lived along the Trinity, Sabine, Angelina, and Neches. That put this thriving people across a wide area of what is today Northeast Texas. They had lived there for centuries before Europeans began recording history to paper.

One thing modern people are likely to equate with the Caddo are grassy mounds. Like their Mississippian neighbors, the flat-topped mounds that appeared throughout Caddoan landscapes were used for ceremonial and religious purposes and sometimes served as platforms for temples. They were community centers for a culture that was stratified into social classes with religious and political leaders, who generally inherited their positions, at the top. The Spanish recorded that compared to the hunting and gathering tribes, the Caddo were "highly organized and civilized."

There was one major difference between the Texas – Louisiana Caddo and the tribal groups along the Mississippi Valley. The easterners lived in fortified villages and fought many bloody battles with the Spanish interlopers. In Texas, the Caddo did not fortify their communities. They relied on a reputation as top warriors, cooperation among bands, and distance between various settlements. The physical layout of the communities was large, too. People often lived out among their fields and gardens.

The Caddo Indians were excellent farmers, and they made the rich land of the Neches, Sabine, and Angelina River valleys work for them. In earlier times, they cultivated maize, beans, and squash alongside native plants of maygrass, amaranth, and sunflowers. But the archaeology shows that by around A.D. 1300, maize had become the biggest part of their diet. They planted different varieties at different seasons of the year.

There was "little corn" harvested in July and "flour corn" harvested in September. Deer was the primary meat, but the Caddo also made use of bison and bear for meat, fur, and hides. When horses, introduced to the continent by Europeans, became available to them, the Caddo began to undertake bison hunting trips. As the Caddo Nation themselves puts it, "We are the descendants of agriculturalists with an intimate understanding of the world, the stars, the sky, the earth and the world below the earth, from which we emerged."

When the French and Spanish arrived, Caddo people inhabited everything from individual homesteads to small villages to large civic and cultural centers. Their houses were fashioned with a precise circular plan of bent poles and horizontal lathing covered with grass. Construction was carried on as a community event: men raised the poles, and women thatched the structure. This skill and knowledge has been passed down to a few Caddo who can practice it today. Visitors to the Caddo Mounds State Historic Site near Alto will find houses constructed under the eyes of those craftsmen.

Texas Caddo maintained vibrant trade with other indigenous people across a wide area of North America. They exported hides and ceramics and imported copper from the Great Lakes, turquoise from New Mexico, and sea shells from all along the Gulf Coast, including as far away as Florida. When the Spanish and French established regular contact, the Caddo Indians expanded their trade to become partners with them, as well.

One of the biggest products that the Caddo exported was wood from the bois d'arc tree. Today, a drive along rural two-lanes in the middle part of the country will bring up those trees, also known as Osage orange, growing along the fence rows. After the last Ice Age wiped out many of the larger animals, the bois d'arc seeds lost their primary way of spreading – through animal poop. Bois d'arc is the best bow wood east of the Rockies which is why the French explorers gave it the name, and the luck of the draw may well have provided the Caddo lands upstream from today's Texarkana with a virtual monopoly on the stuff.

The other big export was salt. The Caddo operated factory-like operations of evaporation and boiling to create dried salt which they traded for hundreds of miles in all directions. In return it netted hides and dried meat from the Plains and turquoise and shells from the Southwest.

Another thing that set the Caddo apart from other tribes was their pottery. Experts agree that for 1,000 years it was the finest east of the Rockies. One 20th century ethnographer dryly wrote, "In Caddo ceramics the art of the Southeast easily reached its apex, for while there are specimens of pottery from the Middle Mississippi region and Moundville which show as high technical excellence, there are none that, upon the whole, exhibit equal artistic feeling."

Caddo pottery is widely varied both in design and materials. Local clays produced unique and readily traceable colors. Over the course of that millennium, Caddo women "executed countless variations on a great many themes." The looseness of community connections also made for distinct local designs. The women artists who created the ceramics taught their daughters and nieces.

The fineness of their work unfortunately contributed to the destruction of their tangible legacy. It was bad enough that archaeologists of previous centuries looked upon Caddo burial sites only in the name of science and without regard to the great violation of the people entombed. The sheer value of beautiful Caddo pottery made the sites prime targets for looters and grave robbers. Some misguided folk might style themselves amateur archaeologists, but that hardly matters when they cart off items for personal collections or surreptitious sales.

Burial practices were in either mounds or flat ground, and the departed were interred along with belongings to help in their next life. The Caddo potters made both coarse ware for daily utilitarian use and fine ware, items meant to be decorated, polished, and admired. Some were used as serving pieces, dishes for company, and others accompanied the dead on their journey. The other part of the equation of destruction is opportunity. The Caddo were forced off their land two centuries ago, so there were no longer people nearby to protect the resting places of the departed.

The Caddo were certainly not alone in being dislocated from their land, and, like tribes across North America, the writing was on the wall long before they were gone. Scientists believe that as almost soon as Europeans carried new diseases onto the Atlantic beaches, epidemics spread westward before them. It did not require the Europeans themselves to make contact with tribes, only for viruses and bacteria to which the Native Indians had never built up resistance to infect a handful of people who unknowingly carried it among the tribes. The best bet is that between 1691 when the French stayed for a time among the hospitable Caddo until the 1830s when Texans started to actively push them off their thousand year tribal homelands, the Hasanai population had declined by 95%. They adapted, but the die was cast.

The Texas Caddo, diminished by disease and attacks from other tribes like the Osage, consolidated previously distinct bands out of necessity. By about 1800, they faced another obstacle. A giant mass of fallen timber and debris created a natural dam on the Red River, built up across hundreds of years. It was called the Great Raft, and it stretched as far as 165 miles. The epic logjam forced waters from the riverbed to cover the surrounding land, and flooded areas continued to expand. Seeing their village would soon be inundated, the Caddo moved to a spot on what is now known as Caddo Lake, a body created by the raft in the first place. They called their town Sha'chahdínnih, meaning Timber Hill.

Members of the Coushatta and Alabama people came into the new Caddo territory. As for the Caddo themselves, they numbered only about 450 adults by 1805 after smallpox and measles brought catastrophe at the start of the 19th century. Still, in that year, an Indian agent and doctor at Natchitoches named John Sibley wrote that the Kadohadacho warriors were "looked upon somewhat like the Knights of Malta, or some distinguished military order. They are brave, despise danger or death, and boast that they have never shed white men's blood." That agency asked Caddo Chief Dehahuit to serve as a roving peace ambassador to other tribes in Texas and Louisiana.

By 1830, a cycle of droughts and floods had destroyed crop after crop for the Caddo. Other tribes and the new American settlers had overhunted wild game. The people were starving. A tribal historian wrote that, "The village on the lake became a place of crying."

The Great Raft had forced that last band of Caddo from their longtime homes, but, by preventing river traffic on the middle Red River, it also isolated and protected them from further encroachment. That safety ended when Whites undertook plans to clear the Raft. A battering ram steamboat was devised. It took two years of work, but by

Spring of 1835, the river was cleared all the way to Shreveport, and the American invasion of Caddo land around Timber Hill, the final vestige of a millennium of living, heated to a level beyond endurance.

A removal treaty was signed on July 1, 1835, and the Caddo scattered. Some went north into the Choctaw and Chickasaw territories. Many Texas Caddo went west into the upper Brazos Valley. The stay there ended in the middle 1850s when the U.S. War Department forcibly placed the shrinking Caddo population with Waco, Anadarko, and Tonkawa people on the Brazos Reservation near the Salt Fork of the Brazos River in present-day Young County. It offered protection from the hostile bands of the Comanche, and the majority of surrounding Whites left the reservation Indians alone. Several men from each of those tribes found work as Army scouts.

Among the exceptions to tolerance was one of the most despicable mass murderers in Texas history – John R. Baylor. That man had at one time been the agent at the Upper Comanche Reservation, home to many Penateka Comanche and near the Brazos Reservation, but he was fired from that post. Blaming everyone but himself, Baylor and two others started a newspaper in Jacksboro. It was called *The White Man*, and it preached and agitated against the presence of the two North Texas reservations. Hatred was soon spreading with each passing stagecoach.

As was the practice on the reservations, a group of 17 braves from Brazos was given permission to go hunt in Palo Pinto County in December 1858. Under cover of night, they were attacked. Seven were killed in their blankets. Governor Hiram Runnels issued a warning that area Whites should leave the Indians be, but no indictments ever came against the attackers of Choctaw Tom and his party. Preparations began to peacefully remove the Caddos and all others out of Texas, but the chance never arose.

Six months later, Baylor led several hundred men into the heart of the Brazos Reservation demanding certain people be handed over and vowing to kill any Army personnel who tried to stop them. While delivering his message, Baylor killed an old Indian man and a woman working in her garden. Warriors quickly massed and chased Baylor and his men to the nearby Marlin Ranch. A gun battle lasted all afternoon.

The man in charge of all Indians in Texas for the United States Army was Robert Neighbors. He had served in the Texas Army under Jack Hays, was kidnapped to Mexican prison by the Woll Invasion of 1842, and served as a state legislator. Most importantly, in his turns as Indian agent, Neighbors earned the trust of the tribes. Knowing that John Baylor would soon regroup and come back seeking to massacre the inhabitants, Major Neighbors quickly rounded up all the Indians at the Brazos Reservation and hurried them north of the Red River. After two weeks of traveling, the refugee caravan was deposited at the Wichita Reservation on the Washita River.

The Texas Indians, now forever gone from the state, set up villages. Early in the Civil War, pro-Union warriors came south to attack the pro-Confederate Tonkawas, and as a result of the unrest, the Caddo mostly went to Kansas until the fighting ended. By 1867, they were back on the Wichita Reservation, and it was another seven years after that before a space of their own was defined and all bands were unified into a single Caddo Nation. In 1902, each tribal member got a 160-acre allotment, and the rest of their reservation was opened for White settlers.

The official Caddo Nation history recounts the cooperation that their ancestors offered to Europeans and Americans who came to their lands and then reminds the world that "Sadly, this initial respect did not spare the Caddo from the common fate of so many of the native societies who came into contact with European diseases, guns, land dispossession and desires. In less than two centuries, the mighty Caddo were reduced to a few hundred refugees who were assigned tiny parcels of land in the Oklahoma Indian Territories, several hundred miles northwest of their homeland."

For well over a century, the accepted story was that the name Texas itself came from the Caddo word for friend, but new scholarship makes an alternate case that the word derived from an archaic Spanish name that might have been attached to cypress trees encountered by the first entradas. From the way they were treated, it would be irony indeed if their word for friendship was adopted as the name of the place and people who ran the Caddo from their generational home.

Firmly ensconced on the reservation near Binger, Oklahoma, a chief with the unfortunate name of Whitebread became a primary source on the Caddo culture for ethnographers George Dorsey and John Swanton who became recognized as experts on the tribe thanks to such conversations. Back in 1888, before Dorsey and Swanton emerged on the scene, and when the taste of recent history lay more bitterly on his tongue, Whitebread offered these words: "My people live with the Wichitas, the Ionies, Anadarkoes, Tawakonis, Kechies and Southern Delawares. Each one of these tribes once had a country and homes of their own. Each tribe once had a country where their ancestors had lived for generations and to which they were attached by ties and associations as sacred and dear as those that cluster in the memories and inspire the hearts of the white man for his country and home. We have none now... The story of our wrongs and suffering is too long to be told you now. I will not attempt it."

Chapter Forty-Five

Raymond Hamilton

We have come to expect it of screen stars, musicians, and prima donna athletes, but there was a time when wanted killers carried on public rivalries and jockeyed for the best press. The Great Depression was the last gasp of national outlaw fandom that started with Old West dime novels and the *Police Gazette*. Americans were hurting financially, and millions of them believed that anyone sticking up the man deserved to be cheered. In the 1920s, people were horrified at the bloody antics of swarthy Al Capone, even if they did willingly flock to his nightclubs, but during the decade of hard times, outlaws like John Dillinger and Pretty Boy Floyd could often count on an abetting public. Some people clipped newspaper images of most wanted murderers and found a vicarious escape from their troubles behind the barrel of somebody else's gun. Those attitudes were especially strong in Texas with a populist streak wider than the Brazos.

Bonnie Parker and Clyde Barrow met their physical end when their smallish bodies were blown apart by six lawmen in Bienville Parish, Louisiana in May 1934, but they were already riding a wave of myth that lingers still. On any given day, newspapers from Alpine, Texas to

Valdosta, Georgia to Ypsilanti, Michigan might each run a definitive
account of a local man who, with knees knocking, leaned into the
window of a V-8 Ford and gave directions to the desperados. During
their three year run of mayhem that started upon Clyde's early release
from Eastham Prison Farm, the duo were spotted more times than Elvis'
ghost at a Dairy Queen.

Thanks to almost a century of media presence, the world today knows
Bonnie and Clyde, but at the time they were active, reporters were just
as likely to call them the Barrow Gang. Though theirs was a story from
West Dallas, the nexus of the gang was unquestionably Eastham Prison
Farm outside of Lovelady in Houston County. "The Ham" opened in
1917 in woods about a mile and a half east of the Trinity River. Inmates
had been carving farmland out of those East Texas acres ever since.

Clyde Barrow first went to Eastham in September 1930, and on the
way there, chained around the neck inside a rolling cell called the One
Way Wagon, he met Ralph Fults, a 19-year old who had just escaped
from the place, though not for very long. Barrow soon learned that the
Ham was a hell hole by design. The man in charge had been fired for
abusing prisoners, but when Lee Simmons took over the Texas prisons,
he hired the same man back. Simmons wanted physical abuse because
he thought it was the best way to keep prisoners in line. He ordered
inmates to be whipped with a long leather strap until they lost control
of their bowels and passed out. He encouraged hard beatings for all
transgressions. When small prisoners like Barrow were regularly raped by
bigger ones, that was no concern of Simmons' guards. There were also
plenty of stories that on the second escape attempt from The Bloody

Ham, guards would not bother with the beatings. They simply shot the rabbiting inmate in the head.

Both Barrow and Fults made it out of Eastham in just over a year. Clyde cut off his own big toe with an axe to be sure, though he need not have bothered. His mother had begged a pardon from the governor. Fults got released first, and while biding his time he smuggled hacksaw blades into the McKinney jail where a younger acquaintance named Raymond Hamilton was locked up for car theft. After Hamilton cut his way out, he owed Fults a big favor.

One of the things that kept Fults and Barrow occupied on the farm was dreaming a mass prison break from Eastham during which they would kill several guards out of revenge. To make their dream real, they needed money, and, after being tossed from a succession of jobs for being sketchy ex-cons, Clyde and Ralph decided a life of crime was the only avenue to get there. To fortify their new gang, the duo added Raymond Hamilton. After Clyde's first target, the safe at a small West Dallas oil refinery, turned out to be empty, friction between Hamilton and Barrow started to build.

Both Hamilton and Barrow were eaten up with "Little Man Syndrome" that made them cocky and confrontational. At 5'3", Raymond was two inches shorter than Clyde. They managed several small stickups and then successfully robbed a bank in Kansas, but when Fults and Barrow decided to spend their shares outfitting for the tantalizing raid of Eastham, Raymond declared, "I don't care about no cons at no prison farm." He took his share and split for his father's place in Michigan. Clyde told Ralph he hoped Hamilton "chokes on that wad of money."

Circumstances changed, however. Raymond Hamilton got laid off the construction crew he had been working in Bay City, Michigan and

headed back to West Dallas and the bulk of his family. While he was
away, his sister and one of the Barrow sisters had become best friends, so
the hatchet was buried between the two boys. They even rented a place
together in Wichita Falls, and Bonnie moved in, too. The only fly in the
ointment was that Hamilton, thanks to police assumptions, was now
wanted for a murder he did not commit. It did not deter Barrow and
Hamilton from resuming their robbery spree. To make things worse,
the duo and another man they had recruited, stopped at an outdoor
country dance in Stringtown, Oklahoma where they called attention
to themselves by drinking and asking local girls to dance. Rather than
submit to a friendly arrest on the drinking charge, knowing that their
murder warrants would soon come out, they killed a deputy and shot the
county sheriff six times. The murder of a lawman ensured a bad ending
for both Barrow and Hamilton no matter what came next.

Trouble cascaded as it always does after bad decisions. A stolen car
in New Mexico led to the kidnapping of a policeman then a narrow
two-car escape at the river bridge in Wharton. That was followed by
stealing Browning automatic rifles from a state guard armory. Hamilton,
who still did not get along with Clyde, decided it was time to go back
to Michigan. Though he considered himself an equal to Barrow, it was
Clyde who always got top billing in the news stories. The press knew
who Raymond was, but he was still just a small timer who had never even
been inside the state prison system. He decided he did not need Clyde
Barrow.

To prove it, Hamilton quickly returned to Texas and, with a series of
partners, robbed a bank in Cedar Hill, then one in La Grange, then the
same bank in Cedar Hill again. With a bankroll in his pocket, he once
again headed north to Michigan. Trouble was that 19-year old Raymond
could not keep his mouth shut. He bragged to a girl at a skating rink

that he was one of the most famous criminals in Texas. The next thing he knew, state police surrounded the place, and Hamilton and cohort George O'Dare were being extradited back home. It took some time, but Raymond Hamilton ended up chained in the same One Way Wagon headed for Eastham. His cumulative sentence was 263 years including 99 for the Hillsboro murder that took place while he was a thousand miles away near Lake Huron.

There had been no change at places like Eastham, and no epiphany of grace for Prison System Manager Lee Simmons. There were, though, reformers in Texas, and one of the most vocal was a chain-smoking, foul-mouthed *Houston Press* columnist named Harry McCormick and his editors, Marcellus Foster and Royal Roussel. Mack, as his friends knew him, had come to Houston from Denver and was soon penning exposes about the rampant brutality in the state prisons. Using jail chaplain Father Hugh Finnegan as intermediary, Mack gained street cred on the P-farms and had a network of correspondents that included Ralph Fults, Raymond Hamilton, and Clyde Barrow. It was a relationship that helped both sides.

Raymond picked cotton and chopped wood same as all the other cons at Eastham, but from day one he was also bragging that he would not be there long. Meanwhile, he made friends. One was Joe Palmer, an asthmatic bank robber who was ten years older than Raymond. Another was James Mullen, a skittish burglar with a drug problem. When Mullen got released, he went directly to Raymond's brother, Floyd, with a plan for Clyde to spring Ray. Mullen also carried the promise of $1,000 when he made good.

Clyde did not like the plan, nor did he like Mullen. He was afraid Raymond would do his usual bragging and word would get back to the guards. Floyd Hamilton argued the since his brother was doing 99 years for a murder committed by Clyde's gang, Barrow was obligated. In the end, they honed a plan for the long-awaited Eastham breakout.

Floyd Hamilton and James Mullen slipped through the barbed wire at the edge of the prison farm and placed an inner tube in a drain culvert. It held two Colt .45s and plenty of ammo. Floyd visited his brother to fill him in, and one of the trustys at Eastham Camp 1 retrieved the stash and brought it to Joe Palmer who had feigned sickness to stay in his bunk. The next morning, in a cold ground fog, Palmer, Hamilton, and two others – Henry Methvin and Hilton Bybee – made their move. Palmer took the opportunity to shoot down one guard who had been especially nasty to him. They took off running and piled into a car where Clyde, Bonnie, and Mullen awaited.

The group headed north. The first big job was to rob a bank in Rembrandt, Iowa. Bybee left the gang at that point, but Barrow, Methvin, Palmer, and Hamilton hit a bank in Poteau, Oklahoma. Palmer was actually a non-factor since he was incapacitated with respiratory trouble, and it rankled Raymond that Joe, and Bonnie for that matter, was getting an equal share. At one point, Hamilton pointed a pistol at sleeping Palmer's head but never pulled the trigger.

The gang dropped Raymond off in Amarillo, and when they met up again, he was with Mary O'Dare, the wife of Hamilton's one-time associate who was banged up in jail for 99 years. She had been working as a prostitute until Ray picked her up in Amarillo. His brother, Floyd, described her as a "short girl with plenty of curves and a hard face covered by enough makeup to grow a crop." Mary became a chief catalyst for Hamilton leaving the Barrow gang, helping Ray steal money from the group's haul and suggesting to Bonnie that she dump Clyde. In early March 1934, the split was done. Hamilton and Barrow went their separate ways for good.

On top of every other complaint against Mary, she could not drive. When Raymond came running from the State National Bank in the town of West with a take of $1,900, Mary O'Dare was behind the wheel of the getaway car. She made it only a few miles before she ran the car through a ditch, knocking herself out in the process and breaking Ray's nose. Now they needed a replacement.

The first vehicle to happen along was Mrs. Cam Gunter of Mexia who was passing by with her four-year-old son. When she stopped to render aid, Hamilton pulled his gun, put the young boy out of the car, and told Mrs. Gunter to head south. They arrived in Houston around sunup, but not before the machine gun-toting Hamilton pulled off into some woods near Conroe and allowed the two women to catch some sleep. Mrs. Gunter told HPD that she had been treated "nicely." Hamilton left his kidnap victim with $30 "to have her car fixed up." After posing in hammy pictures for news photographers, including one in which she held a machine gun, Mrs. Gunter returned to Mexia and her family.

Hamilton considered himself a gentleman bandit who was above the small-time gas station stickups that marked much of the Barrow gang's work, and he sent out angry public statements to make his reputation known. Clyde Barrow reciprocated. Each Hamilton letter or telegram was marked with a fingerprint to show that the missive was "on the level."

When Bonnie and Clyde killed two more lawmen in Grapevine over Easter Weekend, Ray Hamilton sent his lawyer a letter postmarked from the Lafayette Hotel in New Orleans. Hamilton denied killing anyone, stressing that he hadn't been with the Barrow Gang "since the Lanster Bank Robbery," meaning the four grand the gang stole at Lancaster near

Dallas. "I was in Houston Wednesday, April 4," wrote Hamilton. "And have been (in New Orleans) since Thur. even. April 5."

Clyde responded with multiple fiery rejoinder telegrams. At first, he tried to pin the Grapevine murders on Ray, not knowing his rival had an ironclad alibi. He also wrote that Hamilton was "too dum to know how to put a clip in a automatic," and saying that it made him "sick to see a yellow punk like that playing baby."

Raymond heard about the killing of the famous Bonnie and Clyde while he was cooling his heels in Huntsville. He was captured after he and a "chance companion" robbed a bank at Lewisville. Sporting over 360 years of prison sentence, Ray went back into the system, this time on death row.

It was only days after the ambush that Hamilton received a letter in his cell written in Bonnie's hand and signed by Clyde. In it, Barrow offered more enmity and wrote that he'd been looking for Hamilton with the intent to kill him, something that should have happened earlier. Barrow also added that when he busted Raymond out of Eastham, Ray was not the changed man he expected, just the same "boastful punk."

Not quite two months later, Raymond Hamilton finally become the most wanted man in Texas. On Sunday afternoon July 22, 1934, the vast majority of inmates at the Walls in Huntsville were in the stadium watching their beloved Prison Tigers baseball team battle the semi-pro powerhouse Humble Oilers. Prison general manager Lee Simmons was in the crowd. A tough habitual criminal named Charlie Frazier, someone who already carried lead from two other escapes, and the aptly paired

Whitey Walker and Blackie Thompson, had picked this time for an escape. Hamilton and Joe Palmer came with them. Some didn't make it, but three busted out of the death house and onto the front pages.

Dorothy and Estelle Davis, or Dot and Stella as most called them, were the contacts on the outside. They had hooked up with a whole string of desperados. Stella had even been married to one, "Baby Face" Earl Joiner, who had robbed the First National Bank in Cleveland the previous fall and once escaped from Louisiana's Angola Prison with Charlie Frazier. After the Cleveland bank heist, which included a full-on downtown gunfight with local townspeople, newspapers reported that Stella and her sister were the "actual brains of the operation."

For the "sensational" Huntsville break, the women delivered $500 cash and three .45 pistols to prison guard Jim Patterson at a local café. They also drove the two black Ford getaway cars away from the southwest corner of the Walls. When a guard entered Frazier's cell to bring food, Frazier pulled a gun on the man and took his keys. He then headed to the death house, freed the others, and gave guns to Hamilton and Palmer. Ray held a guard hostage as the men ran to a ladder taken from the carpentry shop, then the shootout began. Whitey Walker was shot off the wall. The others took fire on the ladder, but Hamilton, Palmer, and Thompson made it over. Ray pulled a rifle from the back of one car and wounded the guard in the tower before they sped away.

Palmer made it three weeks before being captured in Kentucky, and Thompson went out in the proverbial hail of bullets in Amarillo, but Hamilton's run lasted longer, and the Davis sisters, who sometimes used the name of their hometown of Houston as an alias, stayed in touch. They also became close to Harry McCormick over the next few months. Mack served as their taxi, bought them beer, and took them for meals

at the drive-in. Meanwhile, Raymond reunited with an old friend for a
robbery spree through the Mid-South – Ralph Fults.

One Monday evening in March 1935, one of the Davis girls called
Harry McCormick's home phone and told him to come take the sisters
out, but first we need to "pick up five chicken dinners." Mack drove
to the corner of 11th and Shepherd. As he pulled to a stop, Dot Davis
jumped in beside him and said, "Tail my sister."

They headed west on 11th Street then turned right on Hempstead
Highway. Around the little community of Satsuma, the lead car
pulled down a dirt road and flashed its lights to another automobile.
McCormick walked to the third vehicle and slid into the back seat next
to Raymond Hamilton, the most wanted man in Texas. Belying the
automatic rifle on his lap and the small arsenal on the seat, Hamilton
doffed his hat. This was the interview Ray had promised before he pulled
off his big escape.

Ralph Fults was behind the wheel with Stella behind him and Dot
bringing up the rear of the caravan in McCormick's car. The rolling
interview continued all the way to Hempstead where the three cars
turned north onto Highway 6. Along the way Fults and Hamilton spilled
the beans about the death house escape and an ambush in McKinney
that had almost ended their lives. Hamilton wanted "the people of Texas
to know" his side of the story: he'd never killed anybody. The last act
of the meeting was giving Harry two thousand dollars to pass to Joe
Palmer's lawyer.

"We hope it'll buy a stay of execution," Ray told him. "It's the least we
can do."

Around 4:30 in the morning, in a pasture near the community of Retreat, the outlaws bound and gagged Harry McCormick and carried him back to his own car. They busted out the headlights and cut the wire to the horn. Raymond then left a full set of fingerprints on Harry's hood, dash, and windshield. The idea, Hamilton said was "to keep the feds off you, we best make out like we kidnapped you and held you against your will." Almost 25 years later, in a magazine story, McCormick was still distorting the facts to avoid any potential prosecution.

Raymond Hamilton's prison holiday ended not long after the staged McCormick abduction. He was surrounded in a rail yard at Ft. Worth and gave up without a fight. He allegedly told the lawmen, "Don't shoot boys, I'm fresh out of guns, ammo, whiskey, and women."

In the end, he was reunited on Death Row with Joe Palmer, the man he once plotted to shoot in the head when the two were still riding with Clyde Barrow's gang.

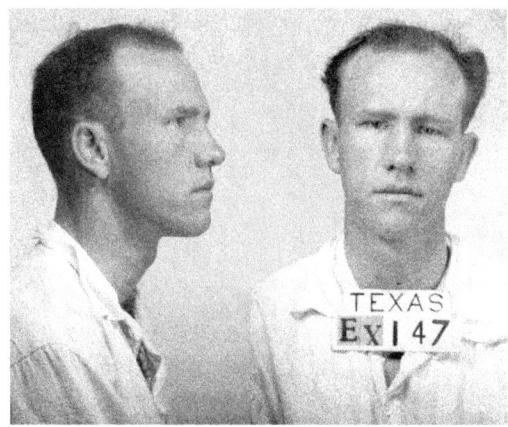

Raymond Hamilton. Texas Department of Criminal Justice

Ralph Fults was dragged from a wrecked car by deputies in Denton less than two weeks after Hamilton's recapture. When they brought him to Huntsville, prison officials were under embarrassing fire over the horrible brutality going on under their watch. In turn the prison bosses looked for a scapegoat, and their top target was Harry McCormick. They had already banned him from all prison facilities. Officials worked over Ralph Fults with a combination of threats and promises. They wanted him to give up Mack for a harboring charge.

"Sure as I'm standing here," Fults told the man. "We kidnapped Harry McCormick."

Joe Palmer and Raymond Hamilton both breathed their last in the Texas electric chair in the first minutes of May 10, 1935. Palmer died first, and then Hamilton "made a brave showing after cracking earlier in the day." Joe Palmer comforted Hamilton when he had lost control at the prospect of his death. At the end, 22-year old Raymond thanked Father Finnegan, then added "Goodbye to all." Three blasts of electrical current, a "sizzling noise," an eerie screech of the dynamo, a clenching of his hands, and he was gone. Among the witnesses was Harry McCormick.

Chapter Forty-Six

Morris Sheppard

There is not much trace of Wheatville, Texas anymore. There is a White cemetery and a Black cemetery. A literal handful of farms stand nearby, and the poultry population outnumbers the humans by maybe 100,000 to 1. The post office has been closed for almost 150 years. Yet, Wheatville was the hometown of a father and son duo of politicians, the latter of whom shaped the United States for almost half a century. His name was Morris Sheppard, and during all his years in Congress, he was one of the most reliably progressive members in that entire body. But he was also a strident segregationist and is best remembered today for one of the most oppressive pieces of legislation in American history.

John Levi Sheppard moved to Northeast Texas from Alabama after the Civil War and ran a general store while he studied the law. His mother's family, the Morrises, were already there. The Morrises were extremely religious Protestants, and family lore holds that Reverend Samuel Morris ordered several of his enslaved farm workers to hew lumber and build four churches across what is now three counties. Using those connections, Sheppard got himself elected district attorney. Six years later, he became district judge. During that decade he served as a delegate to the state Democratic convention and then the national convention where he full-throatedly backed William Jennings Bryan. In 1898, John L. Sheppard got himself elected to Congress.

All of this made quite the impression on his oldest child, Morris. As his father moved the family around the area, Morris attended small schools in Pittsburg, Daingerfield, Cumby, and Linden. After high school, young Sheppard went to the state university and got both a bachelors and law degree there in Austin. His up-and-coming father wanted more for the boy, so Morris went east and completed a master of law degree at Yale, graduating the same year as the judge got elected to Congress. Morris came home to East Texas and joined his father's law practice in Pittsburg and Texarkana. He was also active in the Woodmen of the World, a popular fraternal organization founded as a life insurance company. With the Woodmen, Morris became known as a "silver-tongued orator."

Then, to paraphrase the great philosopher Rick Blaine, destiny took a hand. John Sheppard developed kidney disease. He had been renominated for his congressional seat, but in early October he died. Speculation almost immediately turned to his son. In a hastily called election to fill the remaining months of the current term, young Sheppard defeated three other top men without a runoff. The Mexia *State Herald* called Morris "a wheel horse when it comes to pulling a crowd and a gladiator in a debate."

Speculation was that the election would earn the winner but a few lame duck months in office, but by the end of November it was reported that Morris Sheppard had gone to Washington with a stack of election certificates from every county in the newly reconfigured First District that covered the next session of Congress, as well. The *Mineral Wells*

Daily Index wagered "there is some question as to the legality of it, but... it is presumed he will have no difficulty being seated at once."

There was little pressure on Sheppard to deliver. His Democrats were outnumbered in the House almost 2 to 1. Still, the newest member, only 27-years old, jumped in with the kind of Progressive Era ideas that would have pleased his father and tickled his friend William Jennings Bryan. In his first few years, there was legislation to insure small bank deposits and to provide other forms of low-cost credit for needy groups. Both would become law a few decades later, but in the business-dominated early 1900s, they both lost. There was also another pet cause of Morris Sheppard. He proposed a law to prohibit the shipment of alcohol into dry areas. That one lost, too. Industry lobbyists were strong as iron at the start of the 20th century.

Despite not seeing a lot of legislative success to help the little man, Morris Sheppard became very popular as a speaker and as a colleague. Personally, he was mild-mannered and polite with an ever-sunny outlook. His speeches were ranked among the very best in all of Congress. He knew his Shakespeare and loved to insert lines into his talks. Above all, he was entertaining. Because Texas was a one party state, come election time Sheppard was a shoo-in, so by the end of the decade he was crossing the country stumping for fellow Democrats.

One of the two U.S. senators from Texas was Joe Bailey who had been dodging various credible charges of corruption for years, but they all caught up to him in 1912. Senators were selected by state legislatures at the time, and it became clear to Bailey that he did not have support to win again. So, Bailey resigned at the start of 1913, and the governor appointed Rienzi Johnston, publisher of the *Houston Post*, to take his place. Johnston's term in the Senate lasted 29 days, the second shortest in American history. That year of 1913 also marked the start of popular election of senators in the United States thanks to the 17th Amendment. When the State of Texas held two elections at the end of January, one for the unexpired term of Bailey and one for a regular six-year term to start that March, Morris Sheppard won them both.

Sheppard's ascent to the Senate also coincided with Woodrow Wilson taking the White House, and it finally meant that his priorities fell on the winning side. He sponsored rural farm credit programs, child labor laws, and beefed up antitrust legislation. The Democrats, now in the majority, also lowered tariffs, a policy topic in which Sheppard had immersed himself. Almost from the time he had arrived in Congress, Morris had been in favor of women getting the right to vote, and that finally inched closer to reality.

Like many men who backed women's suffrage, Sheppard came at the issue from the angle of prohibition of alcohol. Women's groups were a major part of the Temperance Movement. Sheppard did not drink personally, and, like those women, he saw the abuse and proliferation of booze as a threat to civilized society. In 1913, in the Senate, Morris helped draft the Webb-Kenyon Act. It stopped interstate transport of liquor if doing so violated "any law of [any] State, Territory, or District of the United States." The Temperance Movement had been gaining ground since the late 1870s, and roughly half the states had already imposed prohibition on a state level, so regulating import from a neighboring "wet" state was a major win. So, too, was the Sheppard Bone-dry Act that he got passed in 1916. It banned all hooch in the District of Columbia. Privately, many tippling members of Congress stewed.

In April 1917, Morris Sheppard again proposed a constitutional amendment to ban the manufacture, sale, and transportation of alcohol.

It was his third try at such an amendment. The first two times he had split sponsorship billing with a flamboyant House member named Richmond Hobson from Alabama. The timing of their first attempt coincided with the new federal income tax offsetting the long-running argument that government needed the money from liquor taxes. The spectacle of a raucous parade to the Capitol steps drew a crowd, but the bill died inside the building.

In 1917, now as the primary face of the movement, Sheppard chose to introduce it on the same day that Congress declared war on Germany. The split of opinion was closer than ever, but just as vehement, and debate raged on through the summer with no solution in sight. Finally, in an effort to bring the matter to a vote of the full Senate, Sheppard offered to tighten the window for states to ratify the new amendment. Even after the measure passed, conventional wisdom was that it would fall short of approval in three fourths of the states, but that conclusion proved wrong. The 18th Amendment surpassed the threshold early in 1919 and the entire nation went dry to start 1920. Eventually 46 of the 48 states signed on to the plan. Rhode Island and Connecticut were the only ones who showed any foresight.

The Temperance Movement was led by hardcore Protestants, of which Morris Sheppard definitely was one, but the morality behind Prohibition was always a moving target. Much more numerous than "dry-drys" were "wet-drys," elected officials who drank personally but wanted Prohibition. They were less reliable when it came to legislating against sin, but Morris Sheppard was the real deal. Years later, William Cabell Bruce, a Maryland senator who was a leader of the wets, listed Sheppard as one of only three members of the Senate who actually did not drink.

Under the politics of the day, support for Prohibition was considered a Progressive cause because it was thought to improve life for the masses. Modern philanthropists like John D. Rockefeller, Jr. and Gifford Pinchot supported it for just that reason. Opposition to the idea often had little to do with drinking per se. It was conservatives who believed that government's only two functions were "to preserve order and protect private property." Some of the most adamant opponents were also head-shakingly reactionary. One outspoken wet was South Carolina's Cole Blease who not only loved a good whiskey but opposed any form of education for Blacks because it "could ruin a good field hand and make a bad convict."

With Prohibition the law of the land, there was still the matter of enforcing this edict. Congress came up with the Volstead Act. That law defined prohibited drinks as anything above half a percent of alcohol and lined out all sorts of measures to stop its creation and consumption. President Wilson, who did not particularly like the 18th Amendment, vetoed the Volstead Act. Morris Sheppard was a leader in whipping the votes in the Senate to override the veto.

Sheppard considered the passage of the 18th Amendment as such a great achievement that every year, on the January anniversary of the vote, he rose in the Senate to commemorate the moment. He was also sure that the law would remain in place forever. In 1930, he stated, "There's as much chance of repealing the Eighteenth Amendment as there is for a hummingbird to fly to the planet Mars with the Washington Monument tied to its tail."

The same year that the Prohibition Amendment went into effect, the Republicans won elections that put them back in charge of the government. Sheppard's profile in the Senate was lowered, and his few successes came as part of a bi-partisan bloc from agricultural states. He did have one major Progressive win during the first year that the majority swung. It was the Sheppard-Towner Act which provided for government-run maternal and pediatric clinics and for an investigation of infant and maternal mortality. Republicans let the law lapse at the end of the 1920s, but some portions returned during the New Deal. Sheppard also rose within the Senate when he became the Democratic whip in 1929.

Earle Mayfield & Morris Sheppard, the two Texas senators for most of the 1920s. Mayfield was a strong supporter of the Ku Klux Klan. Library of Congress.

Most all the ideas that the Progressive Era brought to the country were aimed to help White citizens only. Just as Woodrow Wilson was the most racist president of the 20th century, many progressive senators and congressmen felt the same way. Those hateful views came to a head when new First Lady Lou Hoover arranged the traditional series of White House teas for Congressional wives. One of the invitees was Jessie De

Priest, wife of a new African American representative from the South
Side of Chicago. Much of Washington and the rest of America exploded.
The Hoovers clarified that it was an official event and not a private
invitation. They even arranged a separate smaller tea to segregate Mrs.
De Priest from any Southerners, but dozens of Congress members called
it a disgrace. The Texas Legislature voted to censure Mrs. Hoover for
her actions, and Mississippi, Georgia, and Florida did the same. Morris
Sheppard was dignified in his language, but the content of his character
on the matter was anything but.

"I regret the incident beyond measure," he said. "It is recognition of
social equality between the white and black races and is fraught with
infinite danger to our white civilization."

As the 1920s progressed, any optimism that Prohibition would make
the nation a better place was rapidly evaporating. Morris Sheppard
failed to understand how much Americans liked to drink, but he most
certainly did not forecast the consequences. By all accounts, drinking
had actually increased. The proliferation of urban speakeasies and rural
blind tigers turned some occasional drinkers into regular customers.
The New York City police chief estimated that the number of drinking
establishment in his town doubled during Prohibition. Bootleg spirits
were also killing large numbers of people. Moonshiners sometimes
created poisonous products accidentally, but the federal government
purposely added poisonous compounds into industrial alcohol that
wound up in people's hooch by the thousands. Enforcement of the laws
was spotty, sometimes barely existent, and definitely prone to bribery.
The loss of tax revenue did indeed turn out to be significant, and the
elimination of the eighth largest industry in the country was a disaster

for the job markets. The biggest problem was crime, both organized and individual. Violent crime increased by a quarter in the largest U.S. cities with murder up by two-thirds.

By 1932, with the Depression at its lowest point yet and Hoover and the Republicans doing little to help, the nation voted for the Democrats and Progressives in one of the biggest landslides in history. The new Franklin Roosevelt administration fit Morris Sheppard's belief in protecting the public welfare like a well-worn glove. He backed FDR's New Deal programs to the point that some back home criticized him for being a rubber stamp for White House desires.

Their one glaring difference was over the repeal of the Prohibition Amendment. Public sentiment, so strong and optimistic in 1919, was now overwhelmingly against the idea. In February 1933, Senator John Blaine introduced a joint resolution for the 21st Amendment to overturn the 18th. Morris Sheppard rose the next day for a good old-fashioned filibuster. He spoke against repeal for a solid eight hours. Not a single other senator joined him. The Blaine Act passed the Senate 69-27 and cleared the House by a similar margin. With the next move being ratification by the states, Sheppard got into a Ford truck with a platform and loud speakers in the back and traveled more than 5,000 miles of Texas two-lane asking his constituents to say no. The state legislature voted to ratify the 21st, and 63% of the citizens voted to allow 3.2 beer in Texas. The full return of liquor took until 1935, when voters overturned the state ban on booze. By then Morris Sheppard was a lonely voice pushing for repeal of the repeal.

Morris did not lose his sense of humor over matter. Legend has it that some years later, he was at a D.C. party when Representative Sol Bloom of New York jokingly handed Sheppard a cocktail. With a smile, Morris walked to the buffet and returned with a ham sandwich for the Jewish

Bloom. Meanwhile, Sheppard continued to commemorate Prohibition on the Senate floor every January.

In 1934, Morris introduced the Federal Credit Union Act. Well more than half of the states already provided for some form of non-profit lending co-ops, but Sheppard's bill made it uniform and nationwide.

Three years later came a tipping point in the New Deal. The ultra-conservative Supreme Court, a remnant of 12 straight years of Republican rule, had shot down several of Roosevelt's programs including the National Recovery Act, a minimum wage, and the Agriculture Adjustment Act. The White House's desperate answer was a plan to "pack" the court by adding one new justice for every sitting Supreme Court justice over 70 years old. It could potentially increase the court to as many as 15 members.

Texans in Washington had an inordinate amount of power, and most of them used it to go against FDR. Roosevelt's vice president was John Nance Garner of Uvalde, a man who was already on the outs with the more liberal president, and he began to no-so-secretly organize opposition to the court plan. Representative Hatton Sumners, a successful lawyer/politician from Dallas, saw to it that the plan stayed bottled up in the House. The two Texas senators were split. Tom Connally, normally a reliable New Deal vote, believed the idea was unconstitutional, but Morris Sheppard backed the president. In the end, the court packing notion never made it out of committee.

In his third term, Sheppard became chairman of the Senate Military Affairs Committee, and he used the post to increase defense spending as he watched war break out in Europe and Asia. While other members of Congress dug in on isolationism, Sheppard pushed bills to build up the

Army Air Corps, increase the number of West Point cadets, and assist veterans. He backed Lend-Lease and, with fellow Texan Sam Rayburn, fought to pass a military draft. The renewal of that Selective Service Act just squeaked through.

It was not long after that Morris Sheppard suffered a brain hemorrhage and died seven months before the attack on Pearl Harbor. The following year, his wife Lucille to whom he had been married more than 30 years, married the other Texas senator, Tom Connally, a widower.

Chapter Forty-Seven

Babe Didrikson Zaharias

M ildred Didrikson was the brash, audacious daughter of a Norwegian immigrant seaman, and she cussed as artfully as many men. When she rose to fame, it was wearing a thick bark of rough Texan-ness. She rarely hesitated to self-promote, an attribute that generally annoyed her competitors. It might be a stretch to call those other women peers since Didrikson usually left them far in her wake. She accomplished a wider array of athletic success than any person, male or female, before or since, and along the way she created the role of woman sports star and the controversy that often goes with it.

Didrikson's father, Ole, also did carpentry work, and he built a backyard gymnasium for the family's seven children. Both parents encouraged the kids to make full use of the rudimentary equipment. From an early age, Mildred began playing sports with the neighborhood boys, and when she hit five home runs in a single baseball game she was forever after known as Babe, after the greatest ballplayer in the world. It was a nickname she whole-heartedly embraced.

The 1915 Hurricane that hit the upper Texas Coast chased the Didriksen family from Port Arthur to Beaumont when Babe was four, and it was there that she learned to best the boys in most any sport she tried. At Beaumont High School, she became the star of the girl's basketball team and played tennis, baseball, volleyball, and swam. On the classroom side, she fared worse, and Didrikson left school without a diploma.

At the start of the 1930s, companies across the United States used sports teams as marketing. Semi-pro baseball was enormous for men, and scores of businesses fielded women's basketball teams, as well. Babe was hired by Employer's Casualty Insurance in Dallas, ostensibly as a secretary, but the real reason was to play basketball. She was 5'6" and slender, but her talent and work ethic were huge. She led the company team to the national title in the Amateur Athletic Union, the premier organizing authority in amateur sports.

The AAU oversaw most everything, and that included Olympic qualifying in track and field. The games in 1932 were coming to Los Angeles, only their second time in North America, and the country was enthralled. Women's Olympic Trials were held at Dyche Stadium at Northwestern University in Evanston, Illinois. Employer's Casualty entered a team, but it had only one member – Babe Didrikson. When she was introduced, she ran to the team's place jumping and wildly waving her arms. If anyone thought it was a grand joke, they were soon disabused of the notion.

Over the course of three grueling hours, Babe competed in every individual event offered except the 50 and 220-yard runs. Three of the women's AAU events – long jump, shot put, and baseball throw - were not offered at the Olympics. Babe won them all. Her titles in long jump and baseball throw were repeat championships. She had taken gold in those in 1931. Her baseball throw in '32 was well shy of her 296-foot world record from the year before. In Olympic qualifying events, she did just as well. She failed to make the finals in the 100-meter run, but in three of the other four events, she won. She was largely unfamiliar with proper technique for discus, but she finished fourth.

The high jump was a tie with Pennsylvanian Jean Shiley with both women setting a new American record. The javelin and 80-meter hurdles, Babe won outright. She would represent her country at the Olympics in those three events, the most a single athlete was allowed to enter. Babe, all by herself, also won the AAU women's track team title with 30 total points. The second place team, representing the local state of Illinois, scored 22.

A few weeks later, Babe Didrikson found herself alone at the 10th modern Olympic games. None of her family could make the trip to watch her. She had no coach; her training had been self-led. Her first experience with hurdles had been jumping hedges on Doucette Street in Beaumont.

Olympic track and field events were held in the nine-year old Los Angeles Coliseum. Didrikson won the javelin throw with a new Olympic record, and, in a repeat of the trials, she barely edged fellow American Evelyne Hall to take another gold in hurdles. In the high jump, Babe again tied with Jean Shiley and the two women moved onto a "jump off." Both women cleared the bar at 5' 4 3/4", a new world's record, but judges ruled Babe's technique illegal because her head went over the bar before her body. She was awarded the silver medal.

Didrikson came home to Texas and a hero's welcome. There were parades in both Dallas and Beaumont. Then her three Olympic medals went in a drawer. She still had to make a living, and though she was now nationally famous, none of that translated into money for women athletes in 1932. Lucky for her, self-promotion was never an issue. One car advertisement and a new Dodge cost her spot on the Employer's Casualty basketball team because she was no longer deemed an amateur. She made some money at professional pocket billiards, led the touring Babe Didrikson's All-Stars basketball team, and did exhibitions in tennis, bowling, and diving. There were vaudeville appearances where she played the harmonica and did calisthenics.

She was still the most famous and versatile woman athlete in the world. She was cross-training long before that was in vogue. In March 1934, she went to baseball spring training to face the major league men. Baseball was by far the dominant sport of the era, and Babe's fame demanded she take part. She stopped in Hot Springs, Arkansas where she got some tutoring from National League pitcher Burleigh Grimes then it was on to Florida. Her first exhibition was throwing an inning for the Athletics against woeful Brooklyn. She put two runners on before inducing the Dodgers into a triple play.

Trouble came two days later. Throwing for the Cardinals against the Red Sox, Babe gave up three runs before manager Frankie Frisch walked out and pulled her from the game. Babe rounded out the week by pitching for the Cleveland Indians against their double-A farm club the New Orleans Pelicans. This time she threw two scoreless innings and stroked a line drive out in her only plate appearance. Didrikson followed up spring training by joining the bearded, barnstorming House of David showmen for baseball exhibitions, sometimes even playing while riding donkeys. They paid her $1,500 a month which was worlds better than the $75 clerical pay she was earning for her basketball play at the insurance company back in Dallas.

One story from that summer hit the press when a woman in the stands pointed at the long beards on all the other players and asked Didrikson where her whiskers were.

"I'm sitting on them, sister," Babe said. "Same as you are."

Babe Didrikson had played a little golf during her high school years, but never committed to it. After her big win at the 1931 AAU track championships, the City of Dallas had gifted her a set of clubs, but nothing suggests they got much use. Yet it was a golf game just after her triumph at the L.A. Olympics that had raised her profile, for good and bad, more than anything else. She joined four of the biggest sportswriters of the day for 18 holes at the invitation of Grantland Rice. The others were Paul Gallico, Westbrook Pegler, and Braven Dyer. On the first tee, Babe went to drive the ball off the deck before Rice stepped up and placed her ball on a tee. She then smacked it 240 yards down the fairway. Grantland Rice, the most-read sports newsman over the first half of the 20th century, became her lifelong friend that day, and Paul Gallico, whose misogynist tendencies were only exacerbated after he was humbled by Didrikson on the golf course, became her enemy.

Gallico wrote for the *New York Daily News* and considered himself a man's man. In his quests for a good story, he caught Dizzy Dean's fastball and got knocked out by heavyweight champ Jack Dempsey. In his initial article about Didrikson and her three Olympic medals, he called her a "muscle moll." In 1937, Gallico retired from sports writing to become a novelist, but for the five years prior, he was especially relentless in publishing his distaste for Babe. He called her mannish, a "boy," and an unattractive woman who was unable to get a man. The word lesbian was rarely used in the 1930s, but the whispers and innuendos that accompanied women's sports grew to a hot flame under Paul Gallico's attacks.

Though her exterior had always been that of an unapologetic tomboy, the criticism bothered her. She began wearing hats and better dresses. She started using lipstick, nail polish, and perfume, things she had previously dismissed as "too sissy." Gallico and other writers still ridiculed her looks and her failure "in the sport of man-snatching."

"I know I'm not pretty," Didrickson said. "But I try to be graceful."

Grantland Rice began suggesting that Didrikson concentrate on a career in golf as soon as he saw her natural ability in Los Angeles, and she decided he was right. Like her other pursuits, the famous Babe told the press that she would soon be national woman's champion, but early results did not bear that out. George Aulbach, golf pro at the Dallas Country Club, gave her lessons beginning the month after the Olympics. He pronounced her a "difficult golf pupil."

"She wants to compete instead of practice," Aulbach told reporters. "She has no proper golf swing. Getting her to follow through after connecting with the ball has been a problem. She listens to too much advice from fellows who shoot around 120 or worse. Her judgment in the selection of clubs...is bad. But I'll say this in her favor, she is trying her best, and she plans to stick with the task until she has accomplished her purpose."

She was still pursuing paychecks through baseball, billiards, and basketball, but Babe kept practicing golf when she could, gradually working up to competitive play. In April 1934, she shot almost 100 in a tournament at Galveston, but at the same time was carding in the high 70s during practice rounds at Beaumont Country Club. Employer's

Casualty was backing her for golf appearances around Texas, as well. In a stop at Abilene, her play around the greens was "ragged," but her drives brought oohs from spectators, and she drew the largest golf crowds in the city's history.

Golf is one of the toughest games to master, and coming into it competitively at age 24 is very late for most players, but once she decided to go full time, Babe leaned into it like all her other pursuits. She practiced 10 hours a day, hitting between 1,000 and 1,500 practice balls until her hands were blistered and often bleeding. In the spring and summer of 1933, she stayed in Los Angeles and took lessons from Stan Kertes. The two also found time for a public exhibition at the Pico Fairway driving range. Though she was not yet particularly good, she was still big news.

Didrikson won her first tournament, the River Crest International at Fort Worth, in 1935. Golf was very much a country club sport, and the Texas wives believed that while Babe was a woman, she was decidedly not a lady. Their complaints to the U.S. Golf Association resulted in Didrikson losing her amateur status, not for taking money to play golf, but for getting paid to play baseball and basketball. That meant her disqualification from almost all tournament play.

Babe responded by booking a traveling tour with Gene Sarazen, one of the top men's golfers in the world. It was not uncommon for her to outdrive him. She played in exhibitions with Hollywood stars like Bob Hope, Bing Crosby, and fellow Olympic star Johnny Weismuller. In January 1938, with her game improving, Didrikson received an invitation to compete with the men at the Los Angeles Open on the course at Griffith Park. It was undoubtedly a move on the Professional

Golfers Association to boost attendance, and it worked. Babe shot 84 and 81 in the first two rounds, missing the cut. The most notable thing that happened is that she met her future husband.

George Zaharias was a hulking pro wrestler from Colorado. He was nicknamed the "Crying Greek from Cripple Creek" or "The Greek Hyena." He played a sore-losing villain on the incredibly popular wrestling circuit. Zaharias, whose birthname was Theodore Vetoyanis, was 30 years old and had an announced wrestling weight of 300 pounds. On the surface, he and the slight Didrikson could hardly be more different, but they began seeing each other. Before the end of the year, they were married at a friend's home in St. Louis. Several members of baseball's Cardinals attended. Brooklyn Dodgers infielder Leo Durocher and his wife served as best man and maid of honor.

The couple moved to a farm near Denver, and Zaharias quit competitive wrestling to manage his wife's career as well as promote wrestling matches and run a Denver cigar store. The marriage also put a stop to talk about Babe's sexuality. When Babe was not traveling, she played at area country clubs. She used the men's tees and faced male club members. There were usually wagers, and she usually won. Officially, Babe took no money for golf, and under the USGA rules of the time, her amateur status was eventually restored in 1942.

Because of travel restrictions during WWII most large golf tournaments went dark, but as soon as they resumed, Babe Didrikson began winning them. She took the Texas Women's Open in 1945. It was the first of three straight wins at that tournament as an amateur. She won it twice more once she turned pro. She captured the U.S. Women's Amateur Championship in 1946, the tournament she had cavalierly bragged about well over a decade before. The following year, Babe became the first American to ever win the British Women's Amateur. At one stretch in those two years, Didrikson won 13 consecutive amateur events. She claimed the number was 17, but she conveniently omitted a loss in Spokane from the string. Still, 17 out of 18 tournaments in a row is not too shabby.

Through George, Babe met Fred Corcoran. He was the man credited with bringing professional golf into the sports limelight. He expanded the men's tour by adding pro tournaments in warm winter spots. Corcoran also had great connections in baseball and acted as the unofficial agent for Ted Williams. He became the agent for Didrikson Zaharias. She was regularly booking appearances at Major League stadiums to throw pitches and swing both a bat and a golf club pregame. She made a joint appearance in Florida driving golf balls with Ted Williams. Under Corcoran, she also started getting $1,000 appearance fees on top of her golf tournament winnings.

Babe Zaharias, Fred Corcoran, and several other women golf professional started the Ladies Professional Golf Association in 1949. There were not many women getting paid to play competitive golf, but now there was a structure of tournaments that crisscrossed the country. Babe was the leading money winner for the first four years of the new tour's existence. The following year she took all three of what were then the women's majors - the U.S. Open, the Titleholders Championship, and the Women's Western Open. Overall that year she won two-thirds of the tournaments on offer. Her total LPGA winnings that year were $14,800. The Associated Press named her the Best Female Athlete of the First Half of the 20th Century.

She was the leading money winner again in 1951, and in typical Babe fashion she was not afraid to remind everyone of the fact. She was known to walk into the clubhouse and announce, "Babe's here! Who's gonna finish second?" Resentment among some of the other women built with one or two openly disliking her. Most, though, understood that Didrikson Zaharias was the drawing card. Her booming drives and easy banter with the crowd was what people paid to see. It was entertainment when she stepped to the tee box and told the cheering galleries that she was about to "loosen my girdle and let it rip." Envy be damned, people were there for Babe.

Babe Didrikson Zaharias at Pinehurst, NC

Her LPGA winnings were small beer compared to her lucrative endorsements. She was getting ever increasing fees for various exhibitions, and her name was branded on golf equipment. She was pulling down $100 grand a year. There was even a highly billed role in the Spencer Tracy and Katherine Hepburn movie *Pat & Mike*. Babe played herself, but only agreed to do it after a script change. She refused to lose even to a fictional character. In real life, she pronounced Hepburn "arrogant."

In 1950, at a tournament in Miami, Babe met a young Texas golfer named Betty Dodd. They quickly became close, and were soon rooming together on the road. At first the press referred to the woman as Babe's "protegee," but the old rumors about Didrikson's sexuality emerged again. Thanks to the mores of the time, we are left to assumptions. Neither Babe nor Betty ever spoke of lesbianism, but the two women were most definitely inseparable. Within a year after their meeting, Betty had moved into the house with Babe and George. Though it is easy to assume that it was a physical relationship, no one, including George, ever spoke about it.

George noted that during 1952 Babe had begun to get tired during golf tournaments. There were incidents of rectal bleeding, but still Babe put off going to the doctor because of her pressing schedule. She told her husband, "Just let me get a good hot bath and a rubdown, and I'll be ready to bust loose again in the morning."

She finally made it back to Beaumont and won her namesake golf tournament. Afterwards she visited her hometown doctor, W.E. Tatum. He told Babe she had advanced colon cancer. The only option was surgery. She was told that her days of competitive golf were over. Babe Didrikson had her colostomy in April 1953. At one point after the diagnosis, she reportedly tried to give her golfs clubs away, but she soon made a public vow to return. She insisted that her golf clubs be in the recovery room so she could see them.

As she worked her way back, Babe and Betty Dodd made an appearance on the Ed Sullivan Show. Babe played her harmonica, and Betty accompanied her on guitar. It took only 14 weeks before Didrikson Zaharias was swinging a golf club.

Cancer was a tough thing to talk about in 1953, but Babe was her usual outspoken self. She openly discussed the disease and used her fame to raise funds. She became a spokesperson for the American Cancer Society and declared that a cancer diagnosis did not mean a death sentence. There was even a visit to the White House where she spread her message of positivity.

Babe's accomplishments in sports were legion, but her two nieces believe that her comeback in 1954 was her proudest moment. She won five tournaments that year. The biggest came at Salem Country Club in Peabody, Massachusetts, the site of the U.S. Women's Open. Newsreel announcers spoke of Mrs. Zaharias' battle with cancer. Footage shows that after hitting a still powerful drive, she reached up to adjust her colostomy bag. In the end, she was "so far ahead that other golfers could not see her with a telescope." She won the Open by 12 strokes. When the winning putt dropped and made it official, Babe did not perform her usual hijinks such as leaping into George's arms. Instead, she bowed to the cheering crowd and thanked both her doctors and "the thousands of cancer patients who had written to her and rooted for her."

The 1955 LPGA season started well. Babe played in eight events, winning two, but her back was bothering her. When she went for surgery for a ruptured disc, doctors found that her cancer had not only returned, it had spread to her spine. She spent most of the next year and a half in John Sealy Hospital in Galveston. George and Betty were both there. Betty changed Babe's colostomy bag and shaved her legs. Babe and George established the Babe Didrikson Zaharias Fund to finance a tumor clinic at UTMB. When Babe died in late September 1956, President

Eisenhower opened his regular press conference with a warm tribute to "her gallant fight against cancer."

The Associated Press voted Babe Didrikson Zaharias Athlete of the Year six times, and in 1999 named her the greatest female athlete of the 20th century, but the public has mostly forgotten the Texan who was the first ever woman superstar. There is a museum dedicated to her on the feeder road of Interstate 10 in her hometown of Beaumont, but few people stop to see her medals, golf clubs, and congratulatory telegrams.

Top athletes today likely don't know the name Babe Didrikson Zaharias, either. What they do still follow is one of her regular mantras: "I don't see any point in playing the game if you don't win. Do you?"

Chapter Forty-Eight

Texas Café Firsts

Spirited and sometimes litigious debates over who invented a certain food item span the globe, but those foreign arguments are small fries compared to a long-running dispute over one of the most popular culinary staples on this planet or the next. Many Texans know that the Lone Star State is the birthplace of Dr. Pepper, fajitas, the frozen margarita, and Fritos. A smaller number are conversant with the ins and outs of the feud over the first hamburger, a squabble that has raged for well more than a century.

Frank X. Tolbert was a respected *Dallas Morning News* writer and co-founder of the annual World Chili Championship at Terlingua. He was a smart man as evidenced by the fact that he laid down the law of "no beans in chili" in his book *Bowl of Red*. While that's a position no self-respecting Texas can argue with, his research into the origin of the hamburger has its modern day detractors.

In 1983, Tolbert wrote a famous story backing the claim that Fletcher "Uncle Dave" Davis made the first hamburger at his food stand on the courthouse square in Athens, Texas. In his article, Tolbert cited the existence of a *New York Tribune* article mentioning the new-fangled

hamburger being sold by an unnamed vendor at the 1904 St. Louis
World's Fair. After diligent research, the *Morning News* scribe backed
the case that the king of all American food started with Davis in
Henderson County about 1884. It was enough of a case to convince the
folks at McDonald's Hamburger University to honor Fletcher Davis as
their official pioneer and, presumably, spirit guide.

The story about Uncle Dave ruffled some feathers in other parts
of the country. Three or four lesser places also made claims as the
inventor of the hamburger. Louis Lunch, which sprung from a New
Haven, Connecticut lunch wagon, was trumpeted by the *New York
Times* as having invented the burger in 1900. Others touted "Hamburger
Charlie" Nagreen and gave a date of 1885 in Seymour, Wisconsin.
Hamburg, New York also offered a claim that was frankly murky beyond
the name similarity.

There is little dispute that the word itself is drawn from Hamburg,
Germany. One modern day food historian wrote of a 19th century dish
in Hamburg made from minced beef and onions that made its way to
the United States with German immigrants. Still, none of that placed
it between slices of bread, let alone anywhere near pickles, tomatoes,
and mustard. At least two oldtimers from Athens handed down tales of
"Uncle Dave" Davis' food counter offering up a sandwich of delicious
ground beef with sliced pickles, onions, and mustard on homemade
bread. Their word origin story was that St. Louis locals likened it to the
German concoction, not always in a positive way.

As often happens, historians do some research and ruin a great story.
Two of the modern food experts tried in vain to find the 1904 *New
York Tribune* dispatch from the St. Louis Fair. It seems no one alive,
including Frank Tolbert, ever saw it personally. One of those historians
flatly denied that Fletcher Davis ever went to the 1904 Fair, but his

descendants produced a book of his vendors tickets to prove otherwise. A slight hitch was that the artifact listed Davis as a "pottery turner" which was his day job. His modern family says that the pottery work got him in the door, but that he went to the fair specifically to cook and sell hamburgers on the Midway. Another Athens man in the pottery business told Tolbert stories of Davis moving from very near St. Louis to Texas to work for his family, and that when times turned lean, Fletcher Davis opened his lunch counter. That gentleman, Kindree Miller, not only remembered the details of his parents and the Davises at the world's fair, he could remember eating those ground beef sandwiches as a child on the Henderson County courthouse square.

Those Fletcher Davis descendants do suggest that Tolbert got the dates of his lunch stand wrong. They have a newspaper article about his famous sandwiches, but it is from 1896, two years after they place his arrival in Athens. The fact is that those other claims have even bigger problems. Indications are that Louis Lunch in Connecticut was serving a tasty steak sandwich and that "Hamburger Charlie" in Wisconsin was a meatball vendor who sometimes stuck one between bread slices. Close, but no tomato slice.

One of those food historians found a reference to "hamburger sandwich" in an 1893 edition of the "*Reno Evening Gazette*," but there is no way to know what was in the thing. Later claims touted by others are just that – late. A different book writer credited a grill in Wichita, Kansas, but not until 1915 or 1916, and he also gave originator chops to White Castle in 1921. Clearly there were what we know as burgers well before those dates. An Oklahoma claim is based on their short order cook being the first to use a bun as opposed to a bread slice which sounds akin to saying the paper sleeve is the most important part of a vinyl music album.

Officially, in 2007, the Texas Legislature proclaimed Fletcher Davis of Athens to be the inventor of the hamburger. The town stills holds the Uncle Fletch Hamburger Festival, complete with a cookoff.

Where would the burger possibly be today without the drive-thru? There is another Texas claim to having invented that American staple, as well. Or at least pointed the way.

Jesse Kirby and Reuben Jackson opened the first Pig Stand at what is today Davis and Chalk Hill Roads in Dallas. At the time, in late 1921, it was outside the city limits but on the major thoroughfare connecting Dallas and Fort Worth. Their signature dish was a very un-Texan barbecued pork sandwich with sour relish. They dubbed it the Pig Sandwich. With success came a second location at today's Colorado and Zang Streets. In September 1923, they sold the original and began expanding to other parts of Big D. Their seventh location was in Houston, the first outside of Dallas.

The Pig Stand's boom coincided perfectly with the rapid rise of the automobile. When their restaurant opened, there were a total of 440,000 cars registered in Texas. In less than four years, that number had doubled. People loved their new driving machines, and they did not necessarily want to get out of them. Kirby and Jackson's idea was to bring the food to them. Their Pig Stand restaurants pioneered the car hop. Not exactly the first drive-thru, but certainly the first drive-in eatery. By 1924, they had ten locations in Dallas alone and more in six other states plus other Texas cities. Advertising that year said that they were selling 50,000 Pig Sandwiches a week just in Dallas.

The Great Depression caused their operation to shrink back within Texas, but at the same time a slew of imitation Pig Stands, blatantly ripping off the name, had popped up around Texas and Oklahoma. After losing their lawsuits over the name infringement, the Pig Stands answered with a unique architectural design for their newer restaurants. They added 24-hour service in the 1930s and 40s. By their 40th anniversary, there were only 23 Pig Stands left thanks to increased competition from other car hop establishments and newer eateries.

Pig Stand's design 1920s

The list of firsts claimed by Pig Stand is a long one. The first onion ring, Texas Toast, and chicken fried steak sandwich are attributed to them. The onion ring may be a reach. A British cookbook from 1802 included a recipe for something similar to an onion ring but with lard and dipped in butter, and some valid claims in the United States seem to date as early as 1914. As for Texas Toast, that seems almost certain to be the brainchild of a Pig Stand franchisee in either Beaumont or Denton.

Texas Monthly scribe Daniel Vaughan wrote in 2015 that the Pig Stand also deserves credit for being the first franchise restaurant chain. Most American food history books credit Howard Johnson's with that honor, but Vaughan points out that the second HoJos arrived in 1932.

By that time, there were several dozen franchised Pig Stands. Kirby and Jackson had begun offering franchise opportunities in 1925 when Kirby told one prospective owner: "Give a little pig a chance, and it will make a hog of itself."

For good measure, if you have failed to get enough guilty cuisine so far, there is the Texas origin of the corndog. Immigrant German butchers in Texas, of which there were many, found that not everyone loved daily sausages as much as they did, so they dipped them in corn batter and fried them. It was a short step from sausage to hot dog wieners. Though they are credited with the invention of the idea, there were a couple of non-Texan patents on machines to make them. They were not deep fried, however. They were made like waffles. As to who first impaled such a fried, meaty confection on a stick, the popular claim goes to the Fletcher Brothers, Carl and Neil, who started selling Corny Dogs at the State Fair of Texas between 1938 and 1942. A claim for Pronto Pups invented in Oregon in 1942 also gets wide attention, but Texans certainly know the truth.

Acknowledgements and More

In Undertold Texas Volume 1, I used this space to talk about research, and this volume follows the same pattern. I pulled dozens of sadly dusty books off my own shelves and rooted around in various files that date back to the early 2000s when I was doing a regional history show on a now long gone TV station in Houston. I also leveraged three of my previous books and revisited a few hundred files I compiled for those. In each case, the other books contain more detail than this Volume 2 does, so if you want to know more on the corresponding subjects, please hunt down copies of *A Fire to Kindle* about Harris County schools, *Houston Baseball: The Early Years*, or *Murder & Mayhem in Houston*. You can find the last two on my website, and all three are available online. I rewrote most everything, but there are a couple of cases where I reprised my own words for phrases I liked the first time through. Also in each case, I added some new material not found in the earlier works.

I'm still utilizing research I did at places like the Texas State Library and Archives, Houston History Research Center, and the Harris County Archives. And no Texas historian should fail to thank the hard working people at the Portal for Texas History. That online resource diligently maintained by the University of North Texas is priceless. Ditto for the Handbook of Texas Online and the newspaper access through Houston Public Library.

Thankfully I have built up a little network of history friends, and I could ask them questions or if they had a favorite anecdote about someone they'd written about. Chuck Chandler sent me an entire series of articles he wrote for the Baytown Sun, and it led me to two terrific quotes about Ashbel Smith. The Texas Historical Commission's Bryan McAuley, my buddy for (gasp) 30 years now, talked to me about William Wharton who spent plenty of time at San Felipe de Austin, a stellar state historic site Bryan ran for years. I asked Michael Bludworth about the Texas Airline War, and he pointed me to some cool stuff. Light Cummins and Stephen Hardin gave me nice quotes about Eugene Barker. Steve has graciously talked a lot of early Texas with me over the years working on the Birth of Texas documentaries. Several people at the Laffite Society were helpful on that piece, and a special shout out to Helen Mooty for helping with a couple of refinements in language.

Of course, writing about the Chili Queens made me sad thinking about my departed friend John Nova Lomax. I sure do miss the hours-long phone calls to talk history or bitch about Longhorns football.

I visited a few sites related to these stories and highly recommend you do the same. Langtry is a bit out of the way for most of us, but the Roy Bean museum is worth a stop. Same with the Glider Museum in Lubbock. Fort Clark Springs might not be completely accessible, but it is a terrific visit if you can manage. If you do, don't forget the nearby Seminole related stops.

Lastly, some personal thanks. The people at Rice University's Glasscock School of Continuing Studies are giving me a chance to do another course in Spring of 2026 based on this book. I've been teaching there on and off for 14 years now, and it's forever fun. As always, my good friend, Chris White, is a huge and continuing help on most things publishing. And my wife continues to provide great work in proofreading, though with inflation, her price has gone up.

Sign up for the newsletter at the bottom of any page at www.mikevancewriter.com

If you want to know more about any of Mike's books, whether fiction or non-fiction, the website is the place to go. You'll find loads of extras, plenty of biographical details, and dozens of interesting photos and videos.

Please follow MikeVanceWriter on Patreon, Facebook, YouTube, and Instagram.

Don't forget that one of the biggest favors you can do for any author is, if you enjoyed their books, leave a positive review of those books. Thanks so much for your support.